Evangelical Missiological Society Series
no. **18**

SERVING JESUS WITH INTEGRITY

ETHICS AND ACCOUNTABILITY IN MISSION

Other Books in the EMS Series

No. 1   *Scripture and Strategy: The Use of the Bible in Postmodern Church and Mission*, David Hesselgrave

No. 2   *Christianity and the Religions: A Biblical Theology of World Religions*, Edward Rommen and Harold Netland

No. 3   *Spiritual Power and Missions: Raising the Issues*, Edward Rommen

No. 4   *Missiology and the Social Sciences: Contributions, Cautions, and the Conclusions*, Edward Rommen and Gary Corwin

No. 5   *The Holy Spirit and Mission Dynamics*, Douglas McConnell

No. 6   *Reaching the Resistant: Barriers and Bridges for Mission*, Dudley Woodberry

No. 7   *Teaching Them Obedience in All Things: Equipping for the Twenty-first Century*, Edward Elliston

No. 8   *Working Together With God to Shape the New Millennium: Opportunities and Limitations*, Kenneth Mulholland and Gary Corwin

No. 9   *Caring for the Harvest Force in the New Millennium*, Tom Steffen and Douglas Pennoyer

No. 10 *Between Past and Future: Evangelical Mission Entering the 21st Century*, Jonathan Bonk

No. 11 *Christian Witness in Pluralistic Contexts in the 21st Century*, Enoch Wan

No. 12 *The Centrality of Christ in Contemporary Missions*, Mike Barnett and Michael Pocock

No. 13 *Contextualization and Syncretism: Navigating Cultural Currents*, Gailyn Van Rheenan

No. 14 *Business as Mission: From Impoverished to Empowered*, Tom Steffen and Mike Barnett

No. 15 *Missions in Contexts of Violence*, Keith Eitel

No. 16 *Effective Engagement in Short-Term Missions: Doing it Right!* Robert J. Priest

No. 17 *Missions from the Majority World: Progress, Challenges, and Case Studies*, Enoch Wan and Michael Pocock

About EMS
www.emsweb.org

The Evangelical Missiological Society is a professional organization with more than 350 members comprised of missiologists, mission administrators, teachers, pastors with strategic missiological interests, and students of missiology. EMS exists to advance the cause of world evangelization. We do this through study and evaluation of mission concepts and strategies from a biblical perspective with a view to commending sound mission theory and practice to churches, mission agencies, and schools of missionary training around the world. We hold an annual national conference and eight regional meetings held throughout the United States and Canada.

Evangelical Missiological Society Series no. 18

SERVING JESUS WITH INTEGRITY

ETHICS AND ACCOUNTABILITY IN MISSION

EDITORS
Dwight P. Baker
Douglas Hayward

WILLIAM CAREY PUBLISHING
Available at missionbooks.org

Serving Jesus with Integrity: Ethics and Accountability in Mission
Copyright © 2010 by Evangelical Missiological Society

No part of this book may be reproduced, stored in a retrieval system, or transmitted in any form or by any means—electronic, mechanical, photocopy, recording, or otherwise—without prior written permission from the publisher, except brief quotations used in connection with reviews in magazines or newspapers. For permission, email permissions@wclbooks.com. For corrections, email editor@wclbooks.com.

Published by William Carey Publishing (formerly William Carey Library)
10 W. Dry Creek Cir | Littleton, CO 80120 | www.missionbooks.org

William Carey Publishing is a ministry of Frontier Ventures
Pasadena, CA | www.frontierventures.org

Hugh Pindur, interior design
Mike Riester, cover design
Cover art: Joseph and Potiphar's Wife, by Sawai Chinnawong; acrylic on canvas, 2004, 25 × 31 ½. Used by permission.
Rose Lee-Norman, indexing

ISBN: 978-1-64508-528-7 (paperback)

Printed Worldwide
27 26 25 24 23   2 3 4 5 6   IN
ISBNs: 978-1-64508-528-7 (paperback); 978-0-87808-839-3 (ePub)

Library of Congress Cataloging-in-Publication Data

Serving Jesus with integrity : ethics and accountability in mission / editors, Douglas Hayward and Dwight P. Baker.
    p. cm. -- (Evangelical Missiological Society series ; no. 18)
Includes bibliographical references and index.
ISBN 978-0-87808-023-6
  1. Missions. 2. Christian ethics. 3. Missionaries--Professional ethics. I. Hayward, Douglas James. II. Baker, Dwight P.
BV2063.S42 2010
241--dc22
                    2010030968

Contents

Introduction
  Dwight P. Baker xi

Contributors xix

Part I: Integrity in Message, Finances, and Relationships

1. Reconstructing an Ethic of Evangelism for Twenty-first-Century Congregations
   Fran Blomberg 1

2. An Approach to Financial Accountability in Mission Partnerships
   Mary Lederleitner 27

3. Seeing Through a Glass More Clearly: The Moral and Evangelistic Imperative of More Accurately Representing Other People's Religions to Ourselves
   Edwin Zehner 49

Part II: Integrity in Personal Morality

4. Ethics and Accountability in the Mission Community
   William D. Taylor 75

5. Internet Pornography and Missions
   Steven G. Edlin 105

6. The Dynamic Relationship Between Ethical Compromise and Ministry Effectiveness
   Jon Freeman 127

Part III: Integrity in Institutional Practice

7. "Deleadered": Ethical Removal of Leaders in Mission Organizations
   David Broucek 155

8. Seven Stealth Ethical Issues Flying Under the Radar of Many Mission Agencies
   Gary R. Corwin 179

9. Organizational Justice: Perceptions of Being Fairly Treated
   David R. Dunaetz 197

Part IV: Integrity in the Field

10. Ethical Guidelines for Church Planters: A Suggested Proposal
    J. D. Payne 225

11. Some Ethical Considerations About Short-Term Mission
    Gorden R. Doss 243

12. Sustainable Missions: Ethical Principles for Holistic Practice in a Broken World
    John R. Wood and Michael P. Ferber 259

Part V: Integrity in Recruitment and Representation

13. Truth and Storytelling: It Is Important to Get the Facts Straight
    John McNeill 289

14. Ethical Issues in Missionary Filmmaking: Cinematic Tropes of Power and Perspective
    Curtis A. Wilkinson 309

15. The Missionary and the Camera: Developing an Ethic for Contemporary Missionary Photographers
   Gabriel B. Tait *321*

Part VI: Integrity Through Intentional Accountability

16. Holding Missionaries Accountable: A Proposed Code of Ethics for Missionaries Based Upon the Code of Ethics of the American Anthropological Association
   Douglas Hayward and Paul E. Langenwalter II *343*

Index *375*

Introduction

DWIGHT P. BAKER

The very word "ethics" carries with it an aura of a multiplicity of questions, of countervailing views, overlapping claims, uncertainty of footing, seductive attractions, and diverging paths. Ethical guidelines come into play—or are put forward—where clarity is attenuated and additional light may prove useful. If we knew the right course to take inherently and nonreflectively, by virtue of some inner touchstone of good intentions, ethical guidelines as instruction would not be necessary. If we unfailingly did the right that we do know, ethics as injunction—"Do to others as you would have them do to you" (Matt. 7:12 NRSV)—would be superfluous. But ethical formulations and ethical instruction in themselves are not sufficient. Viewed simply as adherence to rules, ethics falls short. Even apart from our human penchant for evading or overstepping rules, we simply cannot manufacture rules enough. Situations are too numerous and too various for us to be able to supply a rule tailored to each one. We need to be changed, to become new creatures, if our practice is to change fundamentally.

Seductive Attractions

Some issues are very clear, as clear as the horizontal versus vertical axes in Sawai Chinnawong's striking painting, *Joseph and Potiphar's Wife*, that graces the cover of this book. At the same time—because they find deep within us an ally that responds to the tug of their blandishments, because they involve our relationships, commitments, and obligations to other people, and because they bring to the fore our standing before God—the issues can be as complex as the interplay of triangles that gives this painting its core structure.

Potiphar's wife reclines on the couch, legs akimbo, breasts upthrust. A come hither smile lights her face as she tugs on Joseph's cloak, exuding allure, holding out promise of delectation.

But Joseph will have none of it. Upright and resolute, he pulls away, even as his jacket slips from his shoulders. Face set, he turns to the door and, with lengthening stride, exits the scene. What decisiveness, what manly resolve, what firmness of intent and purpose. Not for him the convenient liaison or fraudulent pleasure thrust in his path.

For someone acquainted with Chinnawong's artistry primarily through the book of his art *Christ on the Bangkok Road*,[1] the question arises: Are sanctity, creativity, and fecundity primarily curvaceous, replete with exfoliated contours? Is temptation—and its ultimately self-defeating sterility—sharp edged, angular, pointed? But then, is Joseph's jaw too firmly set? Can it be that his back is held too straight? Is he touched more deeply and in a spot more vulnerable than he dares to acknowledge, even to himself?

Evangelicals have possibly a reputation for being prissy about sex and awkward in coping with moral failure. But is the reputation wholly deserved? They may be reticent to speak about pornography, but evidently they are not reticent to consume it online. Steven Edlin states that U.S. evangelicals, including pastors and missionaries, track fairly closely with the general populace in percentage addicted to pornography on the Internet. More encouragingly, the works he cites show that evangelicals have produced or avail themselves of multiple resources for breaking addiction to Internet pornography. Further, in calling for restoration rather than condemnation, he gives evidence that evangelical mission agencies have moved beyond the stereotype of judgmentalism, "one strike and you're out," of years gone by, if indeed such was ever the case. Edlin shows that pornography is also a pastoral issue that is being addressed in intentional ways by evangelical mission agencies.

More than Personal Morality

If this volume lays to rest the canard that evangelicals have nothing to say about sexual temptation beyond the prohibition "Do not," it also undoes the suspicion that personal morality exhausts the scope of evangelicals' ethical interests and commitments.

Evangelical missionaries *are* concerned about personal morality, about sexual purity, and about financial integrity—and rightly so. Besides Edlin, see the chapters by William Taylor and Mary Lederleitner. Taylor's treatment of moral failure encompasses less easily demarcated issues of personal missional integrity as well as gross sexual faults. How do the missionary's personal life and private practice match up when compared with her or his public persona? From extensive international experience, Lederleitner develops a framework for dealing with the ever sensitive and frequently incendiary issue of financial accountability in international mission partnerships. But the areas of concern in this volume extend much wider than simple personal morality. One chapter enjoins missionaries to be careful to be informed and accurate when speaking or writing about the beliefs and values of other religious traditions (Edwin Zehner). Another lifts up care for creation as a missional concern, a topic heretofore given inadequate treatment by evangelicals (John Wood and Michael Ferber). Gorden Doss asks for integrity in the conduct of short-term missions and in representing them to supporting constituencies.

Several writers focus on institutional and organizational aspects of mission agencies. Gary Corwin is concerned with the way mission boards operate and with the organizational matters that occupy their attention—or slip past their view. David Broucek addresses the sensitive subject of "deleadering" someone, responsibly removing a mission leader from a position of authority. David Dunaetz examines perceptions within an organization that the leadership, and hence the organization, is or is not acting fairly and justly toward personnel.

Those who think that evangelicals see the world only in black and white and are wholly oblivious to stresses imposed by moral ambiguity in cross-cultural missionary service will find Jon Freeman's discussion enlightening.

Between the Times

In serving Jesus, we live a paradox. We yearn for, long for, look forward with anticipation to a new being, but we live and act as the persons of mixed motive and alloyed performance that in the present we now are. We long for a time when our inner person and our outer persona are in sync and harmonious. A time when who we are, what we want to do, and how we go about doing it are transparent to one another and in unreserved accord. A time when motive, method, and mission equally can bear scrutiny and be commended not just as blameless, but as worthy. A time when in union with Christ our Savior and as the overflow of a pure heart, under the guidance of his Spirit and in community with all the saints, our thoughts and impulses and our words and deeds redound wholly to the praise of God the Father.

We yearn for and strive toward that state, but we would be foolish—indeed, self-delusive—to think that we have reached it just yet. Our motivations are often murky or opaque, even to us. The darksome glass still intervenes and prevents us from seeing clearly. Self-interest and will to power skew our attitudes and our actions toward others, even at our noblest and even in mission.

As we push ahead between the times, what resources do we have? Certainly, as evangelicals we acknowledge the magisterial role of Scripture and the guiding and renewing presence of the Holy Spirit who illumines our minds and makes our understanding fruitful. We have the testimony of the community of faith, both the immediate faith community to which we belong and the larger community of faith, the church through the ages, as it has lived and testified to the hope that has sustained it. We have the example provided by servants of Jesus in all ages, showing through their lives in diverse and changing circumstances what faithfulness to the upward calling in Christ Jesus might look like. We cannot replicate what they achieved or the answers they reached. Our day and the challenges we face are different. But we can replicate the intention to be faithful that they exemplified.

We have, also, both in the local congregation and in the church as a whole an interpretive community. Rightly carried out, our reflections—whether in this book or elsewhere—are not meant for ourselves alone as individuals, nor are they intended merely for our clique or branch of the church. They may be specific to a certain function (e.g., photography, Gabriel Tait) or to a certain facet of missional activity (e.g., promotional publications, John McNeill, or video productions, Curt Wilkinson), but they are always offered, in Jesus' name, to the church as a whole. Therefore, they always have, do they not, an inherent impulse toward comprehensiveness. Not that they are always lengthy or elaborate or that they attempt to provide answers to all the issues of life and faith. Some are comprehensive in scope; many are limited; some are very narrowly focused and specific. Though a set of ethical guidelines may apply only to a single function or be drawn up for the guidance of a limited group of specialists (e.g., church planters, J. D. Payne), in the community, the body that is the church, the benefits of ethical conduct and faithful service accrue to all.

Finally, evangelical statements on ethics cannot live in a ghetto. They must be informed by interaction with the insights of the wider Christian church. For the profit of all Christ's followers, they must also, at least by implication, speak to every branch of the church. They must be open to and seek response and responsible critique from other traditions.

Community and Practice

The previous statements lead to two fundamental points. First, ethics is neither a solitary enterprise nor solipsistic. It is a group exercise, not an individual project. As noted by Fran Blomberg, an ethical vision is grounded in and grows from life in community, for community lies deeper and is more basic than individual being. Second, also noted by Blomberg, ethics is at its base something lived; it is a practice. Words and formulas are important, but forms and patterns of life that embody care, concern, rectitude, equity, justice, and accountability are fundamental. As we look forward to the new being and to the new—or renewed—community, ethical formulations are our servants, aides-de-memoire until upright behavior becomes habitual, reflexive, and simply the "natural" or normal thing to do.

Until that day, we wisely profit by instruction, guidelines, and codes worked out by informed and thoughtful missionary practitioners, whether they be limited to a particular facet of missional behavior or provide comprehensive codes for missionary practice. Building on the American Anthropological Association's Code of Ethics, Douglas Hayward and Paul Langenwalter offer a comprehensive code of missionary ethics. But, as they write, this code is a starting point, not an end point: "To be effective, these guidelines need to be discussed in depth by mission executives, taught in missionary training curricula, and further refined and perfected utilizing the shared wisdom, experience, and goals of a host of missionaries and mission agencies engaged in furthering the cause of the Gospel of Jesus Christ."

Ethical instruction is vital and necessary, but each of the authors included in this volume would attest that serving Jesus with integrity—though enriched and strengthened by ethical instruction and ethical reflection—runs richer and fuller than can be engaged if one stays merely on the conceptual level. What is in view in this statement involves thought, yes—long, deep, and hard mental effort; but more, it ushers us into the realm of practice, into a life and heart that are captivated by the character of Jesus Christ and energized by the concerns that exercised his heart. It has to do with a heart that resonates with the great themes—love justice, do mercy, defend the fatherless and widow, protect the alien, care for the sick, help the weak, speak up for the downtrodden and maligned—that echo and reecho through Scripture. And, it has to do with figuring out how to live lives of integrity and faithfulness to Jesus and to Scripture in our very different day and circumstances—which brings us back to guidelines, instructions, and injunctions as well as to encouragement to persevere in well doing.

Ethical reflection is never finished. It is an ongoing discussion. In reaching for the ultimate, we are always enmeshed in and struggle with the penultimate, where we need careful thought, consultation with peers and fellow followers of Jesus, and guidelines if we are to make our way reliably and with integrity. As products of mature ethical reflection, codes and guidelines are useful implements in instructors' hands, assisting us in becoming people "whose faculties have been trained by practice to distinguish good from evil" (Heb. 5:14 NRSV).

Invitation

Take up and read. Put into practice the wisdom to be found in the chapters that follow, and may your missionary practice be enriched. But also question, reflect, and respond. Not all questions have been answered; critical issues remain to be examined. Join the discussion of ways that together we can improve our mission policies and procedures and, most importantly, our missionary practices so as to insure that we are serving Jesus with integrity.

Note

1. Sawai Chinnawong, *Christ on the Bangkok Road: The Art of Sawai Chinnawong* (New Haven, Conn.: OMSC Publications, 2007).

Contributors

Dwight P. Baker is Associate Director of the Overseas Ministries Study Center, New Haven, Connecticut, with responsibility for oversight of the center's seminars and community life. He is also Associate Editor of the *International Bulletin of Missionary Research*, which is edited and published by OMSC. Previous to coming to OMSC in 2001, he served for seven years at the U.S. Center for World Mission, Pasadena, California, where he worked in curriculum development as director of the World Christian Foundations study program. He was a consulting editor and contributor to the *Encyclopedia of Mission and Missionaries* and a coeditor of *Speaking About What We Have Seen and Heard*. He earned an M.A. in English (Bemidji State University), an M.Div. (North Park Theological Seminary), and a Ph.D. in anthropology (Purdue University).

Fran Blomberg is a member of the pastoral staff at Scum of the Earth Church, a church primarily serving youth subcultures in urban Denver, Colorado. She is also Adjunct Faculty in Intercultural Ministries at Denver Seminary. Fran is pursuing a Ph.D. in contextualized missiology at the International Baptist Theological Seminary in Prague, Czech Republic, studying the effects of consumerism on young adults' ability to form and sustain Christian community.

David Broucek serves as International Ministries Director for South America Mission (SAM), Fort Mill, South Carolina. From 1978 to 1994 he served with TEAM in the Republic of Trinidad and Tobago in biblical education, church planting, and leadership development, followed by fourteen years in TEAM's home office, Wheaton, Illinois, coordinating and promoting the personal and professional development of missionaries. He holds a Ph.D. in intercultural studies from Trinity International University.

Gary R. Corwin currently serves as Missiologist with the International Office of Serving in Mission (SIM). He is also Associate Editor of the *Evangelical Missions Quarterly*, for which he writes a regular column. Since 1981 he has served in leadership training in Ghana, in various staff roles with SIM's International Administration, and since 1994 in broader mission leadership, editing, and writing roles. He is a graduate of The King's College (New York) and holds postgraduate degrees from East Stroudsburg University, Trinity Evangelical Divinity School, and Northwestern University.

Gorden R. Doss was born in the United States but grew up in Malawi. His service includes five years in the pastorate in the United States, sixteen years in pastoral education in Malawi, and eleven years teaching world mission at Andrews University. He has earned a D.Min. from Andrews University and a Ph.D. from Trinity Evangelical Divinity School. Cheryl, his wife, is a fellow missiologist who trains missionaries for the General Conference of Seventh-day Adventists.

David R. Dunaetz served as a church planting missionary in France for seventeen years with WorldVenture, starting two multicultural churches in the eastern suburbs of Paris. He is currently an Instructor of Psychology and Adjunct Professor of Management at Azusa Pacific University. His field of research is conflict resolution in voluntary organizations, such as churches and missions.

Steve Edlin is the Counseling Office Director for TEAM, overseeing their Global Member Care Team. He is licensed as a counselor in Illinois and California. In addition to TEAM he has served with Campus Crusade and Asian Access, including seven years in London, England, training missionaries. He teaches at Moody Graduate School as an Adjunct Faculty and is a member of the Christian Association for Psychological Studies and the American Association of Christian Counselors.

Michael P. Ferber is Assistant Professor of Geography and Director of the Environmental Studies program at The King's University College in Edmonton, Alberta. Michael has served as development director of World Vision Appalachia, adjunct professor at Regent University, and instructor of urban geography and urban and regional planning at West Virginia University. He received an M.Div. from Asbury Theological Seminary in 2001, an M.A. in education from West Virginia University in 2003, and a Ph.D. in geography from West Virginia University in 2010.

Jon Freeman is an ordained minister, husband, and father of three who currently serves as a missionary with TEAM. He has worked with churches, pastors, and missionaries in over twenty countries, primarily in the area of leadership development and church planting. Prior to joining TEAM, he served for fourteen years as a minister in the United States in the areas of youth, missions, and church planting. He has a Th.M. from Dallas Theological Seminary.

Douglas Hayward is Associate Dean and Professor of Anthropology and Intercultural Studies in the Cook School of Intercultural Studies at Biola University, La Mirada, California, where he has taught for over twenty years. Before coming to Biola he served for twenty years with CrossWorld as a missionary in West Papua (formerly Irian Jaya). There he worked as a church planter and discipler among the Western Dani. He has published three books on the Dani, including *Vernacular Christianity Among the Mulia Dani: An Ethnography of Religious Belief Among the Western Dani of Irian Jaya, Indonesia* (Univ. Press of America, 1997), as well as several book chapters and journal articles. He is a graduate of Moody Bible Institute (certificate), Westmont College (B.A), School of Intercultural Studies at Fuller Theological Seminary (M.A.), and University of California at Santa Barbara (Ph.D. in anthropology).

Paul Langenwalter II, Assistant Professor of Archaeology and Anthropology at Biola University, specializes in the archaeology of California and the American West. His research focuses on human adaptations, ethnicity, animal use, and culture change. As a professional archaeologist, he works with the Native American community, project archaeologists, governmental agencies, and landowners to relocate cemeteries and culturally sensitive features threatened with destruction, while addressing the legal, ethical, and moral issues attendant to the process.

Mary Lederleitner is a Cross-Cultural Consultant for Wycliffe International and a Ph.D. student at Trinity Evangelical Divinity School. She has a master's degree in intercultural studies from Wheaton College, where she occasionally serves as an Adjunct Professor. She is the author of *Cross-Cultural Partnerships: Navigating the Complexities of Money and Mission* (InterVarsity Press, 2010). Prior to entering missions she worked for the Internal Revenue Service as a certified public accountant.

John (Jack) McNeill is Professor of Anthropology and Intercultural Studies at Providence College, Otterburne, Manitoba, where he has been teaching for the past ten years. During that time he has continued his previous involvement in education projects in a variety of settings in the former Soviet region. With his wife Christel he is also very busy with their four daughters and their families, including nine grandchildren.

J. D. Payne is a national missionary with the North American Mission Board and an Associate Professor of Church Planting and Evangelism at Southern Baptist Theological Seminary, Louisville, Kentucky. He is the author of *Missional House Churches: Reaching Our Communities with the Gospel, The Barnabas Factors: Eight Essential Practices of Church Planting Team Members, Discovering Church Planting: The Whats, Whys, and Hows of Global Church Planting,* and *Evangelism: A Biblical Response to Today's Questions.* He is also the founder of the Web-based resource www.northamericanmissions.org.

Gabriel B. Tait is a Ph.D. student in the Intercultural Studies program of the E. Stanley Jones School of World Missions at Asbury Theological Seminary, Wilmore, Kentucky. His research focuses on the impact of photography in cross-cultural missions as well as in constructing and representing cultural identities. He earned the M.A. in Intercultural Studies at Asbury Theological Seminary and the B.A. in Communication with an emphasis on photojournalism at Slippery Rock University of Pennsylvania.

William D. Taylor, author and editor of many publications on mission, lived in Latin America for thirty years. A graduate of Moody Bible Institute and the University of North Texas, he also has a Th.M. in theology from Dallas Theological Seminary and a Ph.D. in Latin American studies from the University of Texas, Austin. He served on the faculty of the Seminario Teológico Centroamericano in Guatemala for seventeen years and then taught for two years at Trinity Evangelical Divinity School. In 1986 he joined the staff of World Evangelical Alliance, working until 2006 as executive director of its Mission Commission. He now serves WEA as global ambassador and the MC as senior mentor.

Curt Wilkinson is Associate Professor of Communication at Moody Bible Institute in Chicago, where he has been teaching filmmaking, video production, and photography for the past twelve years. Previously he served as a missionary in Latin America working in the area of media development and video production. He is a Ph.D. candidate at the University of Exeter, researching participatory filmmaking strategies.

John R. Wood is Professor of Biology and Environmental Studies at The King's University College, Toronto, and Academic Dean for The Au Sable Institute of Environmental Studies. He is a Fellow in the American Scientific Affiliation. After graduating from North Park University he worked for Job Therapy, Inc., a prison ministry then in Seattle, Washington. His Ph.D. is from the University of California Berkeley, in aquatic ecology and entomology. John's research is on urban ecology, entomophagy (food insects), and sustainability.

Edwin Zehner is a graduate of Houghton College and holds a Ph.D. in anthropology from Cornell University. He has been writing on anthropological and missiological topics for several years, drawing on fieldwork in Thailand, Yemen, and the United States. At the time of writing he was a Visiting Fellow in the Southeast Asia Program at Cornell University and Visiting Teaching Fellow for Southeast Asian Studies at St. Lawrence University.

Part I:

Integrity in Message, Finances, and Relationships

1

Reconstructing an Ethic of Evangelism for Twenty-First-Century Congregations

FRAN BLOMBERG

Significant shifts in worldview are characteristic of the day in which we live. They represent unimagined opportunities for reflecting anew on the ethical underpinnings of evangelism.

The Problem: The Modern Loss of Ethics

In the twenty-first century, evangelicals are heady about evangelistic opportunities, yet impoverished regarding our motivations and presuppositions for this activity. We have reduced ethics to justification of decisions within a pre-existing system and give little heed to analyzing the system itself. As we construct models of mission, we are driven to advance, grow, and "seize the moment"—a drive admirable in its potential to transform lives, but lamentable in its unthinking proclivity for some of the less biblical qualities of our culture.

In this chapter I focus on the ethics underlying the performance of evangelism, particularly within today's U.S. context. By ethics I mean *the virtuous character and lived convictions of a community that give the community its identity, give continuity to its story, and on these bases guide its morality and practices.* Ethics is not simply what we *do* after we decide what we know; ethics is the dynamic *process* of discerning and then practicing what the Holy Spirit teaches the Christian community. Ethics navigates conditions of uncertainty and choice. Therefore our practice of ethics begins with our manner of understanding and learning.[1]

Modernity told us that we could discover meaning with absolute certainty; postmodernity exploded this notion with its own (certain!) claims of the relativity and incommensurability of worldviews. Modernity constructed systems; postmodernity deconstructed them. I propose that we welcome the opportunity to disencumber our faith and practices by casting off linkage to either modern or postmodern constructs for thought.[2] We will then be able to reconstruct our beliefs, practices, and institutions with greater humility and perspicuity.

Before beginning such reconstruction, let me locate our current ethical stance regarding evangelism. Beginning in the eighteenth century as the role of Christianity in culture came under scrutiny, Christians scrambled to one of four tenuous positions to maintain a sense of worth in modernity:

First, biblical criticism and apologetics strove to show concord with scientific reasoning and to prove the intellectual respectability of Christianity. As important as these studies have been, critical realism and emerging global theologies demand the exercise of humility in conclusions put forward.[3]

Second, the church capitulated and accepted the role of chaplain to society.[4] Her usefulness depended on her willingness to support the prevailing values of the dominant culture. In such a role, the prophetic voice of the church was stifled, and an evangelistic call to faith "deteriorated into a technique for maintaining Christian America."[5]

A third perspective allowed that Christianity did not have scientific rationale, but could remain a useful "vendor of religious goods and services"[6] by offering society a discourse for expressing human longing and intuitive morality. Such emotivism merely expressed preference or feeling, with no rational grounds for making judgments.[7] The assumed incomparability of worldviews meant that debate became an exercise in rhetorical persuasion and coercive argumentation, adversely affecting the ethics of evangelism.

Fourth, by accepting modernity's lie that "freedom means autonomy," the church supposedly liberated people from restrictive communal bonds and antiquated traditions. Salvation became a private affair with Jesus accepted as personal Savior, a "voluntaristic soteriology"[8] in which each one was sole agent of self-actualization. As communal accountability and support waned, people were forced to find their own destiny in terrifying isolation.

Evangelism done within these distortions became an embarrassing appendage to the church rather than an integral part of its identity and nature. Without a concern to challenge modernity's deepest values—consumerism and individualism—such "free-market evangelism"[9] has had adverse effects on the credibility and integrity of evangelism.

Such evangelism promotes a spiritual consumerism of "whatever works" for the individual. One constructs a pastiche of

Christianity based on convenience and self-gain as much as conviction and self-donation.[10] Anticipated obsolescence and a constant search for new experiences subvert lasting commitment to Christ and his community. Rather than finding foundational security from being in Christ, the spiritual consumer is left with a fragmented life tenuously held together by "one accident of choosing after another."[11]

A focus on meeting felt needs misses the power of the Gospel to *change* felt needs. Salvation and participation in the community of believers should alter the meaning of people's experiences as they have understood them and should introduce new ways of responding to these situations.[12] Simply meeting felt needs carries no guarantee that sin will be addressed and militates against abiding satisfaction in one's relationship with a sovereign and loving God.

Evangelism reduced to a program rather than being integral to the nature of the church is highly prone to becoming an instrument merely for increasing the numbers in the congregation regardless of the means by which such "converts" are gained or the quality of faith they attain. Ethics demands that the methods of evangelism must be consistent with the character and methods of Christ, and the proper goal of evangelism is faithful witness, not a quantifiable number of converts or church members.

Evangelistic techniques can be exploitative, self-serving for the evangelist, and insensitive to human dignity—improperly imitating unscrupulous power structures. "If we are aggressive, manipulative, abusive, underhanded, lacking in integrity . . . confrontational, insensitive, distorting and provocative in our witness, then we are offensive."[13] Improperly motivated or practiced evangelism can in fact be sin.

The Proposal: Reconstructing an Ethic of Evangelism

To repeat, ethics is *the virtuous character and lived convictions of a community that give the community its identity, give continuity to its story, and on these bases guide its morality and practices.* Much, including foundational principles, is embedded in this definition.

From the outset, ethical evangelism must be construed as a practice and not reduced merely to an assemblage of discrete activities. Practices are complex, coherent, comprehensive, and corporate performances with "rewards" internal to the very doing of the practice, apart from any external benefit that might accrue. Evangelism as a practice has as its internal reward faithfulness to God, apart from the external benefit of converts, church growth, or other quantifiable markers. Ethical evangelism will call for conversion but never measure its success by more than faithfulness in witness. Evangelism as a practice recognizes that Christians are inherently *martyria* (witnesses) prior to engaging in any specific evangelistic task. As representative of God's kingdom the church body is a corporate witness to a watching world. The life and example of such a community are themselves robust arguments for the truth of Christianity.

Christians live as a convictional community in which cognition, affect, and volition combine with integrity.[14] Ways of doing must be consistent with the claimed outcomes of the actions; ways of being must be consistent with the claimed nature of the community. Under this rubric, holism in evangelism does not mean a democratically proportioned combination of proclamation and social action; it means a seamless meld of character and action that unabashedly and habitually shapes the community in Christlikeness.

Faithful evangelism points toward the kingdom of God, characterized by "righteousness, peace and joy in the Holy Spirit" (Rom. 14:17 TNIV). Living toward justice, righteousness, and *shalom* requires rightly fulfilling the obligations of relationships[15] and precludes any disingenuous attempt to make converts by means or methods not characteristic of God.

The convictional community must live virtuously, thirsting for integrity. Developing virtue requires a community of support and approbation; a Christian community without virtue may quickly degenerate into a self-justifying and self-sustaining institution without transformational ability.

Evangelism as a Practice

How does a virtuous convictional community ethically practice evangelism? Thinking of evangelism as a practice invites a number of observations.

Evangelism as invitation. Sarah Wenger Shenk asks, "How should we shape the Anabaptist village so it becomes an inviting home for those who wander homeless through the dead-end streets of post-modernity?"[16] Her question is significant for all Christian traditions. Evangelism can be measured by the community's proactive preparation to receive the wanderer, the outcast, and the obstinate. If the invitation is genuine, the faith community will have to be quite intentional in making room for those who respond, whose presence may well provoke challenges and changes in the community itself. Evangelism is successful when the invitation is issued to come and see how truth is lived out in the community of faith.

Evangelism as witnesses, not salespersons. The logic of being *martyria* is core to our identity as Christians. The faithful community, able to stand in contrast to the world and offer a viable way of living, is the most potent witness. Relationship, rather than "closing the deal," reflects the ongoing work of God in our lives and therefore should be the basis of our outreach in his name. Brad Cecil of Axxess Church in Texas puts it this way: "We have decided to measure success by other means, such as, how long do relationships last? Are members of the community at peace with one another? Are relationships reconciled?"[17] Christianity does not need to prove its intellectual superiority or its ultimate usefulness to society; it proves itself as it is lived authentically in the community of the church.

Evangelism as peaceful means toward peaceful ends. Isaiah declares the beauty of the one who brings good news and proclaims peace (Isa. 52:7). It is imperative, if we claim our goal is reconciliation of people to God, that we employ methods of reconciliation like those God himself uses. "The true people of God, the true family of Jesus, is not allowed to impose anything through force— *neither internally nor externally.*"[18] A misguided sense of urgency encourages us to use any means possible to compel people into the kingdom, but faithfulness to God's character requires us to leave open the door for rejection much as he does. Pacifism in evangelism is not apathetic, but intentionally chooses forbearance and hope over the allure of efficiency and notable external results.[19] As long as evangelism is thought to have conversion as its goal, urgent salesmanship will engender coercive rhetoric. Slick performance strategies will compete with the performances of the world. Faith will remain domesticated by the values of modern marketing culture.

Evangelism as offering a countercultural alternative. Ethical evangelism must offer an alternative to the society's status quo and its dominant idolatries. In the United States today evangelism must stand against individualism and consumerism, and certainly cannot employ these idolatries in its methodology. Ethical outreach offers an invitation to the unwanted to become part of a community, not limited to a "personal relationship with Jesus." Countercultural evangelism does not compete with the resources or productions of the world, rather, it boasts in the cross and the cruciform sacrifice of the community on behalf of outsiders. Such evangelism makes its mark by "such deviant practices as sharing bread with the poor, loving enemies, refusing violence, forgiving sins and telling the truth."[20]

Evangelism that offers the kingdom cannot do so by allowing people to remain friends with the world (James 4:4). In the modern cult of narcissism "lies the root of all other forms of idolatry: we deify our own capacities, and therefore make gods of ourselves and our choices."[21] Those genuinely ready to consider commitment to Christ must be encouraged to disavow allegiances to the world, to willingly limit choices to those that set them apart in holiness.

Evangelism as embracing patience as resistance and suffering as triumph. Patience is a powerful form of resistance that declares that exploitation and guile are unworthy means for demonstrating the grace and power of God. Patience in evangelism declares that the *imago Dei* in each person imparts dignity worthy of respect and that God woos by reconciliation and peace. How hard it is for those of us who possess resources, strength, and acumen to submit to patient witness rather than to manipulate the situation to ensure "winning" the lost on our terms. To be patient in evangelism chafes. Yet ethical evangelism cannot "prey on weakness, nor does it victimize those in need by trading its help for their 'conversions.' It does not ask for sacrifice from those who have already been sacrificed by the world."[22] It is for the evangelist to suffer for the lost, not for the potential convert to become useful to the evangelist.

Evangelism as worship and proclamation. "Seeker-sensitive," safe worship is about far more than a well-prepared bulletin explaining the service; it must be a sanctuary where the wounds of hurting people are recognized and regarded with gentleness. In more private situations, these wounds can be exposed, their sources uncovered, and their deadliness addressed. Worship is an invitation to a costly healing and visible proof that healing has occurred in the lives of others who have braved the debridement of their wounds. The proclamation of the Gospel, the Good News, is altogether necessary as an explanation of, but never as a replacement for, the embodied witness of a faithful community living out its convictions in Christlikeness.

Words are powerful. We evangelicals must bear in mind that our ease while listening to people speak with intense conviction, our quick defense of truth, and our swaggering confidence in the face of multiple lifestyle and faith options do not typify society at large. Our cohabiters in this culture are more comfortable with open-ended dialogue, conversation, and questions that invite reflection without forcing answers. We must acknowledge how overbearing we can seem to those who are not accustomed to our methods of engagement, especially those who have been raised in a postmodern milieu where all opinion counts equally, regardless of age, expertise, or coherence.

Evangelism as rightly remembering the story. Reconstructing an ethic of evangelism in no way requires selling short the message of the Gospel; rather, insisting that the Gospel be wholly lived as well as wholly proclaimed increases the rigor of outreach. Our haste to promote and reinvent the church comes with "a peculiar form of amnesia in which the witness of Scripture, Christian tradition and the practices of the church itself are forgotten."[23] Therefore, an important first step in recapturing holism in evangelism is remembering.[24] Remember by reaching back before the false dichotomies of modernity overtook us, before the empires of Christendom delineated all aspects of faith. Remember when the good news included the unlikely and the unwanted—the leper, the Moabitess, the aliens who fled Egypt with God's newly formed people. Remember that we too were once "separate from Christ, excluded from citizenship in Israel and foreigners to the covenants of the promise, without hope and without God in the world" (Eph. 2:12 TNIV). Remember that we are participants in a grand metanarrative of God's grace. Strive to remember the whole story, not selected bits compatible with the dominant culture.

Remember that we are sent in peace, as the Father sent the Son (John 20:19). We easily remember Jesus' "go and make disciples" (Matt. 28:19 TNIV); he also commanded holistic evangelism with "go and do likewise" (Luke 10:37 TNIV).[25] The first often allows us control as we teach others to be like us. The second could be demeaning and humbling as we stoop to embrace the ill, the unsightly, and the wounded. In a culture addicted to "new and improved," remembering seems an antiquated and even wasteful experience, easily confused with nostalgia. Remembering with boldness requires virtues and disciplined practices such as hope, faith, and humility.

Evangelism as abundant inclusion. Ours is an age of increasing isolation and loneliness. We find people in porous relationships, frenetically seeking, physically and mentally nomadic, unwilling to commit to something good for fear of missing an even better opportunity. Raised without trust or a sense of permanence, young adults especially look for a trustworthy link to community and are more likely to participate in church when a friend sensitively mediates the bond. Relational connections precede any interest in information. Thomas Reynolds expresses it this way: "The basic question of human existence, then, is whether there is welcome at the heart of things. Will I be received and embraced? Is there a voice behind all other voices that says, 'You are precious and I will be there for you'? Our heart's deepest impulse hankers after connection with a trustworthy creation—a purposeful macro-context that bathes our lives in meaning and value, thus cultivating a sense of being at home."[26]

As Jesus fed the multitudes, the Eucharist teaches us to set the table for many. The kingdom of *shalom* is one of abundant inclusion in which the provision of grace never runs short. *Shalom* is God's aim and his means. It is offered to the world through his socially embodied, generously welcoming people.

The body of Christ must always include the weak, ill, and broken. Acceptance of weak members does not weaken the body; in dependence on Christ the church is strengthened through its selflessness and willingness to be a vessel of grace to the needy. If the church community, however, tries to construct a pristine hothouse environment for itself, it weakens its ability to exist in a world in which disease is pervasive. We are designed to combat illness, not to live in a bubble.

Evangelism as sharpened, not threatened, by pluralism. In the twenty-first century, U.S. Christianity has been displaced from a central position in society. We have much to learn from Christians of other locales and times for whom a position at the margins is a familiar habitat. In such a mixed environment, convictions are honed as adherents of other religions (and of no religion) speak with and challenge the faithful. Dialogue first and foremost accepts the responsibility of being sharpened by the other religion and only secondarily takes up the challenge of peacefully demonstrating to the other tradition that it is insufficient in its own claims. The severity of differences or opposition does not negate the fact that Christianity cannot be imposed. The task is to be faithful in character, words, and actions; obedience is its own internal reward.

Evangelism as welcome to the family. In offering a home, ethical evangelism must offer a family. As much as fragmentation and alienation characterize today's pilgrims, the opportunity to convert is wholly unsatisfactory if it is only an offer of cleansing *from* the guilt of sin; conversion *to* kingdom community and reconciled relationships with God and others is essential to overcome shame. Salvation "is a making whole, a healing of that which sunders us from God, from one another and from the created world. The idea of a salvation that is a completed experience for each of us privately, apart from the consummation of all things, is a monstrous contradiction in terms."[27]

We are children made human in relation with others. We need to share the story; we need to find our place in God's metanarrative of redemption. "Deprive children of stories and you leave them unscripted, anxious stutterers in their actions as in their words."[28] In this sense the third-century statement of Cyprian of

Carthage remains true—*extra ecclesiam nulla salus*—there is no salvation outside the church. But the church that offers salvation is not an institution requiring adherence to a prescribed set of doctrines or demanding a standard of conformity to behaviors; it is the Body of Christ itself, embodied in local communities which mediate the message and demonstrate the reality of the present reign of God.

Evangelism as belonging before believing. In state churches in Europe, or in parish-structured denominations in America, one may officially belong whether or not one believes or attends. In "country club" churches, one may belong without ever being confronted with a challenge to believe. In churches with bounded sets, believing is prerequisite to belonging, not just in the sense of official membership, but also in the unwritten code of the church. Centered set churches offer porous boundaries which encourage seekers to enter, participate, experience, and choose increasing levels of commitment based on genuine belief.[29] In America, among accusations of antiquated standards of morality, mythical beliefs, hypocrisy, and authoritarianism, such opportunity to "come and see" gains import. Simply put, "one cannot understand the truth of Christianity as an outside observer. One needs first to experience the embodied truth in community."[30]

The witness of the body must be whole, penetrating, and available to the seeker. In community we are seen to share generously, live simply, forgive, and show hospitality and gratitude. We are seen as free from power struggles, greed, aggression, self-interest, and fear. The welcome of the community as the welcome of Christ attracts and provokes questions that can lead to belief.

Evangelism as the continuing conversion of the evangelist. For too long both mission and evangelism have been unidirectional activities in which transformation occurs only in the recipient of the message, while the communicator remains inviolable in his or her exactitude. The reality of reciprocal change has been provocatively called the need for continual conversion.[31] Hauerwas refers to the need to continually "transvalue" our past and repent, not because we remain morally deficient, but because God is infinitely big and our own spiritual development requires us to continually receive grace for past failures.[32] These failures can well include transgressions made in evangelism. As our claims are scrutinized and our lives examined for integrity with our message, *we* are transformed in humility, patience, conviction, and thirst for even greater Christlikeness. We suffer with Christ in concern for those who are outside of relationship with God.[33] We cannot remain unchanged; the practice of truth and the performance of evangelism change us individually and change our communities as God's grace includes new participants in his grand story.

The Practice: The Example of Scum of the Earth Church, Denver, Colorado

A concrete example of a church striving toward new levels of integrity in the practice of evangelism is found at Scum of the Earth Church in Denver, Colorado, a community in which I am active and that has become my church home.

Scum of the Earth Church (SOTEC) began in 2000 as the outgrowth of a Bible study serving youth subcultures in Denver.[34] SOTEC serves an eclectic congregation of around 300 college students, young adults, homeless persons, artists, musicians, victims of abuse, addicts, mature Christians, new believers, and skeptics. Colloquially describing itself as "a church for the right-brained and left out," SOTEC draws its name from 1 Corinthians 4:11–13 (TNIV): "To this very hour we go hungry and thirsty, we are in rags, we are brutally treated, we are homeless. We work hard with our own hands. When we are cursed, we bless; when we are persecuted, we endure it; when we are slandered, we answer kindly. We have become the scum of the earth, the garbage of the world."

SOTEC happily defies description as postmodern, emerging, or seeker-sensitive, and was labeled "stylistically nouveau, without any genuine theological transformation" by one disappointed writer on the emergent church.[35] The description pleased SOTEC's firmly evangelical leadership, though had Bader-Saye dug deeper into SOTEC's practices, he would have noticed significant differences from conventional middle-class American evangelical Christian culture.

SOTEC cannot pretend to be an exemplary church, able to boast of runaway success in winning the lost and turning out mature, reproducing Christians. Relationships are fragile; past abuse (including ecclesial abuse) makes trust very difficult; skepticism runs high; the struggles of the mentally ill, addicted, and homeless are ongoing; the youth population is mobile. SOTEC serves a congregation of persons with the odds for "success" largely stacked against them. Many in the congregation are giving Christianity its first—or its last—chance.

Practicing Ethical Evangelism

How then do the principles of ethical evangelism as outlined above play out in a congregation such as SOTEC? The practices of ethical evangelism are an organic bundle, a complex whole. The "elements" that follow are the outworking of what we, by the power of the Spirit, as a committed community in fact seek to be and do.

The church as social strategy. In the milieu of the inner city, SOTEC does not simply offer programs to help people; we strive to be a community that demonstrates a holistic and viable alternative lifestyle, following the claim that "the church doesn't have a social strategy, it *is* a social strategy."[36] Our goal is not to change the world; it is to offer community in contrast to the world that has disenfranchised and deceived so many in the congregation. Our contribution is simply being the church, a visible community with practices and integrity that well represent the King and his reign. Christ is central, the authority of Scripture is upheld, and truth is embodied in lives as well as in words.

Care for the vulnerable. By virtue of lifestyle and socioeconomic status, many at SOTEC are accustomed to being maltreated by "the man" and are particularly suspect of any attempt to impose control on their lives. Pressure to "live up to expectations" can seem to be an aggressive encroachment intended to make people more palatable to middle class society.[37] Evangelism must not be used as a method of foisting lifestyle changes that are not necessitated by the biblical narrative.

The poor experience great frustration at being told to change factors in their lives for which their resources are minimal. The middle class can afford (literally) to reserve church for conviviality and friendship; for the hard living, the family of God needs to be the family of protection and provision. Evangelism that does not offer basic respect and is not accompanied by meeting essential needs is disregarded. SOTEC's weekly dinner is open to all without required attendance at the worship service. Dinner is eaten *with* the homeless, not served *to* them. Over 20 percent of SOTEC's meager budget is returned to benevolence monthly.

While society's "cult of normalcy" values independence, productivity, and soundness of mind and body,[38] SOTEC strives to welcome the needy, marginal, and physically and mentally ill. There is no time limit placed on a person's "getting straightened out"; the church remains constantly vulnerable to the neediness of its family. Lives are messy and love is costly, not just in terms of finances, but also in terms of control and orderliness. Such "holy disruption" could easily be averted if the goal were to manage the ninety-nine,[39] but finding the one lost sheep frequently calls for great risk.

Gentle mutuality is particularly important for victims of abuse. Rather than a pastoral will-to-power, the attitude of a suffering servant who will not break a bruised reed is essential (Matt. 12:19–21). A tangible, humble submission that honors the dignity of the defenseless is a far more vital witness than any forcefully or hastily imposed words.

Radical hospitality. Welcome to the community does not depend on an economy of exchange. Believer and non-believer participate deeply in life together, undergirded by a conviction that holiness is contagious and that locale and event can be redeemed by the presence of the person of faith.[40] Outreach at SOTEC occurs at vegan community dinners, our bike shop, jazz clubs, our art gallery, Bible studies, bars, on the streets, and in homes. Not only are individuals welcomed, but their community and culture, too, are honored. Neither believing nor behaving is prerequisite to belonging. Inclusion itself is healing. Reading the Bible together is not an exercise in the educated instructing the uneducated, but an occasion for mutual accountability in interpretation. With raw vocabulary and great profundity, many of the hard living offer lessons in providence, grace, and the mystery of God's dealings with humanity that rival the lessons of trained theologians.

Importantly, those who lapse in lifestyle or who encounter severe doubts are held fast in community. There is no condemnation for questioning, and honest dialogue sets the boundaries for those whose lifestyle choices are inconsistent with biblical norms. "Don't lose her. The world will never tell her to change. Whatever it takes, hang on to her" is the admonition I have been given by our senior pastor on more than one unfortunate occasion. The pain of "hanging on" can be tremendous—and cruciform.

Intentional chaos. SOTEC's obvious delinquency in planning and its distain for performance and polished excellence fit its witness well. Dinner is served on mismatched plates, posters are handmade, and technology is kept simple. "Deliberate" imperfection mimics street capacities for innovation, on-the-fly living, and crisis orientation. It necessitates interdependence, lavish sharing, and respect that does not demand performance, and it fosters living and ministering generously on a shoestring. Such attitudes incarnate the reality of suffering in an unpredictable world and exemplify perseverance rather than an insistence that things get fixed quickly. A struggling leader can say, "Follow me as I follow Christ," and the connection is credible and authentic.

Evangelism, preaching, and Eucharist. Direct evangelism may not have primacy but always has ultimacy in the ministries of SOTEC. All ministries have evangelistic intent, and many eventually have verbal witness. Staff are not expected to increase church numbers but to faithfully evangelize and encourage discipleship "wherever." Freedom is offered for those who come to explore different churches and Christian traditions. SOTEC has begun a smaller, more participatory and liturgical morning service in an effort to extend its reach, particularly to young families. The group has no illusion that the culture of the larger evening service is one that would appeal to all.

The language used in preaching at SOTEC is raw. As a "community of honest sadness,"[41] we view sorrow and melancholy not as flaws in character but as indications of the struggle to live with integrity in a flawed world. With candor we name our sins and the sins committed against us. Greed, exploitation, gossip, lust, drunkenness, pornography, laziness, sleeping around, substance abuse, and violence are called out as wrongs that have both overt and hidden costs to the community. The pastoral task in preaching is to announce that the horror of sin is far outweighed by the reality of healing and salvation. Preaching goes on to provide a new and hopeful vocabulary and an occasion to forgive sin and reconcile from shame.

Informal, conversational "confession" gives opportunity for assessing one's life and for commitment to a Lord far more powerful than one's transgressors or transgressions. When such a confession is heard, the community "makes the other's story part of his or her own story, and by owning it destroys its power to divide forgiver and forgiven. In this sense, to forgive is truly to love one's offending neighbor *as oneself.*"[42] Taking the sinner's story into the community's story grants him or her reconciliation, and commits the church to caring for and restoring the sinner holistically to health.

At SOTEC, the logic of the Eucharist is that of abundant generosity, offered freely to all who "follow Jesus and wish to participate." The sin of overlooking the poor as the primary disqualification from the Lord's Supper (1 Cor. 11: 21) is taken most seriously at SOTEC. An open invitation to the family table can awaken a greater desire to know the Father. The Eucharist, though meaningful in different ways, is a ritual familiar to many, but as the very diverse congregation is served with identical words of consecration, a unity is felt that bears witness to the sacrifice of Christ for all humanity, all unworthy.

Taking time and more time. With suspicion of institutions and authority, the false bravado of independence, and the deep woundedness of past fractured relationships, the congregation at SOTEC is unlikely to respond to heavy-handed persuasion and urgent appeals for immediate change. Ethical evangelism must move cautiously at the pace of the enquirer, with purpose, but without prerequisites, conditions, or deadlines. A biblical pattern of conversion must slowly dislodge and replace deeply ingrained worldviews of agnosticism, nihilism, and individualism. Transformation takes time, and SOTEC is reluctant to laud a decision prematurely before it has shown itself to be lived out in discipleship, however haltingly that growth may occur.

The irruption of the kingdom now is good news, unheard in a world that quickly discards the broken. We practice and teach eschatological hope and patience that repudiates "instant gratification," the drug of choice in our consumer culture. We realize that we will be hustled by those wanting quick access to benevolence or, sadder yet, by those whose hard lives have convinced them that love is earned by certain behaviors. We renounce any activity or attitude on our part that would reinforce such a lie, and will risk being used or rejected rather than adopt tactics of subtle aggression. We practice "peaceful means toward peaceful ends."

The virtues of an ethical evangelist. Again it must be stated that we at SOTEC struggle for godliness and fall short of our own ideals daily. Yet we believe that "what is significant about us morally is not what we do or do not do, but *how* we do what we do."[43] We emphasize virtues that are not admired by the world and often contradict recommendations for "successful" ministry. *Presence* is simply showing up without an agenda; it is listening and hanging out to show interest and esteem for another.[44] *Courage* is required for truth-telling and for bearing the outcome of its telling. The person spoken to may disagree, attack verbally, reject, or worse. *Patience* refuses to preempt the work of the Spirit; one leader prays, "Lord, don't let him ask what I think until he's ready to hear what you think." *Humility* bears the hustling, the deception, and the sense of failure when time and again our witness is rejected. *Surrender* is a state of constant readiness before God, a willingness to release self-interest to the extent of the cross, welcoming the fact that "God rarely uses a man greatly until he hurts a man deeply."[45] All genuine forms of *nonviolence* require extraordinary training; only those with well-developed internal self-control can risk denying themselves the external protection of verbal or physical aggression or intimidation.

Conclusion

Put in contemporary urban terms: do not pimp the church. Do not reduce evangelism to hasty, disconnected activities apart from commitment to holistic relationship and care. Do not let expediency trump virtue. Do not let the bride of Christ be flaunted as an appealing option requiring no essential transformation of character. She is not an option that simply accommodates our great idolatries of individual, consumer self-interest.

Ethics is not an add-on consideration after we get our ministry in order; it is *how* we get our ministry in order. Ethical evangelism is set in the narrative of God's ongoing redemption of his creation and is practiced in virtuous consistency with his character and the qualities of his kingdom of righteousness, peace, and joy in the Holy Spirit.

Questions for Discussion

1. Do you agree with the author's statement that "Evangelism done within [the distortions of modernity] became an embarrassing appendage to the church rather than an integral part of its identity and nature" and that a return to honesty and integrity is needed today?
2. Should the author's critique of the church be extended, beyond simply evangelism, to the entire process of building community as believers?
3. How might the author's recommendations be extended so as to instill new perceptions and values among students on college campuses, particularly in Christian schools and seminaries where the next generation of church leaders are being formed?
4. What are the dangers of cultural faddism? Is the case study around which this chapter is built a faithful representation of the transformative power of the Gospel? Why or why not?

Notes

1. Sarah Wenger Shenk, "Practicing Truth as a Global Community," in *Practicing Truth: Confident Witness in Our Pluralistic World*, ed. David W. Shenk and Linford Stutzman (Scottsdale, Pa.: Herald Press, 1999), 225.

2. John Caputo, *What Would Jesus Deconstruct: The Good News of Postmodernity for the Church* (Grand Rapids: Baker, 2007).
3. Paul Hiebert, *Missiological Implications of Epistemological Shifts: Affirming Truth in a Modern/Postmodern World* (Harrisburg, Pa.: Trinity Press International, 1999), offers insightful comment on contemporary ways of knowing.
4. Shane Hipps and Brian McLaren, *The Hidden Power of Electronic Culture: How Media Shapes Faith, the Gospel, and Church* (Grand Rapids: Zondervan, 2006), 153.
5. David J. Bosch, *Transforming Mission: Paradigm Shifts in Theology of Mission* (Maryknoll, N.Y.: Orbis Books, 1991), 282.
6. Darrell Guder, *Missional Church: A Vision for the Sending of the Church in North America* (Grand Rapids: Eerdmans, 1998), 84.
7. Alasdair MacIntyre, *After Virtue: A Study in Moral Theory*, 3rd ed. (Notre Dame, Ind.: Univ. of Notre Dame Press, 2007), 11–12.
8. Bryan Stone, *Evangelism After Christendom: The Theology and Practice of Christian Witness* (Grand Rapids: Brazos, 2007), 139.
9. Ibid, 163–70.
10. John F. Kavanaugh, *Following Christ in a Consumer Society*, 2nd ed. (Maryknoll, N.Y.: Orbis Books, 2006), 51. Kavanaugh speaks of the incapacity to be "self-donating" when one perceives oneself and others as utile commodities.
11. David F. Wells, *Above All Earthly Pow'rs: Christ in a Postmodern World* (Grand Rapids: Eerdmans, 2005), 78.
12. Rodney Clapp, *A Peculiar People: The Church as Culture in a Post-Christian Society* (Downers Grove, Ill.: InterVarsity Press, 1996), 168.
13. Marv Newell, "Is Evangelism Ever a Sin? Ethical Evangelism in a Watching World," *Visions: The CrossGlobal Link Newsletter* (June 2009), 2.
14. James Wm. McClendon, Jr., and James M. Smith, *Understanding Religious Convictions* (Notre Dame, Ind.: Univ. of Notre Dame Pres, 1975), 8.
15. James Dunn, *The Theology of Paul the Apostle* (Grand Rapids: Eerdmans, 1998), 341–42.

16. Shenk, "Practicing Truth," 227.
17. Eddie Gibbs and Ryan K. Bolger, *Emerging Churches: Creating Christian Community in Postmodern Cultures* (Grand Rapids: Baker: 2005), 99.
18. Gerhard Lohfink, *Jesus and Community* (Philadelphia: Fortress Press, 1984), 55; italics in original.
19. John Howard Yoder, *The Politics of Jesus*, 2nd ed. (Grand Rapids: Eerdmans, 1994), 239.
20. Stone, *Evangelism After Christendom*, 13.
21. Christopher J. H. Wright, *The Mission of God: Unlocking the Bible's Grand Narrative* (Downers Grove, Ill.: IVP Academic, 2006), 164.
22. Stone, *Evangelism After Christendom*, 211.
23. Michael G. Cartwright, "The Once and Future Church Revisited," in *Embodied Holiness: Toward a Corporate Theology of Spiritual Growth*, ed. Samuel M. Powell and Michael E. Lodahl (Downers Grove, Ill.: InterVarsity Press, 1999), 120.
24. This theme is treated at length in Walter Brueggemann, *Biblical Perspectives on Evangelism* (Nashville: Abingdon, 1993).
25. Michael E. Lodahl, "'And He Felt Compassion': Holiness Beyond the Bounds of Community," in Powell and Lodahl, *Embodied Holiness*, 145–65.
26. Thomas E. Reynolds, *Vulnerable Communion: A Theology of Disability and Hospitality* (Grand Rapids: Brazos, 2008), 51.
27. Lesslie Newbigin, *The Household of God: Lectures on the Nature of the Church* (New York: Friendship Press, 1954), 147.
28. MacIntyre, *After Virtue*, 216.
29. Stuart Murray, *Church After Christendom* (Carlisle: Paternoster, 2005), chap. 1, offers definitions and numerous permutations on belonging, believing, centered sets, and bounded sets. See also Guder, *Missional Church*, chap. 7.
30. Gibbs and Bolger, *Emerging Churches*, 125.
31. George R. Hunsberger, "Acquiring the Posture of a Missionary Church," in *The Church Between Gospel and Culture: The Emerging Mission in*

North America, ed. George R. Hunsberger and Craig Van Gelder (Grand Rapids: Eerdmans, 1996), 292. See also Darrell L. Guder, *The Continuing Conversion of the Church* (Grand Rapids: Eerdmans, 2000).

32. Stanley Hauerwas, *A Community of Character: Toward a Constructive Christian Social Ethic* (Notre Dame, Ind.: Univ. of Notre Dame Press, 1981), 131.
33. Thomas N. Finger, "Confessing Truth in a Pluralistic World," in Shenk and Stutzman, *Practicing Truth*, 218.
34. See www.scumoftheearth.net. See also Bob Whitesel, *Inside the Organic Church: Learning from Twelve Emerging Congregations* (Nashville: Abingdon, 2006), chap. 9, and Michael Sares, *Pure Scum: The Left-Out, the Right-Brained, and the Grace of God* (Downers Grove, Ill.: InterVarsity Press, 2010).
35. Scott Bader-Saye, "Improvising Church: An Introduction to the Emerging Church Conversation," *International Journal for the Study of the Christian Church* 6, no.1 (2006): 13.
36. Stanley Hauerwas and William H. Willimon, *Resident Aliens: Life in the Christian Colony* (Nashville: Abingdon, 1989), 43; italics added.
37. Tex Sample, *Hard Living People and Mainstream Christians* (Nashville: Abingdon, 1993), 55–56.
38. Reynolds, *Vulnerable Communion*, 76.
39. Kimberly Bracken Long, "In from the Streets: When Homeless Christians Join the Worshiping Assembly," *Journal for Preachers* 31, no. 3 (2008): 39.
40. Such boldness, exemplified by Christ, is discussed in Craig Blomberg, *Contagious Holiness: Jesus' Meals with Sinners* (Downers Grove, Ill.: InterVarsity Press, 2005).
41. Walter Brueggemann, *Cadences of Home: Preaching Among Exiles* (Louisville, Ky.: Westminster John Knox, 1997), 4.
42. James Wm. McClendon, Jr., *Systematic Theology: Ethics* (Nashville: Abingdon, 1986), 225; italics in original.
43. Hauerwas, *Community of Character*, 113; italics added.

44. Sean Marston, "The Ministry of 'Hanging Out,'" *SIM Magazine* (February 2009); www.sim.org/index.php/content/the-ministry-of-hanging-out.
45. This saying is often attributed to A. W. Tozer.

2

An Approach to Financial Accountability in Mission Partnerships

MARY LEDERLEITNER

Statistics do not answer all questions, but they suffice to inform us that significant change is sweeping across the global mission movement and that we are entering a new era of partnership in mission. An unprecedented number of cross-cultural partnerships are being formed between funding churches and organizations in the West and indigenous organizations and churches in the Majority World. In the United States alone, between the years 1998 and 2005 the number of organizations that said partnership was a primary strategy for how they planned to engage in global missions increased by a staggering 6900 percent (Moreau 2007, 2007b). In itself partnership can carry a number of meanings, but for many of these partnerships monetary transfers are central, raising thorny and at times contentious issues of oversight, common vision, and accountability at the personal and organizational levels.

Additionally, growing financial regulations and requirements in countries such as the United States and Canada pose a serious hurdle for organizations when funding is sent abroad (IRS 2009; Van Cleef 2003; Canadian Revenue Agency 2009). Fiduciary requirements, often seemingly intense, are being imposed in the very mission contexts where colonialism once reigned and past injustices have never fully healed. Is it possible to adhere to Western ethical and cultural standards when funding is sent abroad without fostering neocolonialism in this next era of global mission partnerships? Is it possible to partner as "equals" when financial disparities are so enormous and one group requires such in-depth accountability for the use of resources shared?

To discussion of these questions I bring an eclectic mix of academic research in the areas of cross-cultural conflict, formal accounting training, intercultural training, and theological reflection blended with personal experience and the fruit of many heartfelt dialogues which have occurred over the course of the past decade. Much of my ministry life has been spent straddling the worlds of missiology and financial compliance. I have felt the internal distress of trying to conduct my life and ministry in a way that is true to both disciplines. Instead of using finance as a trump card to shut down discussion and demand compliance, I have tried to discern whether looking to the heart of God, who values both relationships and accountability, might supply answers that can serve us as we enter the next era of global missions (see the rich resources related to relationships and accountability available at www.cosim.info, the Web site of COSIM [Coalition on the Support of Indigenous Ministries]).

I would like to say that I have emerged from this journey as an expert, ready to answer all questions and settle all debates once and for all. That however has not been the case. Instead, this chapter provides an opportunity to raise questions that have been churning in my heart for some time (Lederleitner 2006, 2010). Often important technical issues of financial compliance must be addressed and we dare not minimize these realities. As I have wrestled with the competing tensions, however, I have often wondered whether the problem is not far deeper. If we examine the issue through the broader ethical lens of the Word of God, might we find more solid ground for agreement? From that place of deeper agreement, might we finally access the grace and capacity needed to deal with the global challenges we are facing?

What Is "Neocolonialism"?

An unending supply of research documents issues related to colonialism and the myriad of effects it has had on cultures and people groups. For this reason it may be helpful for me to clarify what I mean when I use the term "neocolonialism."

Almost since the beginning of time, "foreign" governments have conquered near or distant regions of the world and ruled over them. Even our Lord had to deal with this phenomenon (John 19:12–15). Often the invading governments brought with them new laws and different practices. Under colonial rule some forms of progress occurred. At times roads were built, infrastructure was established, and schools were formed. What we would call "development," however, usually came at the cost of people's freedom. Many who were indigenous to the area being "colonized" lost their voice and their ability to make decisions about what would happen in their own homeland.

A concern for missiology today is how there can be effective cross-cultural partnerships, despite vast amounts of wealth coming from affluent donors and nations, without fostering a new form of colonialism now known as "neocolonialism" (Rieger 2004; Cooper 2005; Schwartz 2006). Neocolonialism implies that although physical occupation by a foreign power may no longer occur, wealth and resources are provided in ways that enable continued domination of others. Some on the receiving end of mission funding feel demeaned and controlled by the process. These partners have the sense that they are losing the right to make their own decisions and that they are losing their voice. Neocolonialism raises concern whether true partnership, the kind that models genuine mutuality, can even take place between funders in the West and recipients in the Majority World, given their vast disparity of wealth.

What Happens in the Dialogue?

As I have sat and listened to people engage in these conversations and debates over the past decade, I have heard two polarizing views expressed. When concern about control or neocolonialism is expressed, wealthy donors often respond with irritation and defensiveness. They frequently articulate a sense that they are not appreciated or manifest a tendency to stereotype fund recipients by assuming they must not be trustworthy, otherwise they would be willing to be "accountable." For the partners receiving funds, I often see a different, almost instinctual, response. When funds are received with all kinds of fiduciary requirements, they will often say that this is "just another form of colonialism" or "evidence of neocolonialism." To them it feels as though once again they are being controlled by elite foreign powers.

Attribution theory explains much about why these misunderstandings are occurring (Elmer 2007; Mitchell and Green 2005; Nickerson 1998). When people come from different cultures and when ministry leaders are juggling many different responsibilities, it is easy to attribute negative motivations and character traits to others. To assume that ideology from the past is the cause for current behavior becomes an almost automatic response. This identification, however, is not always correct; the past is not always determinative. If we automatically impose past meaning on current circumstances without taking time for adequate inquiry or critical reflection, "yesterday's meaning becomes today's dogma" (Senge 1996, x). When that occurs, we find ourselves in a vicious loop from which we cannot escape.

The Role of Meaning

As I reflect upon the tension in the global church surrounding the issues of money and financial accountability, I often feel that, yes, yesterday's meaning is becoming today's dogma. There seems to be inadequate space for true inquiry, dialogue, and deep reflection. A general lack of awareness erects a barrier to recognizing the tacit meanings assigned to financial accountability, whereas in actuality it is the meaning assigned (Berger 1967, 3–28; Hiebert 1985, 141–69; Mezirow 1991, 1–36) and not financial accountability itself which determines if it will be a destructive or constructive force in missions. Yet the global body of Christ as a whole seems anesthetized to its contradictions (Bohm 1996, 5) with regard to this issue. Financial accountability has somehow been assigned, especially by those from Western cultures, as being a "neutral" issue, when it is anything but neutral.

Critically Examining Financial Accountability

Critical thinking is essential if we hope to get to a better place in global missions. When "habits of mind go unexamined, they create limitations and form boxes" (Cranton 2006, 28) that entrap us. We need to discover "how and why our assumptions have come to constrain the way we perceive, understand, and feel about our world" (Mezirow 1991, 167).

Joerg Rieger supplies a starting point for necessary missiological reflection when he writes that "failure to consider our colonial heritage may result in failure to understand who we are today" (2004, 202). "Reading the histories one gets the strong sense that the missionaries meant well.... So why did Christian mission end up as part of the colonial enterprise?" (205). In Rieger's view this happened because colonialism became, for all practical purposes, simply the natural backdrop for life. Many missionaries seemed to be unable to differentiate between "what was" and "what ought to be." Complaints and resistance often arose only when abuses by those in power became especially flagrant (206).

David Maranz, in his superb work *African Friends and Money Matters* (2001), examines money and culture through the lens of cultural anthropology. The book is rich in description of the reasons why Africans and Westerners view money differently. He also explains the process of financial accountability under colonial rule, writing that "during the colonial period African leaders were not accountable to the people under them, but to their colonial masters. These in turn were accountable only to their home governments. The local people were there to be controlled, not informed. Surely this colonial pattern left indelible marks across the continent" (39).

Current worldly standards. Some might say, "Colonialism is long gone. That was another era. It no longer impacts me or how my mission organization operates." We Americans like to put the past behind us quickly and to say that we are working in "new" and "cutting edge" ways, but how does financial accountability work in our current world? Is it not often a power issue? Someone with wealth supplies money to someone with less wealth, often for altruistic reasons. The person with less wealth is now "held accountable" by the person with greater wealth. Almost always the accountability still flows in only one direction. In our current culture accountability is most frequently "upward" to those with financial means and not "downward" to those who have fewer resources. As a result, those with greater resources call the shots. Those with greater resources set the standards. Proverbs such as "beggars can't be choosers" or "the one who pays the piper calls the tune" become unexamined guides to behavior. Those with significant financial resources have "voice" and the greatest ability to determine outcomes. This value system is the foundation upon which most of the Western legal requirements regarding financial accountability are based.

Biblical standards and values. Scripture sets forth a very different value system. Although Jesus uses parables in which people are held accountable for resources entrusted to them by persons of greater financial means (Matt. 25:14–30; cf. Matt. 18:23–27, 20:1–15), he also emphasizes that there will be eternal consequences and that we will be held accountable for our actions toward those with fewer financial resources (Matt. 25:40). The Book of James gives a scathing admonition not to show partiality to the wealthy, for if we do we transgress the law (James 2:1–12). All people are to be treated with dignity and respect. The body of Christ should function in a way that models mutuality and interdependency (1 Cor. 12:1–31). Paul explains that we are all part of the same body and Christ is the head, forcefully showing that one part of the body cannot say it has no need of another. In a human body, every part has a voice and can impact the whole. In the end, God will hold us accountable for all our actions. The searing depth of his judgment will even apply to "every careless word" (Matt. 12:36 NASB).

Why are we surprised? The secular values governing financial accountability that are currently present in Western funding policies quite often reflect a very different set of values than those we see in Scripture. Why then are we surprised that our brothers and sisters in Christ feel demeaned by our financial accountability requirements? If we were to step back and look at the bigger picture, we would find it odd if they did not feel demeaned by the process. If accountability only goes upward to those with greater financial means, how can we think that our ministry processes will ever model mutuality, dignity, interdependency, and voice for all?

Can We Begin to Redeem Accountability Processes?

We know that we have to comply with Western financial regulations. If we do not adhere to these requirements, ministry leaders will incur criminal charges, some will face jail time, we will suffer a profound loss of credibility with our donors, our ministries will come to an abrupt halt, and we will severely hinder the witness of Christ. The news media will highlight stories that will only cause greater cynicism in the hearts of unbelievers and believers alike. In the spirit of Romans 13:1–8, we must adhere to the admonition to obey governmental laws regarding accountability. I believe, however, that love compels us to go further and to do more than merely comply with external regulations.

Where do we begin? Essential to the act of "redeeming" is trying to discern God's true purpose for something. Before we can move forward, we need to begin to uncover the positive "meanings" for accountability. If we start to address the blockages, one of which I believe is the negative or secular meaning of accountability, we can begin to replace them and "create something new between us" (Bohm 1996, 5). Dialogue with our partners is the pathway to finding redemptive meanings.

Satan has distorted accountability. We see him active in the cross-cultural conflict currently present in the global church surrounding legal compliance and accountability for outside funding. He causes us to think accountability can "mean" only that those who are wealthier should hold those without wealth accountable. What other meanings might accountability have? Social science research offers a place to begin our search for alternative meanings. Research indicates that accountability is totally necessary for the growth and maturity of individuals in the workplace (Goleman 1998, 268–74). In this sense accountability is something positive. There are also strong parallels to be found in the growth and development of cultural intelligence (Peterson 2004, 89–90). Research also shows that accountability is a critical component in adult transformation (Mezirow 1991, Cranton 2006, Taylor 1994, 2000). Accountability also prepares us for the final day when we will stand before God and give an account of our lives (Luke 12:35–48). Do we want work environments that will foster deep maturity, growth in cultural intelligence, and lasting transformation? Do we want to prepare one another for the day we will meet God face to face?

Dialogue offers a helpful way to begin uncovering better "meanings" for accountability. We can discuss different types of questions; for example, as we look around in the world—in government, in companies, and in the church—does a lack of accountability tend to bring good or bad outcomes? What happens when there is no accountability? People who have seen or been involved in a setting where theft or fraud has occurred know the extreme damage it does to a community of believers and to Christ's witness in a ministry. How should accountability be seen in light of these things?

Dialogue about this issue is of utmost importance, because accountability has to be everyone's idea. Financial accountability will not work if one partner assumes it is helpful and other partners believe it is only oppressive and controlling. If left solely to the dogma of our own societies, we will never see accountability in its proper light. Without better meanings, it will be impossible to move forward.

Accountability processes and scriptural values. Someone might ask, "Can accountability processes model scriptural values?" The amazing answer to that question is a resounding "yes!" Western governmental regulations stipulate that we have to be able to confirm that funds are being used to accomplish the task or help the people for whom the funds were raised. In theory we all agree to this or we would not be working together. Despite our theoretical agreement, if we stop with giving assent to this overarching value and are satisfied with meeting only that one objective of financial accountability, we will not be likely to model mutuality for the accountability governments require tends to be one directional.

We have in our power, however, the ability to create within our partnerships a web or system of overall accountability that can model holistic mutuality.

Covenant/presbytery model. What might such a system or approach of holistic mutuality look like? First, our system or approach needs to be designed and developed to fit each specific situation. One size does not fit all. John Rowell writes of utilizing a covenant relationship process in his partnership with Bosnians. In this partnership the parties involved have mutual accountability and mutual voice through a presbytery (2006, 160–61). This model can be helpful for smaller church-to-church or smaller church-to-agency partnerships. Use of this model becomes complicated, however, in a large multinational mission organization that has hundreds of diverse partnerships around the globe. Still, although some basic policies regarding financial reporting are necessary or required in larger agencies, it is feasible for individual regions working closely with indigenous partners to create more comprehensive and God-honoring local accountability structures that facilitate mutual respect and voice.

The key to building accountability processes that model mutuality and foster transformation is to work to level the playing field. In these accountability processes, every person has positions of strength and positions of vulnerability. That means that if one party is bringing funding, he or she needs to be accountable in areas of great vulnerability as well. Areas of vulnerability might include needs for personal maturity in various areas, or growth in a professional capacity that the person does not already possess. This broader network of holistic accountability helps to keep everyone honest and to remind everyone in the partnership that all parties are being stretched and are being held to a standard that at times is quite difficult to keep. It is in areas of vulnerability and weakness that partners can pray for one another and stand together as brothers and sisters before their heavenly Father, all in need of growth and maturity.

Mutual pledges. Partners International is an example of a mission agency that is doing great work in cross-cultural ministry partnerships in many parts of the world. Daniel Rickett, in *Making Your Partnership Work* (2002), outlines some aspects of setting up and working through partnerships that Partners International has found helpful over the years. At the end of the book he highlights a pledge that Partners International makes to its overseas partners (131–38). It is a strong move in the right direction in that Partners International is trying to convey clearly that it does not see accountability as a one-directional dynamic. They need for their partners to be accountable with finances, but they are willing to be accountable in many ways as well. This is an excellent step. Having interacted with some of the leaders of Partners International over the past few years, I know that any pledge is developed in a context of rich and engaging dialogue.

The caveat or concern I have is that other ministry leaders in the United States might take this pledge and use it directively, in effect, dictating terms to their partners. Instead of together creating mutual accountability pledges, if not used carefully this pledge might again become an instance of the wealthy partner dominating the relationship and setting all the terms. Dialogue is utterly critical to mutuality. Documents such as this pledge can sometimes be a helpful way to start conversations and design mutual pledges. It is only as we sit and truly begin to listen to and hear one another, however, that we will find Christ in our midst, giving us new ways to solve the complex issues embedded in mutuality and accountability.

A voice for the most powerless. In *Walking With the Poor: Principles and Practices of Transformational Development,* Bryant Myers (2007) does a superb job of highlighting the need for accountability in all directions. He explains that we "mar the identity of the poor" (130) if there is no way for them to have a voice to the process. He focuses the issue as he discusses evaluations, which by nature are a part of accountability processes. It is essential that the poorest persons impacted or affected by a partnership also be able to hold others accountable. If the means for this to happen are not built into the process, we can easily deceive ourselves that our ministries have a greater impact and are more fruitful than they truly are. Also, by including the poor in the process, we better prepare ourselves for the day when God will hold us accountable for how we have treated "the least of these" (Matt. 25:40 NRSV).

How Do We Contextualize Processes?

If the field of intercultural communication has taught us anything (Hofstede and Hofstede 2005; Trompenaars and Hampden-Turner 1998), it is that the same practice in one setting can have a very different meaning in another. We cannot "plug and play" a set of policies or practices designed for one cultural context and assume they will work effectively in another. "One of the goals of cross-cultural training is to alert people to the fact that they are constantly involved in a process of assigning meaning to the actions and objects they observe" (Trompenaars and Hampden-Turner 1998, 201). Direct and indirect communication, status issues, implications regarding the loss or building of face, tolerances for ambiguity, and the like all impact the meaning ascribed to certain behaviors. Individual personalities, leadership styles, and organizational cultures also vary greatly among partners.

If past behavior is any indication, invariably ministry leaders will want to cut this process short, copy what has been done somewhere else, and just "get on with things." The problem with this mind-set is that it circumvents dialogue and substantially increases the likelihood that any new process introduced from the outside will not work or will not be sustainable over the long haul. In missiology we seem willing to invest much effort and time to ensure that our ministry programs or church planting efforts are contextualized. As a whole, however, we seem to have little patience or awareness that the processes by which we "do business" or "achieve financial accountability" also need to be contextualized if they are going to foster good meanings and outcomes.

Developing culturally contextualized processes for each partnership will take more time. For instance, in some partnerships it might be possible for partners to speak directly to one another. In other partnerships it might be wise to have many third-party go-betweens in place so voices from people with differing levels of power can truly be heard. In some partnerships Western accountability processes may be the best solution. In others, these same processes will most likely encourage fraud because they are largely based upon paper receipts, which are worthless in many parts of the world.

Mutually developed and contextualized processes are much more likely to have redemptive meanings and sustainability, but creating them will not be a quick process. Things will need to be tried, evaluated, adapted, tried again, tinkered with, and then adapted further. Lest we tire of the process of dialogue and building accountability structures together, we need to realize that we are establishing a process that has the potential to foster genuine unity and profound growth and maturity for all involved. Building processes is far more than a money issue. It is changing the way we work so that the very processes themselves model the values of the One we follow.

What Can Jesus Teach Us?

Matthew 17:24–27 teaches lessons that can enable us to weather what at times seem to be unreasonable and illogical financial requirements. In the passage people begin questioning Peter as to whether Jesus would be paying the temple tax or not. Using the incident as a teaching moment for his disciple, Jesus inquired of Peter, "What do you think, Simon? From whom do the kings of the earth collect customs or poll-tax, from their sons or from strangers?" (17:25 NASB) Peter responds correctly, stating that this tax is for strangers. Jesus affirms that this is indeed the case. The requirement is illogical and should not apply to them. It is what Jesus says afterwards that is so amazing. "But, lest we give them offense, go to the sea, and throw in a hook, and take the first fish that comes up; and when you open its mouth, you will find a stater. Take that and give to them for you and Me" (17:27 NASB).

Jesus could have responded in many other ways. He could have railed against the people who were requiring financial compliance. He could have said, "I don't have to pay the temple tax! I am God! The temples were made to worship God! This is so stupid!" He also could have ignored the requirement and dismissed it with passive aggressive behavior. He could have said, "I am too busy to be bothered with this!" After all, he was training a group of people who would be leading a global movement. He was healing the sick and raising the dead. He was also preparing to become the sacrificial lamb and die for the sins of all humankind. For heavens sake, he was legitimately too busy to deal with this! Yet how did he respond?

Jesus did not let this governmentally regulated accountability requirement shake his confidence. He did not give the external financial requirement the power to cause him to feel demeaned or disrespected. Jesus stopped what he was doing to address the issue. He seemed to take extra care to "not give offense." Yet we see in earlier chapters that Jesus did not hesitate to offend others under different circumstances (Matt. 15:12–14). He did not seem to waste a moment worrying about whether he was offending the Pharisees. When his disciples asked if he realized he had offended the Pharisees, his response was, "They are blind guides of the blind. And if a blind man guides a blind man, both will fall into a pit" (Matt. 15:14). He seemed indifferent as to whether or not he had offended the Pharisees. Yet when it came to an unreasonable financial accountability requirement, he took care not to give offense.

What does such a passage mean for us? Can knowing who we really are (1 Cor. 12:1–31) enable us to have a new and greater capacity for dealing with frustrating fiduciary requirements? Can an understanding of our connectedness help us realize that if anything we do hurts our partner, it also hurts us and the work of the kingdom? Do financial requirements by governments, in and of themselves, have the ability to demean us? What role does having our identity rooted in Christ play in this overall debate? How might Christ's actions guide us as we seek to work together? What implications do his actions have with regard to what is worth fighting about and what is not? In the end of this story we see that God provided what was needed through a special act of grace. I often think that we approach the thorny issue of financial compliance without first seeking God's grace and provision. This passage gives us hope that Christ understands our struggle and can help guide us through it.

Conclusion

We all recognize that Western governmental accountability and fiduciary requirements are not going to diminish any time in the near future. They are not going to go away. We are living in a post–9/11 era. With a global war on terrorism underway, funds crossing national boundaries are being scrutinized. An economic crisis, caused largely by unethical business practices in the United States that were not caught due to massive deregulation, continues to rock the global financial world. For these reasons, financial regulations will likely increase rather than decrease in the near future, and nonprofit organizations and ministries in places such as the United States and Canada will not be able to give large amounts of unaccounted-for funds across national borders.

If that is the reality of our world, how should we respond? As I consider the situation, all kinds of questions come to mind. Should we just stop sharing financial resources? Is that what God wants—for one part of Christ's body to be rich with financial blessings and for other parts to lack the means to meet their most basic needs? How does that option sync with Psalm 67, which says that God blesses us so the ends of the earth may know him? How does that option sync with our call in 1 Corinthians 12 to be the "body of Christ"? Even the earliest of believers seemed to understand that resources should be shared to meet needs within the body (Rom. 15:26). I then think of the debate as seen from other parts of the globe. Does a good relationship mean no accountability is needed? If so, what does it mean to say that we have a close relationship with Christ, yet that he is holding us accountable? Does trust grow with no accountability? Or rather, does trust grow as we are all accountable and faithful to God and to one another?

Might the way forward be for us to begin to redeem accountability processes so that they no longer mirror worldly values but instead reflect the reality of our own relationship with God? Everything in all of our cultures must be brought to the foot of his cross. If we take our Western secular methods of financial accountability and ways of doing business and simply thrust them into cross-cultural partnerships, our partners will continue to feel demeaned by the process and they will lose their voice. Secular patterns of accountability do not mirror the values and principles found in Scripture.

If our Heavenly Father values accountability and relationships, can he give us the capacity to value both as well? Is it simply not possible to design and contextualize accountability processes that will give everyone a voice and a say in the process? Is it not possible to develop accountability structures that go in both or, better, in all directions? Can we build these processes with an eye not only toward meeting the standard set in Romans 13:1–8 but also as a means to better prepare all of us for the day when we will give a final accounting to our Maker face to face? Are we willing to redeem accountability so it can serve as a tutor to help us all grow in godliness and maturity in Christ?

These are the thoughts that churn in my heart as I think about the issues of financial accountability and neocolonialism. I keep wondering if at this deeper level we might find agreement. If we implement these types of changes might it be possible to begin to resolve the issue of neocolonialism in global missions once and for all?

Questions for Discussion

1. What suggestions do you have for guiding rich donors in the West who are faced with appeals from poorer national church leaders seeking assistance in their ministries? What steps will help to foster healthy partnerships?
2. How can both giving agencies and receiving agencies build bonds of trust while also agreeing on shared standards of accountability?
3. What conditions might turn well-intended financial assistance into hurtful assistance?
4. Inevitably charges of misuse or abuse of funds will be raised. Some will come from envious or misinformed people, but others will have plausibility or be well founded. What might donor agencies do ahead of time to avoid such charges or to address them if they arise?

References

Berger, Peter L. 1967. *The sacred canopy: Elements of a sociological theory of religion*. New York: Random House.
Bohm, David. 1996. *On dialogue*. New York: Routledge Press.
Canadian Revenue Agency. 2009. Charities in the international context. www.cra-arc.gc.ca/tx/chrts/ntrntnl-eng.html.
Cooper, Michael T. 2005. Colonialism, neo-colonialism, and forgotten missiological lessons. *Global Missiology* 2 (2): 1–14; http://ojs.globalmissiology.org/index.php/english/article/view/105.
Cranton, Patricia. 2006. *Understanding and promoting transformative learning: A guide for educators of adults*. 2d ed. San Francisco: John Wiley & Sons.

Elmer, Duane. 2007. IMCO (Inter-Mission Cooperative Outreach) Conference presentations. Saskatchewan, Canada. Available at www.imcomissions.net/pdf/IMCO_Conference_Catalogue_08-09.pdf.

Goleman, Daniel. 1998. *Working with emotional intelligence*. New York: Bantam Books.

Hiebert, Paul G. 1985. *Anthropological insights for missionaries*. Grand Rapids: Baker Books.

Hofstede, Geert, and Gert Jan Hofstede. 2005. *Cultures and organizations: Software of the mind*. 2d ed. New York: McGraw-Hill.

IRS. 2009. Tax information for churches and religious organizations. www.irs.gov/charities/churches/index.htm.

Lederleitner, Mary. 2006. The theology of internal controls. *Evangelical Missions Quarterly* 40 (4): 516–21.

———. 2010. *Cross-cultural partnerships: Navigating the complexities of money and mission*. Downers Grove, Ill.: InterVarsity Press.

Maranz, David. 2001. *African friends and money matters*. Dallas, Tex.: SIL International and the International Museum of Cultures.

Mezirow, Jack. 1991. *Transformative dimensions of adult learning*. San Francisco: John Wiley.

Mitchell, Terence, and Stephen Green. 2005. Attribution theory: Managerial perceptions of the poor performing subordinate. In *Organizational behavior 1: Essential theories of motivation and leadership*, ed. John B. Miner, 184–203. Armonk: N.Y.: M. E. Sharpe.

Moreau, Scott. 2007. Mission trends and implications for cross-cultural partnerships. Presentation at COSIM conference, Wheaton Bible Church, Wheaton, Ill.

———. 2007b. Putting the survey in perspective. In *Mission handbook 2007–2009: U.S. and Canadian ministries overseas*, ed. Linda Weber and Dotsey Welliver, 11–75. Wheaton, Ill.: EMIS.

Myers, Bryant L. 2007. *Walking with the poor: Principles and practices of transformational development*. Maryknoll, N.Y.: Orbis Books.

Nickerson, Raymond S. 1998. Confirmation bias: A ubiquitous phenomenon in many guises. *Review of General Psychology* 2 (2): 175–220.

Peterson, Brooks. 2004. *Cultural intelligence: A guide to working with people from other cultures*. Boston, Mass.: Intercultural Press.

Rickett, Daniel. 2002. *Making your partnership work.* Enumclaw, Wash.: WinePress Publishing.

Rieger, Joerg. 2004. Theology and mission between neo-colonialism and postcolonialism. *Mission Studies* 21 (2): 201–27.

Rowell, John. 2006. *To give or not to give: Rethinking dependence, restoring generosity, and redefining sustainability.* Atlanta, Ga.: Authentic Publishing.

Schwartz, Glenn. 2007. *When charity destroys dignity: Overcoming unhealthy dependency in the Christian movement.* Bloomington, Ind.: AuthorHouse.

Senge, Peter M. 1996. Preface. In *Bohm on dialogue*, by David Bohm, vii–xiv. New York: Routledge.

Taylor, Edward W. 1994. Intercultural competency: A transformative learning process. *Adult Education Quarterly* 48 (1): 34–59.

———. 2000. Analyzing research on transformative learning theory. In *Learning as transformation: Critical perspectives on a theory in progress*, ed. Jack Mezirow. San Francisco: Jossey-Bass.

Trompenaars, Fons, and Charles Hampden-Turner. 1998. *Riding the waves of culture: Understanding diversity in global business.* New York: McGraw Hill.

Van Cleef, Carol R. 2003. The USA Patriot Act: Statutory analysis and regulatory implementation. *Journal of Financial Crime* 11 (1): 73–102.

3

Seeing Through a Glass More Clearly: The Moral and Evangelistic Imperative of More Accurately Representing Other People's Religions to Ourselves

EDWIN ZEHNER

Recently a friend lent me a video documentary that represented itself as "exploring the experiences of five very normal, Christian, American families" to "discover how people of faith handle the realization of having a gay child or family member."

I realized that I could not expect a balanced theological presentation. After all, the video was advertised as a film that "brilliantly reconciles homosexuality and Biblical scripture—and reveals that religious anti-gay bias is based almost solely upon a misinterpretation of the Bible." However, I determined to watch it anyway. Given some things in my friend's background, I expected that lending me this video was less an attempt to evangelize me

49

than an invitation to conversation, so it was important for me to watch it.

The filmmakers' goal was clearly evangelistic. But if the goal was to evangelize theologically conservative evangelical Christians, they could hardly have picked a worse way to begin. The first four minutes consisted of footage of evangelicals, sometimes not very educated, saying extreme-sounding, scary things, interspersed with urbane, reflective clergy and intellectuals expressing opinions like those of the filmmakers. In effect, the film consisted of stereotypes of our own tradition such that, even though they contained a kernel of truth and the video presented a good deal of footage of actual evangelical Christian preachers, the overall effect was almost deliberately offensive.

The problem was not that the things reported had not been said, for the film was showing actual footage of people such as Jimmy Swaggart, Ronald Reagan, Jerry Falwell, and Anita Bryant. The issue was that for the most part it was showing hatred—for example, Jimmy Swaggart saying he would kill a man if he even looked at him "like that"—in contrast to the reasonableness and measured tones of those expressing the filmmakers' point of view.

Many times we evangelicals do the same thing, portraying others' religions or perspectives in ways that make theirs look bad and ours look good. If the purpose is to persuade ourselves that our way is correct, then fine. But if the purpose is to provide insight into the other, then the approach is not as good. The important thing is to be aware of the perspective of the other person and find ways to speak to that.

3—*Edwin Zehner*

A Muslim Leader

Here is another example of how evangelistic outreach went wrong.

Recently I had the privilege of visiting a major Islamic school in a Middle Eastern country. The school had attracted a sizable foreign contingent of students and teachers, many of them from English-speaking countries and most of them eager to win the conversion of non-Muslims like myself. I particularly remember an hour-long conversation with an experienced teacher who told me he previously worked with college students in a major university town in the United States. Expressing concern for my soul, he set out to draw me to Islam by citing proofs of God's existence. Both because I was a guest and because I wanted to learn about Islam as he understood it, I allowed him to talk. Before long I realized he was trotting out the same proofs for God's existence that I had heard while growing up in a conservative Christian church in the midwestern United States. Despite my protests that I already believed in God, he kept going. I kept saying I already agreed with him. He kept going. By the end of his hour-long, one-on-one presentation I resorted to amusing myself by voicing some of the same challenges to God's existence that I had heard others express, just to see if I would learn something new from his answers (I did not; they were mostly the same answers I had heard while growing up).

The result of his efforts? I smiled at the time, and I smiled at him later. But I also did my best to avoid him throughout the rest of my visit. His zeal to convert me had somehow kept him from noticing the person actually in front of him. So he had geared his presentation to somebody else he had imagined, a person who presumably did not believe in a Creator God. Where had he gotten this idea? I could not say. But whatever the reason, his attempt to convert me ended up merely annoying me, to put it politely.

Zeal Without Knowledge ...

Far too often, we evangelical Christians are guilty of doing exactly the same thing to the people we claim to be trying to reach. In the name of evangelism we unintentionally offend the very people we seek to persuade, by misunderstanding, misrepresenting, or too quickly dismissing the very things that are most meaningful to them.

One of my favorite missiologists frequently warns that zeal without knowledge is dangerous, citing Proverbs 19:2 as support. I suggest a corollary: Zeal without knowledge runs the danger of being unethical. It often leads to violating the commandment against "bearing false witness," by misrepresenting the beliefs of the people we are actually trying to win. Worse, it frequently leads to our accusing others, often the people we wish to win to Christ, of some of the very things we do ourselves. And sometimes we end up antagonizing the people we wish to persuade.

Focusing on the Worst

For some reason this tendency becomes most evident in cross-cultural and interreligious discourse. It is far too common to compare our ideal selves at our best to the worst that we imagine in the other religion or culture. Or at times we may do the reverse, idealizing the other's religion while criticizing our own. Even more problematic is the tendency to misrepresent another religion's teachings, emphases, and practices, or the meanings they have for the people who practice that religion. This is problematic whether we do it deliberately or whether we are simply repeating things heard from other Christians or from the media without checking them against more informed sources. In my view such misrepresentation is an ethical problem whether it is done deliberately or whether we are simply satisfied with stereotypes learned from others.

If we are merely passively interested in the topic, ignorance may be excusable. But if we are involved in direct ministry—whether in overseas evangelism, cooperating on a social welfare project, or simply interacting with schoolmates, doctors, or workmates—lack of curiosity, perpetuation of misinformation, or willingness to assume the worst about the other is an ethical problem. Such attitudes and actions are a hindrance to our efforts to show the love of Christ to others, and could be taken as a publicly visible manifestation of the "works of the flesh" rather than the "fruit of the spirit" (Gal. 5:19–23).

Fear of Muslims

Nowhere are these problems more evident than in Christian missions to Muslims. Fear and ignorance of the poorly understood "other" often interweaves with popular images of Muslims as a violently expanding threat to Western civilization. There seems to be far less concern for discovering aspects of the religion that we can reach and touch to find starting points for mutual understanding.

The signs in the media are clear to see. Over the past decade, nearly every Arab or Muslim portrayed in popular media or film, *when the emphasis is on their identity as an Arab or Muslim,* is portrayed as a terrorist. Sometimes, to signal an atmosphere of danger, all the film needs to do is depict Muslims at prayer or provide a soundtrack of someone saying "Allahu Akhbar" (God is the greatest). By contrast, relatively little attention is given to the ethnic or religious identities of Arabs and Muslims who are *not* considered dangerous. How many realize that Ralph Nader, the well-known consumer rights crusader and perennial presidential candidate, is Arab? Or how many realize that Tony Shalhoub, the actor portraying the lovable television character "Monk," is also Arab? Or how many realize that the phrase "Allahu Akhbar" is normally a prayer acknowledging God's greatness and incomprehensibility rather than a call to war and violence? Though it is sometimes used for the latter (much as Christians use the word "crusade" for both war and peace, and much as Christians pray to God for victory over enemies), there is something wrong when this simple prayer is almost invariably portrayed as a synonym for "Kill the Americans" in video and films. It is even more problematic when those desiring to minister among Muslims allow themselves to be swayed by those same images.

Christians who are involved in ministry to Muslims should be taking the lead in correcting the imbalanced picture offered in these misrepresentations, because their effect is to scare Christians while closing doors to ministry and making it even harder for us to reach heart-to-heart across our religious differences. Unfortunately, far too many of us are doing exactly the opposite, sowing the seeds of fear and misunderstanding even as we seek to equip and inspire others for ministry. In our own talk about ministry we often do the same type of thing as was done in the video I mentioned in the opening—presenting the other as "dangerous" and supplying little nuance that would show the complexity and variety of positions within the other religion. Not only is this practically counterproductive, but it is also ethically problematic.

In the examples that follow I cite both "secular" and evangelical Christian examples, because the attitudes are so interwoven, at least in North America and possibly Britain, that it is impossible to disentangle them from each other.

To start with the scholars, there has been much excited talk from the mid-1990s onward about the "clash of civilizations" (Huntington 1998 and the second half of Jenkins 2002), an idea that posits an inherent conflict between globalizing "secular" (or "Christian") capitalism and presumably parochial militant Islam (Barber 1992, 1995). The underlying assumptions of this discourse have been much criticized (Abu-Lughod 2002; Eck 2001; Hefner 2000; Ho 2004; Mamdani 2002; Pearse 2004; Sadiki 2002; Said 1976, 2001), but the notion persists in popular thinking, partly because the underlying ideas are so simple ("us" versus "them") and because they correspond so well with widespread American assumptions about race, ethnicity, religion, and "foreignness."

Popular columnists go even farther. Among the most egregious was a column by Ann Coulter shortly after September 11, 2001, in which she argued that America should bomb the Muslims, invade their countries, and convert them all to Christianity (apparently forcibly), as a way of making America safe from the Muslim threat.

Though few are as violent in their expression, similar notions are common among people seeking to do ministry to Muslims. At one consultation I attended recently, some audience members said in the public question and answer sessions that one of their primary motivations in wanting to evangelize Muslims was because they thought doing so would end the militant threat to the United States. Maybe it would. But probably it would not, because—as in most interreligious conflicts—the militancy and violence are rooted in complaints, resentments, slights, and intragroup identities that are far more complex than simple religious difference.

I was shocked that none of the consultation's leaders, all of whom were deeply experienced, intelligent, and even sympathetic ministers to Muslims, sought to correct the underlying assumption. This disturbed me greatly. Should not evangelistic missions be motivated by love of the other rather than by politics? Would not mixed motives such as these translate into counterproductive ministry styles? And if our missions are motivated by political nationalism, would we not be tempted to perpetuate the very same cultural and nationalistic behaviors that have been so offensive in the past? "Missions" like this runs a danger of making things worse rather than better, both for the local church and for the sending country. But nobody raised the point. They should have done so.

Take another example. An e-mail newsletter I used to receive lists news items dealing with Muslims around the world, ostensibly as a way of inviting intelligent prayer and planning for ministry. Some of the items are drawn from apparently reputable news sources, while others come from unknown or unaccredited sources. Though the stated purpose is to encourage prayer for Muslim ministries around the world, I have often found myself feeling that the overall purpose (or at least effect) is to scare Christians, because most of the stories deal with violence or with persecution of Christians or with supposedly extremist teachings by Muslims in Britain, in America, or in Asia.

Rarely did the prayer letter list an article that might humanize the experience of Muslims, that presented a nonextremist Muslim viewpoint, or that would help readers understand the perspective of an actual Muslim. Though such articles were not entirely missing, they were far outnumbered by news articles that seemed to highlight danger or religiously motivated excess. The overall effect was to perpetuate the notion that Islam and Muslims are dangerous, and the newsletter seemed designed as much to mobilize its readers to political action as to spiritual ministry. Given how often Christians complain of Muslims' tendency to combine the spiritual and the political into a single religious realm, it was distressing to see Christians doing exactly the same thing in their discussions about the danger of Islam. This sort of antagonistic back-and-forth has become so common in Christian-Muslim relations that it is important to point out just how odd it is.

Religious Antagonism and Oppression

Religious oppression is common almost everywhere in the world, both where Christians are a majority and where they are a minority. But Christians, including evangelicals, are just as guilty of this as are people adhering to other religions. Alongside the unwillingness of the Saudi Arabian government to sanction the construction of non-Muslim places of worship, for example, must be listed the efforts of some local American governments to prevent the conversion of vacant properties into Muslim or Hindu places of worship, usually on the grounds of potential "damage" to the community or to property values.

Similarly, alongside Thailand's encouragement for its schoolchildren to recite homage to the Buddha at the beginning of the school day must be set the long-standing efforts of U.S. Christians to enforce teacher-led school prayers even in religiously mixed settings. And Christians' treatment of Jews up until very recently has been nothing short of horrifying. Whenever we have had the chance, we Christians have been just as insensitive to the minorities in our midst as anybody else. For some reason, though, Muslims come in for especially antagonistic treatment at the hands of evangelical Christians and in nations whose culture and politics are rooted in Christianity. Again, it is important to realize just how unusual this is. Similar actions by followers of other religions do not provoke nearly the same kinds of alarmist reactions as they do when practiced by Muslims.

Consider the following parallel. In predominantly Buddhist Thailand, converts to Christianity are sometimes ostracized and worse by their spouses, their families, and even by entire communities. In the 1980s, public speakers were even heard equating the threat of Christianity with the threats posed by Communism and corruption. Yet the churches have found ways to cope, and even grow, without engaging in antagonizing counter-discourses. In Thailand, it has been rare to hear Christian leaders urging the kind of antagonistic responses to the majority religion that are so common in the rhetoric of Christian ministries to Muslims.

In Thailand it is common instead for both missionaries and local church leaders to urge restraint in speaking about Buddhism and Buddhists. The concern is not just to ensure safety (as is often urged in the case of ministry to Muslims), but also to express respect to others among whom the Christians live. This expectation extends across all Protestant denominations, especially including evangelicals. In 2007, for example, when I asked Thai church leaders about their experiences receiving short-term missionaries, one of the most commonly cited problems was overzealousness in preaching in inappropriate places and ways. Thai church leaders argued that it was more important to show respect.

3—*Edwin Zehner*

Deliberate Ignorance

But the problem goes beyond the issue of respect versus antagonism. At least among North American Christians, one finds an almost deliberate ignorance about Islam, along with a tendency to see in it the opposite of our best selves. One often hears, for example, the assertion that Islam lacks the sense of a personal God (or at least the sense of God being close), that it lacks the sense of a loving God, and that it lacks a concept of forgiveness. And it is often said that Islam is a religion founded on works, whereas Christianity (or at least Christian salvation) is founded entirely on God's grace and forgiveness.

None of these stereotypes is totally true or totally false. Just as in Christianity, all of these elements are mingled in various ways with their logical opposites. For example, just as Christianity combines the sense of salvation as a free gift with the notion of the believer's personal responsibility, so also Islam—at least as described to me by Muslims—combines a sense of responsibility with the possibility of God's forgiveness. Notions of the manner by which the forgiveness is provided may differ from person to person, and Muslim notions of divine forgiveness, and the means of its provision, can be very different from evangelical Christian notions of salvation through faith in Christ. Nevertheless, the concept of forgiveness and undeserved grace indeed exists in Islam, and many Muslims remind themselves of God's forgiveness every time they pray.

Similarly, the idea that Islam lacks a close, present, and sometimes directly experienced God is a serious misrepresentation. Not only among the mystical Sufis, but also among the radically anti-Sufi Wahabis and Salafists, the notion of a directly personal

God who hears our prayers, cares about our behavior, and acts on our behalf is very strongly asserted.

Why do these misrepresentations persist, despite having so little basis in fact? One reason may be a tendency for devotees of the two religions to speak past each other. For example, it is common for Christians teaching about Islam to focus on their formal beliefs rather than on their customary practices. Yet for many Muslims (just as for many Christians) it is the practices that reveal the actual beliefs, and it is through the practices that devotees measure and demonstrate their commitment to God.

It is useful, therefore, to know what those practices are and what they mean to those doing them. It is useful, that is, to know how Muslims worship, how they access their own scriptures, and how those scriptures intersect with other aspects of Muslims' knowledge about themselves and God. This knowledge is especially important if missionaries are citing Muslims' scriptures to try to guide them to Christianity (as is being done in some forms of missions to Muslims). Thus, it is not sufficient to engage in "apologetic" teaching about Muslim doctrine, as that tends to miss the point altogether. From the Muslim perspective it might be more useful to consider the measures of our own devotion and humility before God. How do we ourselves measure up, and to what extent can we recognize this same concern in others? Though doctrine certainly matters, the practices and evidence of humility and submission before God matter even more, at least in the eyes of many Muslims.

An additional issue, albeit coming from a different direction, is the assumption among some evangelical Christians that if the other religion would just strip things down to their core, setting aside all the "peripheral" issues and practices, there might be a better basis for conversation. One hears, for example, the assumption that "the problem with Islam" is not the Qur'an but the *Hadith* (generally accepted accounts of the Prophet's teaching and actions) and the schools of law, with the assumption that the "core" of Islam as revealed in the Qur'an is fundamentally more compatible with Christianity. This is only partly true. There is indeed a good deal of overlap between the Qur'an and the Christian scriptures. However, some of the most serious differences between Islam and Christianity are encapsulated in the Qur'an itself, including the claim that Jesus is not God and the charge that Christians have corrupted his message.

Parallel Attitudes Toward Other Perspectives and Religions

I have been talking mostly about Islam. But similar attitudes can be observed toward Mormons, "Darwinists," "secular humanists," "postmodernists," anthropologists, and even creative artists. Some of this concern arises from fear of the new or of groups adhering to later revelations. Some of the concern is certainly justified theologically. Some of it is also motivated, sometimes justifiably, by the need to differentiate evangelicals from people of other backgrounds or persuasions. But when it hardens into stereotypes, the concern about boundaries often creates shields against the wrong enemies, causes us to mis-recognize friends, and leads to lost opportunities for effective public expressions of faith.

To take just one of these examples, "secular humanism" (a term few practicing "secular humanists" actually use) is often attacked as if the "secular" part means "irreligious," when in fact the term is more likely to be an expression of the freedom of religious practice that has been advocated by North American evangelicals ever since the Baptist William Rogers established the colony now known as Rhode Island. Evangelical critics have also been far too slow to realize that whatever perspectives the "humanistic" stance may have expressed regarding conventional religious belief (and some of its leading proponents are indeed critical), the orientation has also inspired adherents to such intense work for the benefit of others as to put many of us evangelicals to shame.

To take another example, "Darwinism" is all too frequently attacked as if it were a monolithic creed, based on a single book (Darwin's *Origin of Species*), that has never changed over time and that (to cite the most outrageous of its critics) is inherently Godless, inherently erosive to faith, and even (according to a video I recently saw) the cause of racist divisions around the world (the filmmakers apparently forgot that the American institution of slavery predated Darwin by nearly 250 years). Creative notions like "punctuated equilibrium," the existence of "theistic evolutionists," and the fact that many supporters of "intelligent design" are people working within the evolutionist framework—all of which are in one way or another exceptions to the stereotype—are overlooked or misrepresented in the efforts to rally the faithful to battle against the intellectual mainstream.

Though these rather radical defenses against so-called "evolutionism" are understandable, in many ways they are actually corrosive to Christian witness, because their misrepresentation of mainstream scientific ideas and methods practically ensures that bright young evangelicals will never truly engage mainstream science—and mainstream culture—in a way that enables a Christian perspective to be truly "heard." Either they will avoid the evolutionary paradigm altogether (except to criticize it in ways that fail to convince others), or else they will begin using the paradigm as a major tool in their work and assume that in doing so they must stop being evangelical Christians. Either way, we miss opportunities for sophisticated, effective public witness, and it is largely our own fault that there are entire fields in the sciences and social sciences where scarcely any Christian voices are heard outside the rarified confines of Christian colleges and universities.

As for "postmodernism" (a term most academics have already abandoned, in our haste to move on), most evangelicals have been very slow to realize that its attack on absolutist visions of knowledge have also re-opened the academy to open expressions of faith, including evangelical ones, so long as we Christians exhibit the same respect for others as is now increasingly being extended to us.

Evangelical Attitudes Toward Mormons

One of the most interesting examples of evangelical attitudes toward other religions occurs in evangelical attitudes toward the Church of Jesus Christ of Latter-day Saints (LDS, commonly known as Mormons, after the name of their best-known additional canonical scripture). Mormonism is, like Islam, a faith that adheres to a new set of revealed scriptures while claiming to revere Jesus and the words of our Bible. This step alone is enough to make evangelicals wary, and for good reason.

In giving credence to a later revelation, the Mormons rightly provoke some of the same concerns as Islam does, but often the expression of those concerns ends up misrepresenting the faith practiced by actual Mormons. For example, when Mormons assert that they believe in grace, evangelicals will assert that they believe in works only. To some degree this is justified, because Mormons do give works a greater role in their understanding of salvation than evangelicals do. But the strong version of this perspective is patently false (some of this was discussed in Zehner and Petersen 2009; also see Millet and McDermott 2007, Chapter 7, especially the section by the evangelical Gerald McDermott, titled "Grace, Faith, and Works").

Intriguingly, similar misrepresentation is happening on the other side, and on both sides such expressions have been sharp and heartfelt ever since the earliest days of the Mormon church (see Bushman 1984 and Shipps 1985, 2000, among others; also see the foreword and introduction in Beckwith, Mosser, and Owen 2002). A fellow anthropologist who is a Mormon has suggested to me recently that part of the motivation for this mutually exaggerated rhetoric, at least on the Mormon side, is over-vigilance about the boundary between us, exaggerating the differences as a way of keeping the faithful within the fold. I am sure evangelical readers can recognize a similar motivation within our own ranks. But my friend went on to say something truly fascinating. He suggested that in their desire to differentiate themselves from evangelicals (or "mainstream Christians," as Mormons call us), Mormons may have nudged themselves away from some of their own early teachings in order to accentuate those emphases that are least like those of the mainstream.

This is a truly arresting thought. If he is right and if the processes he describes are rooted in common human nature, could we ourselves be denaturing and reshaping our faith in order to seem more different? Could it be that, if we truly looked at scripture, we might find that we are more like the humanists and postmodernists than we realize? Could we find some aspects of Mormon teaching with which we might resonate while still noting our differences? And though academic engagement with Mormons is not likely to be affecting mainstream evangelical faith all that much (few of us are likely to be aware of those exchanges), could something similar arise from our ongoing eagerness to differentiate ourselves from Islam?

Whatever the answers to the above questions, the evangelical-Mormon example suggests that there are better ways forward that do not erode faith and that in fact can strengthen it. Over the past decade or more there has been a growing literature comprised of discussions between Mormons and evangelicals at the scholarly level. Some of the most outstanding of these publications include *How Wide the Divide? A Mormon and an Evangelical in Conversation* (Blomberg and Robinson 1997), "Mormon Apologetic, Scholarship, and Evangelical Neglect: Are We Losing the Battle and Not Knowing It?" (Owen and Mosser 1998), and *Claiming Christ: A Mormon-Evangelical Debate* (Millet and McDermott 2007).

So far have these discussions come that when Beckwith, Owen, and Mosser produced a new volume of apologetic work on Mormonism (*The New Mormon Challenge: Responding to the Latest Defenses of a Fast-Growing Movement,* 2002), it was reviewed favorably by a leading Mormon apologist (Ostling, n.d.), who felt that—unlike most anti-Mormon literature—the book accurately represented contemporary Mormon thinking, even while continuing to assert doctrinal points that Mormons cannot fully accept.

That parallel literatures have yet to arise from Muslim-evangelical conversations may indicate just how hardened are the relations between our two religions. But there may be signs of change. When in late 2007 a group of leading Muslims issued a conciliatory letter titled "A Common Word Between Us and You," it was a group of evangelicals led by a study center at Yale University who developed some of the most robust responses, including a public statement signed by 300 Christian leaders, including many evangelicals, and published as a full-page advertisement in the *New York Times* (both "A Common Word" and the Yale response were subsequently published in the Winter 2007 edition of *International Journal of Frontier Missiology,* also known as *IJFM*). This same group then organized a conference at Yale in the summer of 2008 that may have been the first meeting of such an array of Muslim and evangelical leaders in the same place, though evangelicals were hardly the only Christians participating.

True, some of the evangelical signatories were initially criticized for their cooperation with this initiative (see, for example, the articles in *IJFM* by Rebecca Lewis, 2008, and Rick Love, 2008, the latter in response to a critical video by John Piper that was apparently later removed from Piper's Web site). But that the engagement could have been made at all is an indication of increasingly nuanced thinking on both sides. And similar engagements are already being made at the micro-level all the way down to the mission field.

Some Positive Suggestions

The question is how to make these engagements happen at the level of the people in the pew and the pastors who teach them. Not everyone has the chance to read extensively on Mormons and Islam, not all have the time and opportunity to talk with educated representatives of those religions, and not all have the educational background or institutional support to sift through all that material on their own. How does one overcome these limitations while remaining faithful in our words, relationships, and witness?[1]

3—*Edwin Zehner*

I offer here a few practical suggestions and hope that discussions provoked by the questions at the end of this chapter will inspire even more.

- There seems to be general agreement among missions practitioners that it is best to seek common ground in people's meaning systems and ways of thinking as a starting point for further conversation. Often a genuine curiosity about the ways of the other can be a good starting point for learning more.
- Respect is important. It can be difficult to gain a hearing if one is at the same time being overly critical. Sometimes it is important to be able to set aside fear of the unknown other in order to gain rapport. This does not mean a broad license to accept everything that the other religion teaches. But it does mean setting aside the fear of the religion itself and developing respect for the perspectives expressed by particular persons from that religion.
- When writing or speaking about other religions, leave open the possibility of overlaps with our own teachings—not *entire* overlaps, but at least partial ones. One way to think of this is in terms of overlapping circles of meaning. Often it is from the overlaps in conceptual, moral, and practical teachings that conversations can arise. In other words, instead of highlighting just the *contrasts*, it can be useful to be aware also of the points of *similarity* flowing from the ways that people think and from the ways they live their lives.
- Show genuine interest, and be willing to see how people work through the relationships with Christianity. Sometimes they will focus on the differences (indeed, often they will do so). But at other times they will discover interwoven meanings that work for them. I was talking recently with someone

who had been working in the slums of Bangkok. One of the men he had been talking with had been a Buddhist monk for ten years and was now a layman again (this is common in Thailand, and those who leave the "yellow robe" of monkhood behind face no social disgrace). While at first this former monk was not open to the notion of a God in the Christian sense (nor of any God at all, since the Theravada Buddhists of Thailand are not theists), he eventually forwarded the notion, drawing on ideas within his own belief system, that God was timeless, having neither beginning nor end, just as we believe. In this case, it was the Thai person, raised as a Buddhist, who was doing the work of contextualization, and he did so starting with concepts that were experientially and conceptually "near" for him.

As this story suggests, be aware that people often work through their conversions in their own ways, drawing on material they may already have known and believed. I found this to be the case in conversion stories I collected in Thailand for my Ph.D. dissertation. These stories often drew on overlaps between Buddhist and Christian notions of heaven and hell and on overlaps in moral teaching, while linking those concepts with Christian notions of God.

- Always match information from other sources, written or otherwise, with the person in front of you. Sometimes the person matches the information in the books. More often the information gotten from books is merely the starting point of our exploration, while each individual expresses his or her own variants. Though people may share the traditions described in the books, the details that matter come from the individuals, and it is through *them* that we learn about the traditions as they are actually appropriated. And

3—*Edwin Zehner*

it is the traditions *as they are appropriated* that truly matter the most.

I suggest, in conclusion, that the most ethical approach to representing other people's religions to ourselves is to represent them in ways that would be sensible to followers of that religion. How do they experience it? With what meanings do they invest it? Which are the practices that matter most to a person in that religion? Attending to a clearer approximation of truth as seen from the perspective of the other would not only be most ethical, it could also open doors to more conversations.

Questions for Discussion

1. What perceptions do I, or the members of my congregation or ministry, have about (choose a religion or sect) or the followers of that path? Where do those perceptions come from? What are we doing to assess how accurate those perceptions might be?
2. When the followers of another religion or sect express a perspective on their faith different from the ones we expected them to express, do we take this as useful information? Or do we argue that they do not understand their own religion? What are some effective ways to gauge the extent to which we are doing one or the other?
3. When engaging in ministries among people of other religious and cultural backgrounds, whether professionally or as members of short-term ministry teams, what can and should we do to inform ourselves of the others' perspectives and ways of life? In what ways can we use on-field experi-

ences, and discussions of those experiences, to enrich those understandings without engaging in stereotypes?
4. When working with people who are religiously or culturally different from ourselves—whether on the mission field, in our schools and offices, or cooperating in social welfare projects—what are some ways we can use our conversations and work experiences to enrich our understanding? In what ways can readings about their religion help to supplement those conversations, and vice versa?
5. What are some practical ways that we can combine respect with witness?
6. Consider some of your current or earlier conversations with people of a different religion. Were there times when the two of you found your experiences and views resonating with each other? If so, consider when that was happening. Were there particular reasons why those discussions "clicked"? Did those moments help or hinder your public witness as a Christian? Why or why not?

Note

1. Note that I am not advocating that we abandon or weaken evangelical faith or teachings in any way. This point should be obvious throughout this chapter and is stated even more explicitly in my review (Zehner 2009) of *Christian Theology in Asia*, edited by Sebastian Kim, where I noted that some contributors were going so far in the direction of accommodation as to weaken the authority of the Bible, a principle that no evangelical should feel comfortable abandoning.

References

Abu-Lughod, Lila. 2002. Do Muslim women really need saving? Anthropological reflections on cultural relativism and its others. *American Anthropologist* 104 (3):783–90.
Barber, Benjamin R. 1992. Jihad vs. McWorld. *Atlantic* (March).
———. 1995. *Jihad vs. McWorld.* New York: Times Books.
Beckwith, Francis J., Carl Mosser, and Paul Owen, eds. 2002. *The new Mormon challenge: Responding to the latest defenses of a fast-growing movement.* Grand Rapids: Zondervan. See the Ostler entry below for a Mormon apologist's review of this book.
Blomberg, Craig L., and Stephen E. Robinson. 1997. *How wide the divide? A Mormon and an evangelical in conversation.* Downers Grove, Ill.: InterVarsity Press.
Bushman, Richard L. 1984. *Joseph Smith and the beginnings of Mormonism.* Urbana: Univ. of Illinois Press.
Eck, Diana L. 2001. American Muslims: Cousins and strangers. In *A new religious America: How a "Christian country" has now become the world's most religiously diverse nation.* San Francisco: HarperSanFrancisco.
Hefner, Robert. 2000. *Civil Islam: Muslims and democratization in Indonesia.* Princeton: Princeton University Press.
Ho, Engseng. 2004. Empire through diasporic eyes: A view from the other boat. *Comparative Studies in Society and History* 46 (2):210–46.
Huntington, Samuel P. 1998. *The clash of civilizations and the remaking of world order.* New York: Simon and Schuster.
Jenkins, Philip. 2002. *The next Christendom: The rise of global Christianity.* New York: Oxford Univ. Press.
Lewis, Rebecca. 2008. Responding to "A common word": WWJD? *International Journal of Frontier Missiology* 25 (1):43–45.
Love, Rick. 2008. Why I signed the Yale response to "A common word between us and you." *International Journal of Frontier Missiology* 25 (1):46–47.
Mamdani, Mahmoud. 2002. Good Muslim, bad Muslim: A political perspective on culture and terrorism. *American Anthropologist* 104 (3):766–75.
Millet, Robert L., and Gerald R. McDermott. 2007. *Claiming Christ: A Mormon-Evangelical Debate.* Grand Rapids: Brazos Press.

Ostler, Blake. n.d. "Reviews of *The new Mormon challenge.*" Posted online at Ostler's blog titled *FAIR: Defending Mormonism* (www.fairlds.org/New_Mormon_Challenge; accessed July 2009).

Owen, Paul, and Carl Mosser. 1998. Mormon apologetic scholarship and evangelical neglect: Losing the battle and not knowing it? *Trinity Journal* (Fall):179–205.

Pearse, Meic. 2004. *Why the rest hates the West: Understanding the roots of global rage.* Downers Grove, Ill.: InterVarsity Press.

Sadiki, Larbi. 2002. *The search for Arab democracy.* New York: Columbia Univ. Press.

Said, Edward. 1976. Arabs, Islam, and the dogmas of the West. *New York Times Book Review*, Oct. 31, pp. 4–5.

———. 2001. The Clash of Ignorance. *The Nation*, Oct. 22.

Shipps, Jan. 1985. *Mormonism: The story of a new religious tradition.* Urbana: Univ. of Illinois Press.

———. 2000. *Sojourner in the promised land: Forty years among the Mormons.* Urbana: Univ. of Illinois Press.

Zehner, Edwin. 2009. Review of *Christian Theology in Asia*, ed. Sebastian C. H. Kim. *The Journal of Asian Studies* 68, 2 (May):583–85.

———. and Jeff Petersen. 2009. Conflict and conversation in Mormon-evangelical relations: Toward a more ethnographic approach. Presentation at the annual meeting of the American Academy of Religion, Montreal, November.

Part II:

Integrity in Personal Morality

4

Ethics and Accountability in the Mission Community

WILLIAM D. TAYLOR

Before me is a pair of shoes. I have called them "The Old Marathoner's Shoes," for they remind me of life and ministry, not as a sprint, nor even as a mid-range race, but the marathon of our pilgrimage on this earth, following the Living God, attempting to live, serve, and finish well. They belonged to my aging father; I had asked him to mail me a pair of his old shoes, reminders of what it meant to finish well.

The last time he was able to converse with me, before that terrible Alzheimer's finished destroying his brain, was in the extended care facility where he and my mother lived until the end. As the elevator doors opened to their floor, he was there. It was as if he had sensed I was coming and his rheumy eyes caught sight of me. I walked to hug him, and then he said in his wavering, jerky voice, "Bill . . . . you taught me . . . . how to . . . . finish well . . . . and I'm . . . . trying to. . . ."

You will find those shoes on a prominent shelf in my office. They speak, they walk, they challenge, and they encourage me.

And at this latter stage of my own pilgrimage-marathon, I need help to finish well. Too many of my friends and colleagues have not. But the majority have, or are, as of this day. These old shoes offer a physical metaphor of this chapter on ethics and accountability in the mission community.

A few stories come to mind. One is of a student at Moody Bible Institute, too many years ago: a case of cheating on final exams. It is the story of divine intervention through the godly preaching of an old New Jersey pastor and the spiritual sensitivity of Moody's president, who, sensing the work of the Spirit, canceled all classes for the remainder of the day. These led to the conviction of the Holy Spirit and confession of sin in the life of this student. Confessing to God led to the next, hard step—confessing to the dean of students. To the student's astonishment, this elderly man of God ministered God's grace and restoration in the middle of tears, imparting encouragement and shared sorrow. He had to take the case to the Academic Committee, who thankfully did not expel the student, but did put him on academic probation for two years. Yes, I am that student.

I have fresh in my heart and mind the case of a keen young couple, attempting to establish the church among an unreached people group in one of the most demon-infested areas of the world, the Tibetan plateau. Their team of missionaries had acquired a new leader with zero cross-cultural experience and minimal people skills. He applied to missions the same ruthless tactics that made him successful in the marketplace. And in the process, he demolished the lives of too many couples, including two of my personal friends. This toxic leader forced people out of the team who did not fit his management-by-objectives, tangible-outcomes model. When my friends returned to the United States, broken in health and spirit, their restoration took almost three years. But the demonic attacks continue, now aimed at their adolescent daughters.

As my German friend Harry Hoffman, member care leader in a large Central Asian country, says, "There are too many sad stories": broken vows, marriage breakdowns, lost children, financial mismanagement, power games, sexual defeats.

All of us feel the sickness in the pit of our stomachs when we hear or read about or witness yet another evangelical leader who has fallen due to sin. We would do well not to criticize the Roman Catholic Church in their crisis regarding the sexual abuse of children. Rather, we must learn from them, whether positively or negatively.

However, the majority (please, Lord, may it be true!) of our mission community is probably doing better rather than worse, attempting to serve with integrity, growing in the fullness of the Spirit as they develop their unique giftedness in global service.

My gut feeling is that we all want to finish well. Robert Clinton suggests five reasons (to which I add two final ones) why Christian leaders are not finishing well:

- Moral problems
- Financial misconduct
- Serious family difficulties
- Abuse of power
- Plateauing (drifting into mediocrity towards the end of active service)
- Allowing spiritual dry rot to destroy our passion and integrity
- Inability to transfer institutional authority and responsibility to a successor

We all want to finish well by God's grace. And we can if we work at it.

Grappling with the Issues

These written reflections originate from a plenary address given at the meeting of CrossGlobal Link and the Evangelical Missiological Society in Orlando, September 2009. In preparation for that presentation, I wrote a number of my global mission colleagues in different countries, asking questions and requesting some of their internal documents. Many served me well, and some sent confidential agency documents that laid out crucial values and procedures. I am grateful to them all.

My knowledge base does not come only from my forty-five years in cross-cultural ministry, during which I studied Christian leadership the entire time. My own father modeled a high caliber of leadership. We also learned much from the two WEA Mission Commission studies on attrition and retention. Many of our readers are familiar with the research projects on attrition in the mid-1990s, *Too Valuable to Lose: Exploring the Causes and Cures of Missionary Attrition* (William Carey Library, 1997), which I edited, and then ten years later the study of retention and best practices, *Worth Keeping: Global Perspectives on Best Practices in Missionary Retention* (William Carey Library, 2007), edited by Rob Hay et al. Both publications, purposefully given parallel titles, have had an impact on the global mission movement.

Now in the twenty-first century we find new causes of attrition to work through in addition to those explored in the studies, among them Internet pornography, available worldwide. We have a greater sensitivity to demonic backgrounds (both in the Global South and in the North). We grapple with the delicate issue of gender confusion. We continue to grow in our understanding of best practices for mission and church leadership.

Five Arenas in Which Ethics and Accountability Must Be Examined

I have served in most of the arenas within the mission community. Hence, I describe the arenas from both a personal and a historic perspective.

The first arena is the *personal family circle*. Here, we speak of deeply rooted sin or past brokenness (demonic backgrounds, gender confusion); of sexual sin (by both men and women, and by children); of broken family systems that rear their ugly head; of hidden addictions (whether porn or the pathological need to travel, with its toll paid by marriage and children); of abuse of power (toxic leaders are just one example), and of growing violence against spouse and children—primarily (but not exclusively) by the husband/father.

The second arena is the *ministry team*—which includes the mobilizer, church, mission agency/society, or academy leadership—a large and complex conglomerate of diverse mission entities. Much has been written about church leadership ethics and accountability issues, and this overlaps with other entities who form ministry teams.

The third arena is the *national mission movement, network, or association*. The nomenclature varies from nation to nation. Only in the United States do we find the anomalous case of more than one national mission movement. The WEA Mission Commission (MC) is connected to some fifty such movements around the world, and the diversity is vast. But all have some kind of leadership, and with it their own particular challenges, especially when they serve as unpaid volunteers.

The fourth arena includes *other mission entities*, such as professional organizations (e.g., Evangelical Missiological Society, International Society for Frontier Missiology, and American Society of Missiology). They overlap with other arenas, especially with the academy, but there are particular issues that apply to each one in singular ways.

A fifth arena is hard to nail down—*the world of the independent church, including teachers, mobilizers, prayer teams, very small network mission leaders, trusts, and foundations*. Many are one-person or Mom and Pop entities. Many are freelancers. Some are related to an outside system of accountability with a known structure that guarantees their curriculum vitae, their finances, their leadership, their field work, their governance. But many have none of these. These groups, or individuals, are a particular challenge to evaluate due to the unique nature of their autonomy in life, family, and ministry. Today, with generous laws of incorporation in the United States and with the Internet, one can launch what appears to be a huge, global ministry, but that has little in the way of visible accountability structures. In some cases due diligence reveals very little substance.

Recently a young couple that I am mentoring into mission sent me an e-mail about a new agency that they really thought sounded like what they were looking for. I immediately wrote some people who would know. I went to the organization's Web site and studied every link. I tried to discover who had awarded the D.Min. degrees to their leadership, or more about that seminary with such a rich Web site. My colleagues who know much about the mission world wrote back saying they had never heard of the group before. It is not that these entities do not exist, or that they do not (probably) do a good job. It is just that due diligence is hard to establish. It was my task to gently give my report and simply state, "I really think there is a much better agency match for you out there. Let's keep working on it." Thankfully, their response was mature.

The final arena embraces perhaps the *fuzzier entities, global networks, associations, or alliances.* More and more of these are emerging, and the "flatter" they are, the more complex the challenges of accountability. After all, when one extension of a star-fish is cut off, it replaces itself, or that severed part regenerates into a fully new creature. Discipline and restoration of network or alliance partners is tough because the accountability structure is diffused, and in some cases, non-existent. Many servants in this arena operate from home offices, and "punch in" whenever they wish, or not. In some cases, they never leave their office.

These are the arenas of our concern.

Consider Carefully Terms That Characterize Positions, Affirmations, and Documents

Those of us who live now in the United States and Europe have to be increasingly careful of our language, our structures, and our internal documents that guide best practices, disciplinary processes, and financial-legal issues. The United States in particular is a litigious culture, but I suspect that Brussels (center of the European Union) will produce as fast as possible rules and regulations that will apply to all Christian entities.

What are some of these terms?

- Principles and practice, perhaps the oldest language

- Terms and conditions, which we find used in Global Connections, the national mission movement in the United Kingdom
- Policies and procedures
- Codes of best practice
- Codes of conduct
- Best Codes and Standards of Conduct (Global Connections is most helpful; see www.globalconnections.co.uk/codes andstandards)
- Guidelines of discipline (for various causes: moral, family, toxic leadership, theological change, financial mismanagement, abuse of power, conduct unbecoming a Christian leader), redress, appeal, and hopefully, restoration (within or no longer with the organization or school or ministry)
- Covenants, which carry a much more serious language of integrity commitments

Surely many readers can add to this list, and I would appreciate hearing from you.

Lessons of Value from Two WEA Case Studies

In 1992, WEA suffered a body blow with the moral collapse of one of its key leaders. That led to the *Singapore Covenant*. In 2006 the Mission Commission had to deal with a very painful issue of toxic leadership, which led to the *Granada Covenant*. I will address both of these histories and covenants, for, while similar, they are significantly different. To aid further study, the WEA MC dedicated the August 2007 issue of *Connections: The Journal of the WEA Mission Commission* to codes of good practices in the missional arena. Both the *Singapore Covenant* and the *Granada Covenant* can be read or downloaded at www.weaconnections.com/Back-issues/Codes-of-Good-Practice-in-the-missional-arena.aspx.

Both of these documents emerged from the painful reality of personal sin that reverberates around the world: moral failure, family breakdown, financial deception, power abuse, hidden addictions. Both case studies challenged all of us in the WEA and MC community deeply. Both covenants passed through an extended process of draft, evaluation, and consensus to arrive at the final edited document. Issues of language were key, as in some cultures there is no easy equivalent for terms like "partnership" or "accountability," though all cultures have clear dynamic equivalents. Both covenants were applied to a global network with fuzzy boundaries, many offices, too many invitations to travel, and the challenge/danger of working without organizational accountability.

The Singapore Covenant: 1993–95

My assignment to work on this process and document came from Jun Vencer, WEF's international director from 1992 to 2001. When we were shaken to our core by the fall of our respected colleague, Vencer asked me to chair the team to formulate our response.

In 1994 I wrote to a number of personal friends and colleagues, and Chuck Swindoll sent me his strong church-based position on discipline and restoration. In personal correspondence he wrote of a group of men who at that time would meet weekly and ask and answer these seven key questions:

- Have you been with a woman this week in a way that was inappropriate or could have looked to others as though you were using poor judgment?

- Have you been completely above reproach in all your financial dealings this week?
- Have you exposed yourself to any explicit unhealthy material this week?
- Have you spent time daily in prayer and in the Scriptures this week?
- Have you fulfilled the mandate of your calling this week?
- Have you taken time off to be with your family this week?
- Have you just lied to me?

The application of these questions to a global movement such as WEA is encouraging to read and ponder.

My personal mentor since 1967, David Howard, international director of WEF (now WEA) from 1982 to 1992, led me to a marvelous resource. Dave knew of a critical document called "The Modesto Manifesto," which had marked with sterling and long-term quality the leadership of the core Graham team: Billy Graham, George Beverly Shea, Grady Wilson, and Cliff Barrows.

It is vitally important that we understand the four key elements of ethics and accountability that have been crucial to the credibility of the Billy Graham team through the decades. Beyond that team, countless numbers have been impacted by Graham's written document and commitment to purity. I googled "Modesto Manifesto," and Google cited 1,790,000 hits.

The context of this core document emerged from the November, 1948, Graham Crusade. Sinclair Lewis' *Elmer Gantry*, a novel caricaturing an unscrupulous evangelist, and Graham's understanding of the raw power of the media's influence caused Graham and his team to ponder their personal accountability. In his Modesto, California, hotel, Graham called the team together to discuss their ethics, purity, humility, and integrity. Each man then went to his room to jot down the key terms. Returning, they converged on four affirmations.

I have identified the four affirmations in my words, as many documents have different phrases. I compiled these from the Billy Graham Archives of Wheaton College (www.wheaton.edu/bgc/archives/faq/4.htm; accessed May 20, 2010).

- The Graham team would avoid any appearance of financial abuse.
- They would exercise extreme care to avoid even the appearance of any sexual impropriety (from that time forward Graham made it a point not to travel, meet, or eat alone with any woman other than his wife Ruth).
- They would cooperate with any local churches that were willing to participate in united evangelistic effort.
- They would be honest and reliable in their publicity and reporting of results.

Some other sources explain these commitments, but it does not take much to adapt them for today: money (they would not emphasize offerings, would accept a straight salary, and would insure that all accounts were open and certified), immorality (this classic temptation was countered by having hotel rooms close to each other; Graham's vow even meant that a colleague would search his hotel room before Graham entered), exaggeration (no puffing of the numbers; they allowed numbers to be set by local police, fire departments, or arena managers), criticism (they would not even criticize their harsh critics).

I am astonished at the power of this modest Modesto Manifesto, and the way it helped sustain over sixty years of integrity in ministry.

My files—both paper and electronic—contain scores of documents that trace their development to the seminal Graham team document, including the aforementioned documents from Swindoll plus many from other sources. All of these, in addition to interviews, correspondence, reflection, counsel, and prayer, led WEA to a watershed moment in Singapore. The final *Singapore Covenant* emerged as the fifth draft of our collegial work.

On June 3, 1994, I wrote our senior staff the preparation letter. Here are some excerpts.

Dear WEF Colleagues,

Within a month we shall meet in Singapore for our full staff meetings. Jun Vencer has slotted time in the program for me to guide a session for us to discuss again the matter of WEF staff and accountability. During this time I am proposing that we hammer out a final draft of what could be called the *Singapore Covenant*, a statement/affirmation on ethics and accountability that would set a standard for all WEF staff. The International Council might want to evaluate its application to them as key players in the WEF world. What I present here is a fifth draft. I would appreciate any feedback that will allow me to revise this version. That way when we arrive in Singapore we are closer to the same page on the issues and can dialogue more significantly, and hopefully come to conclusion. Nothing which I present here is final decision, although I am making some strong recommendations that will initiate the agenda for discussion.

What is the rationale for a covenant for WEF like this? I believe the reasons can be articulated in the following six factors.

First, God is steering WEF to an historic position of global credibility and influence. This means a much more visible national and international profile for WEF and its senior staff, requiring of all of us unusual commitment to holiness, integrity and accountability.

Second, we are stunned on a regular basis at the moral fall of renowned evangelical leaders. We have a recent specific example that most directly damaged the WEF family.

Third, we as a small senior staff team tend to operate from widely distributed bases, with offices in Australia, Singapore, Philippines, Korea, the U.K., United States (Wheaton, Miami, Austin, Lexington), Germany, Canada, New Zealand, and perhaps other cities. Many of us have our office in our homes and therefore are not in daily contact with colleagues. This requires creativity in our leadership, but also isolates us from ongoing WEF and colleague relationships. We all need each other, but those who office at home must take special precautions to ensure accountable relationships.

Fourth, "Broken moral integrity means the spiritual leader forfeits the right to lead." This document is designed as preventive medicine for our staff team. In our worst dreams we would not want a WEF colleague to forfeit his or her ministry due to a violation of spiritual vows and lost moral integrity.

Fifth, something like the *Singapore Covenant* can become a kind of public model of institutional ethics and personal accountability. If God enables us to draft and sign a statement, we can then go on public record that this is our stance, not for pride's sake, nor as an organizational one-upmanship; rather it is a commitment we make in light of the terrible toll we all feel with the fall of our leaders, as well as our commitment to prevent more falls in our immediate circle.

The senior WEF staff met in Singapore, where our international headquarters were at the time. We spent hours discussing face to face what we had circulated by fax (the prime, rapid international communication mechanism of that time). After extended dialogue and consensus on a final draft, we had a ceremony and signing in Singapore. That document is found at the end of this chapter for your perusal.

An Evaluation of This Process and Document

I believe this covenant had a substantive impact on the staff at that time. Perhaps because I was involved in crafting it, to this day I remember certain exchanges, and the core content is with me. Regretfully though, and honestly, I acknowledge that rather little happened after the Singapore signing. The document itself did not have internal longevity nor application, as it was not central to the top leadership agenda. I wonder and lament whether it was an experiment in vain. I hope not.

For an ethics and accountability document like this to have longevity, the following must take place.

- First, this issue must be central to the top leadership.
- Second, any statement like this must be affirmed by the staff on a regular basis.
- Third, it must be reviewed and revised to sustain its relevance.

However, the 1994 project took on new meaning in 2006 when the Mission Commission came to grips with a different kind of leadership problem.

The Granada Covenant: 2006

The immediate stimulus for the *Granada Covenant* came from a different context and cause than the WEF issue. In the 2006 MC case, a network leader disobeyed the specific counsel of our leadership, abused the position, and was asked to step down. It is important to clarify, though, that this specific case was only one component in the move to a new covenant. The MC leadership had been increasingly discussing what it meant to finish well, and we were probably already moving to some form of document with which to spur each other on toward that good finish.

In light of my experience with the *Singapore Covenant*, Bertil Ekström, MC executive director, tasked me with the creation of a working draft that would be prayed over, edited, and finally released. I am thankful for Bertil's confidence in me, and his competence in chairing this process, along with Rose Dowsett and K. Rajendran (MC chair and vice chair), who placed their imprimatur on the final document.

The WEA Mission Commission leadership converted the core of the *Singapore Covenant*, making adaptations to its own situation. It was submitted by the MC Global Leadership Council to all MC Associates (those formally linked to the MC via annual financial contribution and participation in one of the working teams, networks, or MC units), and a final draft was authorized. Signing the *Granada Covenant* is now a requirement for membership as an MC Associate.

It was crafted to spur all MC leaders to integrity and holiness, to faithfulness in marital vows, to full financial transparency, to personal and corporate transformational discipleship, to serious mutual accountability, and to the honorable treatment of one another as created in the image of God. The degree to which MC leaders fall short may determine their continuance in ministry and as MC Associates.

We again faced the problems that networks and alliances encounter regarding an accountability covenant. Who has the authority to act when the covenant has been broken? To whom do the MC or "docked" ministries belong? How do we work with the accountability team of the problematic person? What if she or he says that their formal accountability leadership has given them permission to act this way? Then what does the MC leadership do?

Let me clarify the difference between the wholly owned MC working teams and what we have called the "docked" teams, networks, and working units. The MC has created a number of its own teams, primarily called task forces or networks. The MC units currently include:

- National Mission Movements
- The Global Dialogue Forum
- Publications and *Connections* team
- International Missionary Training Network
- Global Missiology Task Force
- Global Member Care Network
- Mission Mobilization Task Force–research project
- Continuum—Younger Mission Leaders Task Force
- Missional Churches and Pastors Task Force
- AiM: Arts in Mission Task Force
- JIMI: Joint Information Management Initiative

In a separate category are those networks and ministries that have "docked" with the MC. They identify a win-win relationship with the MC through more formal contact, based on a Memorandum of Understanding crafted by their leadership and that of the MC. These now include:

- ETHNE—global network focused on less-reached peoples
- IPA: Interdev Partners Associates
- RHP: Refugee Highway Partnership
- SEALINK—South East Asia network focused on less-reached peoples
- TI: Tentmakers International

The MC accountability relationship is very different between the first and second groups. In the first category, the top leadership is appointed by the MC's executive director. Thus, the accountability relationship is directly linked with the MC, even if that person has been released by a "parent ministry" to serve with the MC. Therefore, any ethics problem is an MC issue, though it must be acted upon wisely in conjunction with the official leadership of the colleague.

An Evaluation of the Granada Covenant

I sense that this affirmation and challenge has in general been more helpful to the MC than the *Singapore Covenant* was to WEF. The reason is that the MC leadership continues to uphold the Granada document as a key instrument to challenge us all to a higher standard of ethics and accountability. As I will affirm in the final observations, however, ultimately no document, affirmation, or covenant can deal definitively with the darkness of the human heart.

The MC grapples with some of the same problems as the broader WEA family. We live far from each other, meet by Skype on a regular basis, and try to convene twice a year in a central location. None of us, however, punches a clock at a physical office. Our accountability teams are self-appointed, and hopefully they work effectively and pastorally.

Yet this covenant has served to challenge us all and is a continuing guideline for MC Associates. As mentioned earlier, the full statement can be downloaded from the MC Web site.

A Significant Side Note: The WEA Attempt of 2006

The most recent attempt by WEA's leadership to craft an ethics statement took place in 2006, partially in the context of the Ted Haggard scandal. Haggard had been head of NAE, the WEA-related body in the United States. While there were some discussions and exchanges, no final decisions emerged. This is regrettable. Below I share segments of a letter I wrote to the WEA leadership as these matters were being broached.

November 8, 2006

Dear Colleagues,

Thank you for your gracious words on the MC code of best personal practices. But before we go any further, please note that it is something crafted by the Mission Commission leadership for our own MC Associates. This is an idea for our International Leadership Team to consider, but it is not a final draft. It would have to be discussed and revised to become more realistic for the broader WEA family.

Our MC project was not crafted as a knee-jerk reaction to the Haggard case, but as a result of our own MC history and personal commitments before God and our family, and our vows of integrity and fidelity. Let us keep this in mind and then if the Spirit makes it clear, we shall work together to craft something fresh and valid for today's WEA.

No statement of any kind substitutes for personal decisions, integrity and accountability.

William D. Taylor
Global Ambassador for WEA and the Mission Commission

Final Observations and Reflections

Following are eight of my own observations and reflections.

First, I am convinced that no ecclesial stream and its mission structures (whether charismatic or Pentecostal, evangelical or liturgical-sacramental), and no school, or mission agency, or church has a monopoly on integrity, holiness, spirituality, or sin. Neither can any of these streams or structures guarantee the life of the kingdom of Christ. All streams require battle and vigilance, self-awareness, and lifelong transformation. The renovation of the heart requires the commitment to a long obedience in the same direction. Thank you, Dallas Willard and Eugene Peterson, for your example and reflections.

Second, there must be commitment by the top leadership of a mission structure or entity for any ethics and accountability document like the ones I have presented to have longevity. These issues must be central to the top leadership; statements must be affirmed by a staff team on a regular basis; the document must be reviewed and revised to sustain its relevance.

Third, we can have all of the codes, best practices, principles and practices, documents, and covenants possible in our mission structures and life, but if there is no core personal commitment to integrity and holiness in both leadership (modeled by leaders) and the rank and file (motivated by the Jesus life and empowered by the Spirit), it is to no avail. At the end of the day, ethics and accountability are a matter of faithfulness to our vows and willingness to do battle against flesh, world system, and arch-enemy.

Fourth, there is no substitute for the accountability of a very small, tested team of friends and colleagues who have the courage and invitation to speak hard truth to us. Gordon MacDonald, who knows failure, stated that all men who have failed in their marriage vows were not accountable to anybody. Chuck Swindoll said the same in his correspondence with me. And this circle of accountability is rooted in the intimacy and authenticity of the home, of the relationship between wife and husband, parents and children.

Fifth, I believe we agree that the purpose of ministerial discipline is restoration of the person. Restoration is interpreted in wildly diverse ways, however, especially in the lax American version of Christianity many of us live with. We fear lawsuits; we fear being charged with being prejudiced and narrow; we fear the application of a kind of tough love; we do not want to appear penal in our codes; we do not want people to feel bad. I have seen enough cases of serious financial mismanagement by leadership that could have been taken to court, but were not, whether for mercy's sake or for fear of bad publicity or because it would be too much work.

At the same time, for perhaps all of the cases in which I have witnessed firm but loving discipline, the outcomes were painful, but right. And ultimately they heal. Yet this does not automatically restore a person to the same ministry as before. In some cases the person simply must step out of professional Christian ministry. For how long? I do not know.

Sixth, we desperately need models of godliness that are long lasting. I am profoundly grateful to those who have modeled this to me: my father; David Howard (as mentioned, my mentor since 1967); my wife, Yvonne. Will we be that to others, volitionally, consciously? How sad to hear a missionary grieve, "During my fifteen years on the field, I must honestly say that only one person modeled integrity and character to me."

Seventh, we need to open a space for the intercessors and the confessors of our movement. We know about the first, but how about the second, the confessors? We have rightly reacted against Roman Catholic extremes of auricular confession of sin, but have we discarded a virtue and a gift? As a member of an evangelical Anglican church, I am impressed that, particularly on Holy Friday, the pastor stays afterward to listen to confessions. An evangelical! So, who will listen to our sin (besides the psychologist or psychiatrist) and work us through the process of confession and forgiveness?

Finally, can we assume that each agency and institution, alliance and school, team and network, or other group represented by the North American mission movement has written statements of principles and practice, values and behavior, disciplinary and restoration process, appeal process, protection for the whistleblowers, even some kind of covenant for leaders and members? If not, then they should. How are our leaders grappling with the hidden addictions of mission and educational ministry?

Drawing to a Close

I wonder to what degree we have or have not applied the Pauline qualities for spiritual leadership in our mission structures. Are they equally valid for ministries outside of the local church? Why not? What would it mean for them to guide us in our overall spiritual leadership? Even as I draft these ideas, I mull over a perturbing case of an academic leader who has abused his roles as husband and academic authority. Based on Paul's guidelines, the least this person would have to do is to step out of leadership until radical repentance and behavioral change comes.

In his deceptively small book, *In the Name of Jesus* (1988), Henri Nouwen articulates his reflections on Christian leadership. His themes and structure come from the temptation of Jesus. In essence, he affirms and calls for the following shifts in our orientation:

From relevance to prayer:
- The temptation: to be relevant
- The question: "Do you love me?"
- The discipline: contemplative prayer

From popularity to ministry:
- The temptation: to be spectacular
- The task: "feed my sheep"
- The discipline: confession and forgiveness

From leading to being led:
- The temptation: to be powerful
- The task: "Someone else will take you"
- The discipline: theological reflection

4 — William D. Taylor

Nouwen concludes, "I leave you with the image of the leader with outstretched hands, who chooses a life of downward mobility. It is the image of the praying leader, the vulnerable leader, and the trusting leader. May that image fill your hearts with hope, courage, and confidence as you anticipate the next century" (p. 73).

Questions for Discussion

1. What does the author of this chapter mean by the term "toxic leaders," and what examples might you be able to identify from your own experience or your study of the work of missions or the church?
2. How do the seven questions raised by Charles Swindoll apply to missionaries who might work in remote parts of a country in isolation from other team members?
3. How might standards of accountability be practiced by missionaries in the context of national believers as well as their own missionary peer groups?
4. How might the *Singapore Covenant* and the *Granada Covenant* be used to prepare future missionaries to incorporate higher ethical standards in their ministries?

Appendix

The Singapore Covenant
World Evangelical Fellowship

WEF Mission Statement [as of 1994]

World Evangelical Fellowship and member organizations exist to establish and help regional and national evangelical alliances empower and mobilize local churches and Christian organizations to disciple the nations for Christ.

Prologue to the Covenant

In dependence upon the Holy Spirit, fully identified with World Evangelical Fellowship, supporting its mission statement, and in sincere inter-dependent partnership with each other as vital members of the WEF family, we the staff members solemnly affirm these commitments before the Triune God.

1. We commit ourselves to personal purity. We affirm the need for vital personal growth in Christ, with transparency before God and our colleagues. Integrity, holiness must mark our personal walk with God. These are intimate matters, but at the same time we can and must submit them to scrutiny by loving and honest colleagues. We will establish a personal team of fellow servants who will call us to authentic accountability in our private, family and public worlds. When necessary we will submit to and support restorative discipline.

2. We commit ourselves to the spiritual disciplines. We confess that as Christian leaders we have given too little time to prayer and the Word, and we ask God's forgiveness for this inconsistency. We as WEF staff desire that our ministry be marked by personal godliness, not only by competency, strategic thinking, and effective programs. We pledge to encourage and challenge each other, by sharing articles and books that have impacted us directly, by praying for each other and by informing each other that we do so pray.

3. We commit ourselves to our family. We affirm that parents and/or spouse and children are our initial responsibility. May our ministry not be at their expense, producing bitterness, but rather resulting in love and respect. We will seek to maintain a balance between family and ministry to others. We shall submit our travel schedules to our spouses as well as our accountability team.

4. We commit ourselves to a local church. We will seek opportunities for witness and service according to our gifts and time. We will model in our local churches what we in WEF desire to see built in the worldwide Body of Christ.

5. We commit ourselves to financial integrity. We accept our responsibility as stewards of God's resources, and will open our personal financial records to trusted colleagues. Our corporate financial books can be evaluated by competent believers who articulate a valid cause to know how we raise, account for and use funds.

6. We commit ourselves to respect Christian organizations and leaders. We seek to build up the Body of Christ! We confess that too easily we can belittle others. We wish to be characterized as a movement that genuinely affirms other leaders and the ministries they serve. Where there is error, however, we will speak the truth in love.

7. We commit ourselves to honest communication. We will report stories and statistics accurately, without embellishment. We shall give credit to the individuals and organizations involved.

We covenant that our lives and ministry will by God's grace exemplify Scripture: "You are witnesses, and so is God, of how

holy, righteous and blameless we were among you who believed."
I Thessalonians 2:10.

To the greater glory of our God and in anticipation of that magnificent, ongoing worship scene in heaven.

Signed in Singapore, July 5, 1994

Granada Covenant of Best Personal and Ministry Practice
World Evangelical Alliance Mission Commission

Affirmations of the Mission Commission Global Leadership Council created for the MC Associate community

In dependence upon the Holy Spirit, fully identified with the vision, purpose and values of the Mission Commission; in sincere interdependent partnership with each other as vital members of the global missional family; we, the worldwide community known as Mission Commission Associates, affirm these commitments before the Triune God:

1. We commit ourselves to personal purity. We affirm the need for vital personal growth in Christ, of transparency before God and our colleagues. Integrity and holiness must mark our personal walk with God. These are intimate matters, but at the same time we can and must submit them to scrutiny by loving and honest colleagues. We will establish a personal team of 3–5 fellow servants who are authorized to call us to authentic accountability in our private, family and public worlds. When necessary, we will submit to and support transforming repentance, forgiveness, discipline and restoration.

2. We commit ourselves to the spiritual disciplines of transformational discipleship. We confess that as Christian leaders we have given too little time to prayer, the Word, to fasting and meditation, to worship and deeper reflection. We ask God's forgiveness for this inconsistency. We in Mission Commission leadership desire that our ministry be marked by personal integrity and godliness, and not only by competency, strategic thinking, quality research and effective programs. We pledge to help, encourage and challenge each other by sharing valuable sources, counsel, articles and books that have impacted us directly, by praying for each other and by informing each other that we do so pray. We commit to read some of the challenging and even difficult books on spiritual formation that have been produced by women and men of God over the centuries who know what they speak of.

3. We commit ourselves to our family. We affirm that parents and/or spouse and children are our priority ministry responsibility. May our ministry, especially if it requires extensive travel, not be carried out at their expense, producing bitterness and alienation from family and/or faith, but rather resulting in love and respect. We will seek to maintain a balance between family and outside ministry.

4. We commit to invite the intervening and convicting Spirit of God into our interior landscape. He must examine us, our weaknesses and addictions in ministry, some of which we list: abuse of our position and authority, unjust treatment of fellow-workers, excessive travel, weakness in personal morality and temptation, attraction to Internet pornography, gender confusion, struggles with faithfulness to the spirit as well as the law of our marriage vows.

We shall submit our travel schedules to our spouses as well as our accountability team. We will not accept any invitation unless at least 48 hours have gone by. We are fully aware of the subtle craving for extended ministry travel. The price already paid by some of our friends and colleagues is all too clear. When needed, we ask the Spirit of God, and our sisters and brothers, to expose this addiction and help us recover from it.

5. We commit ourselves to a local church. We will seek opportunities for witness and service according to our gifts and time. We will model in our local churches what we in the broader World Evangelical Alliance community desire to see built in the worldwide Body of Christ. We desire to see vital missional churches who truly impact their community and from that base spiral out to the world.

6. We commit ourselves to financial integrity. We accept our responsibility as stewards of God's resources. We will reveal our funding proposals and open our personal financial records to trusted colleagues for their critique. Our corporate financial books will be evaluated by competent accounting firms who can examine our finances and by courageous colleagues who can evaluate our motives and processes as we raise, account for and utilize funds.

7. We commit ourselves to respect Christian organizations and leaders and honest communication. We seek to build up the Body of Christ! We confess that too easily we fall to the temptation to belittle other colleagues and ministries. We wish to be characterized as a movement that genuinely affirms other leaders and the ministries they serve. Where there is error, however, we will speak the truth in love. We will report stories and statistics accurately, without embellishment. We shall give credit to sources as well as individuals and organizations involved and not take credit for that which we have not accomplished.

We affirm these seven commitments as a personal and corporate covenant of best ministry practice, exemplifying the Apostle's charge: "*You yourselves are our witnesses—and so is God—that we were pure and honest and faultless toward all of you believers,*" I Thessalonians 2:10.

To be signed by the Mission Commission staff, Global Leadership Council, and all Mission Commission Associates as one way of demonstrating our commitment to the vision, purposes and values of the Mission Commission.

Note: The signing began in Granada, Spain, November 2006.

5

Internet Pornography and Missions

STEVEN G. EDLIN

A missionary is counseling several men who have an Internet pornography problem. The missionary has never visited a pornographic Web site. He often works late in the evening on his computer. One night he decides to go online to see what the men he is counseling are looking at. He becomes addicted to Internet pornography and now spends his late nights viewing pornography on his computer. One day his assistant discovers pornographic pictures on his computer and the secret is revealed.

Another missionary is a country director. One day he calls his regional director and confesses he has a problem with Internet pornography. He has struggled with pornography since his college days. His wife has caught him numerous times. Each time, he tells her he is sorry and will never do it again. Recently when his wife was out of town he spent eight hours on the Internet looking at pornography. When he confessed it to his wife this time, she told him that if he did not call his director she would.

Can you relate to these situations? How would you handle such a situation? These are composites of situations I have encountered. The temptations of Internet pornography are a present reality. But how big a problem is pornography on the Internet in missions? Are these cases exceptions or do they indicate a growing trend?

Statistics on Internet Pornography

Surveys tend to show little difference in behavior between Christians and the general population in consumption of Internet pornography. They suggest that 50 to 60 percent of Christian men and 30 percent of Christian women have viewed Internet pornography. The percentages for teens are higher than for adults, and the gap between male and female is shrinking.[1]

Though we would like to believe that missionaries are committed to living by a higher moral standard, little if any research has been done just on missionaries, and research on comparable groups gives little cause for complacency.[2] One set of data available to us consists of studies done of pastors. In a 2001 survey conducted by *Christianity Today*, 51 percent of pastors said cyber porn was a temptation, 37 percent said it was a current struggle, and 40 percent indicated that they had visited a porn site.[3] That survey is now dated, and both Internet access and the availability of pornography on it has only increased.

The counseling office of TEAM recently completed a review of the confidential sexual questionnaires filled out by applicants as part of the psychological assessment portion of the application process. We were looking for clues that might tell us how vulnerable TEAM's current workers are. Our assumption was that a person's past history might indicate his or her vulnerability to Internet pornography. The questionnaires were all from missionaries who had been accepted for service with TEAM. While protecting the confidentiality of the questionnaires, we tabulated the number of times certain things were mentioned by 227 missionaries.

The categories we were most interested in were how many had viewed pornography as a child or youth, had viewed pornography recently, had a problem with masturbation either in the past or presently, or were sexually active outside of marriage before or after they became serious about their Christian faith. We found that 45 percent of men had viewed pornography in childhood and 15 percent had viewed it recently. Only 7 percent of the women had viewed pornography in childhood, and none of them had viewed it recently. One of the more significant pieces of information was that 42 percent of the men and 40 percent of the women had been sexually active before marriage.

What can we learn from these statistics? Clearly we need more research to be able to answer the question precisely, but I believe that it is possible to learn something from these statistics about the vulnerability of missionaries. Before commenting though I first want to discuss what is meant by "Internet pornography." Pornography has changed. It used to be a matter of looking at pictures of naked people. With the advent of the Internet this definition is too narrow. So what do we mean by "Internet pornography"?

Definition of Internet Pornography

Internet pornography certainly includes hard-core pornography (there are over 42 million Web sites with hard-core pictures and videos), and soft-core pornography is available at Web sites for magazines such as *Cosmopolitan* or *Maxim*. YouTube has its share of soft-core porn video. Movie trailers and TV programs are online as streaming video. Chat rooms provide opportunity to meet with someone anonymously and have vicarious sex or an emotional affair. For those seeking an emotional affair, e-mail provides a conduit for pictures, video, and chats, and invitations to pornographic Web sites come as spam. Internet pornography is also present on social networking sites; some statistics state that 89 percent of social network users participate in sexual discussion complete with video cams. Users of Facebook may have received an invitation from "Lola," with a sexy picture, wanting to be their "friend." These are just a sampling of what is out there in the way of Internet pornography. Our computers and other electronic devices such as cell phones and iPods now put XXX-rated bookstores, magazine stands, and art theaters at our fingertips, along with topless bars, prostitutes, and mistresses—and the list goes on.

Internet Pornography and Missions

Using this broad definition of Internet pornography, we can draw some conclusions from the statistics. First, missionaries are vulnerable. This conclusion seems reasonable in light of the responses made by missionary applicants to TEAM's confidential sexual questionnaire. A high percentage of applicants have been sexually active before marriage. When this fact is considered along with the high percentage of Christians in general who have viewed pornography, it is reasonable to conclude that missionaries are as vulnerable as most other Christians and, as will become clear in a moment, maybe more vulnerable. Counselors who work in this area say that persons who admit to having viewed pornography once are likely to have done so a number of times.

Particularly is this true of the Christian population, because so much shame is attached to the admission. In general, in answering a confidential questionnaire people are likely to understate or minimize the facts. I believe this is even more likely to be the case for missionaries, since admitting to this behavior could cost them their missionary career.

A second conclusion is that the percentage of those in missions who struggle with Internet pornography is probably higher than we would at first be inclined to suspect. Why? For one reason because our data are too imprecise. TEAM's sexual questionnaire, for example, is not precise and is being revised because the definition of pornography has changed. If an applicant has not been looking for pictures on the Internet, he thinks he has not been involved in pornography. But as Ken Williams of SIL observes, "Our human capacity for self deceit is virtually limitless and nowhere is this truer than in the area of sexual sin."[4] Another reason is that we tend to think that missionaries are somehow more spiritual than the general run-of-the-mill Christian and therefore less vulnerable. In fact, those who are attracted to missionary work have traits such as risk taking and a drive to succeed that may make them more likely to act out sexually, even those who have not been sexually active outside of marriage before becoming missionaries.

Archibald Hart, former dean of Fuller Theological Seminary's Graduate School of Psychology and someone who has long studied missionaries and Christian workers, states, "I've seen sexual impropriety in two categories of pastors: at one end, those who have struggled and failed a lot, who then turn to sexual immorality to make them feel better, and at the highly successful end of the spectrum, those for whom great success no longer brings pleasure. At both those ends, there is a risk of which pastors need to be aware, and take measures to protect themselves. And I am not talking about pastors who are not living godly lives, who aren't sincere in their spirituality!"[5]

A third conclusion is that the problem is likely to get worse. If the statistics on growing teenage use of Internet pornography are accurate, this seems to be a logical inference. The teenagers who are on the Internet today will be joining our organizations very soon. In the last ten years I have seen an increase in applicants who are joining TEAM who have sexual issues. I expect this trend to continue in the future.

Internet pornography is as anonymous, available, and addictive for the missionary as for anyone else. Patrick Carnes, perhaps the leading expert in the area of sexual addiction, speaks of Internet pornography as the "crack cocaine of the twenty-first century." What happens in the brain of a person viewing Internet pornography is so powerful that it can be as addictive as crack cocaine.[6] If this is true, then it is urgent for mission organizations to have a plan that addresses the issue.

Mission leaders are often chosen because they are good at developing strategies for reaching the world. The same caliber of strategic thinking is needed for addressing the issue of Internet pornography within mission organizations. An appropriate organizational strategy will address at least three large domains: prevention, policies and procedures, and response.

Building an Organizational Strategy: Prevention

In an organizational strategy focused on the problem of Internet pornography the initial domain to be addressed needs to be prevention. Organizations as well as individuals often address the problem backwards. They develop ways to deal with individuals who have fallen rather than thinking about prevention. A good organizational strategy will help the individual missionary be wise in how he or she uses the gift and resources of the Internet. It may seem that policies should come before prevention; however, policies and procedures will be more relevant and practical if they are informed by prevention strategies. The goal of an organization's strategy is to enable missionaries to use the Internet wisely within appropriate boundaries.

A common though insufficient strategy for prevention is avoidance, along the lines of the "bruised and bleeding Pharisees," a strict sect of Pharisees who to avoid even looking upon a woman would cover their eyes—and as a result bruised themselves by running into walls. Though solely a defensive strategy, avoidance does have a place. But a proactive strategy is likely to be more successful, for prevention is about more than avoidance. It is about the creation of positive attitudes, relationships, and practices to fill the spaces into which use of pornography might otherwise seep. It involves, first, the creation of a robust environment; second, education; and third, judicious use of the assessment tools at the disposal of mission societies. These three preventive measures are, in turn, composed of a number of building blocks.

Creating a robust environment as prevention. As a preventive strategy, building a robust environment calls for establishing openness, building relationships, and fostering a positive view of sexuality.

Creating an environment of openness in communication demands intentionality. I learned about sex on the street and in church. The church basically said that everything I learned about sex on the streets was dangerous and bad. This condemnatory response shut off communication. It led on my part to thinking of sex as sinful, sexual sin as really bad sin, and therefore something I did not dare to talk about. Attitudes may be changing, but many missionaries have been raised in the type of environment I have described. Unfortunately, what cannot be talked about cannot be dealt with. Since sexual sin thrives in an environment of repression and secrecy, mission organizations need to be intentional about changing the perception that sexual sin cannot be discussed.

Sexual sin goes hand in hand with secrecy. For mission organizations that want to prevent problems of sexual sin from arising, transparency and vulnerability are key issues. Is it okay to be honest about struggles or is openness a one-way ticket back home? Is there grace, compassion, and a commitment to restoration, or is the emphasis on retribution? An environment where it is safe to be transparent and vulnerable makes it easier for missionaries to admit to having a problem and to seek for help.

Relationships are integral to building a robust preventive environment. Organizations need to see relationships that support growth in godliness as a normal part of the Christian life. TEAM asks each missionary to have a personal growth partner. When people have supportive, growth enhancing relationships, they have someone that they can talk with honestly about struggles and temptations. Is it assumed in your organization that everyone will have a close relationship with someone of the same sex with whom he or she can share honestly and openly? Is it clear that this should not be a spouse, but someone outside the marriage and family?

Fostering a positive view of sexuality within an environment of openness and healthy relationships helps to preempt opportunities or inclinations toward unhealthy sexual behavior including viewing of Internet pornography. The best view is that sex is good because God created it, but we must use it wisely. If discussions

5—*Steven G. Edlin*

about sexual matters focus primarily on the dangers of sexual sin, a message will be sent that sex is bad and that we must avoid sex—or else something really bad will happen as punishment. We are, however, sexual beings and we will have sexual feelings. Our message must be that there are wise and appropriate ways to respond to sexual feelings, and there are sinful ways to respond. These are not easy discussions to have but they are necessary if we are to create a healthy environment as a resource for missionary personnel.

Education as prevention. The second main measure in a prevention strategy is education. This includes education about the nature of Internet pornography as well as what Ken Williams calls the "dynamics of sexual temptation."[7] He points out that Christians need to understand the dynamics of sexual temptation as well as their own vulnerability.

Education begins at the top. Do the mission's top leaders see themselves as vulnerable to sexual sin or Internet pornography? What steps are they taking to educate themselves and the inner core of the mission's leaders before they try to educate the rest of the staff? Does the topic figure in the ordinary flow of conversation and reports or only in extraordinary circumstances when moral failure becomes known? Does one hear at a leadership team meeting, for example, remarks such as "I just went to a workshop that talked about Internet pornography; here is what I learned"? Some questions mission executives may want to consider include: Has the mission's top leadership discussed the problem of Internet pornography among themselves? Does the mission's leadership development program include this topic? Is the topic addressed at field conferences, furlough institutes, or other organizational meetings? Is past sexual sin addressed in the application process? What help and counsel does the mission agency provide for those who evidence potential for problems in this area? Is the topic addressed specifically in candidate orientation? Does the mission provide resources for people who are struggling in this area as well as for parents who want to protect their children? Could you as a mission leader ask each member of your organization to read and discuss one or two books you have chosen that clearly outline the issues of sexual sin?

Missionaries may not be part of the inner leadership within their mission agency, but they have roles as leaders in the setting where they are assigned. That is part of what being a missionary entails. Apart from personal vulnerability to sexual temptation, what steps has the mission agency's educational program taken to alert staff to the special vulnerability that comes with being a leader? To quote Archibald Hart again: "There is also the risk that church planters become addicted to their adrenalin, which comes with risk-taking and 'highlight experiences.' There is a lot of novelty associated with church planting, and you become very quickly adapted to this adrenaline surge, which biologically impacts the brain's pleasure center quite significantly. . . . In the beginning of a church plant there are lots of ups and downs, which can build into an addictive process. . . . You might be winning and then suddenly appear to be losing. With a new church, the first time you get 20 people is a high! But later on, if only 20 people come you go into deep depression."[8] Does this sound like missionaries you know? Does this sound like you? Missionaries may in fact be at more than ordinary risk. No one who has fallen ever believed it could happen to him or her. As Ken Williams states, "No one falls into sexual sin, they slide into it."[9] We are all vulnerable in some way.

Education about Internet pornography needs to be addressed in candidate school but must be carried through as part of member training and care. Education as prevention should include review of the dangers of the Internet. It should include discussion of the environmental issues mentioned earlier, including secrecy and healthy sexuality. Education should incorporate brainstorming to generate creative ideas for maintaining integrity in Internet use, such as no Internet use past a certain time or positioning computer screens in the house and office where anyone can see what is being viewed. It should encompass research on helpful resources and computer software strategies. There should be education by example; field missionaries should be told, for instance, what steps the home staff is taking. Some missions are using Covenant Eyes (www.covenanteyes.com); TEAM is in the process of implementing its use for all missionaries.[10] Finally, education should ensure that people know your organization's philosophy if someone falls. Hopefully it is a philosophy of restoration rather than one of retribution.

Assessment as prevention and means for early intervention. The assessment of new applicants which occurs at the very beginning of a missionary's relationship with an agency is an important third means available for an effective prevention strategy. TEAM does a thorough psychological assessment of new applicants. The assessment includes a confidential written sexual history as part of its life history questionnaire. This part of the application (used for the survey discussed above) is seen only by a licensed counselor and does not become part of an employee's file. Answers to the questions give clues to future vulnerability, but they also enable TEAM to identify people who may already have a problem, which provides an opportunity to intervene right at the beginning. Any concerns that arise from the questionnaire are discussed with the candidates, and developmental growth steps are set out to help candidates deal with the issues before they go overseas.

Building an Organizational Strategy: Policies and Procedures

Policies and procedures constitute a bridge between the domain of prevention and the domain of response in a mission organization's overall strategy related to Internet pornography. As suggested by Bob Hodge, one place to begin is with an appropriate Internet use policy.[11] TEAM's employee handbook for the administrative office has such a policy, but to my knowledge nothing similar exists for TEAM's missionaries. At a minimum, a policy makes missionaries aware of the issue.

Policies are often incorrectly thought of as a way to control behavior or as the solution to a problem. In reality they are like speeding laws; they may control the behavior of some but probably not very many and possibly of even fewer missionaries. In the nature of the case, missionaries are given both wide-ranging responsibilities and wide latitude in deciding how they will carry them out. What policies can be helpful for is in conscientizing: raising the issue and alerting missionaries that the organization sees it as a potential problem. While many missionaries may not need to be told this, a formal policy does reinforce the fact that this is an issue that the mission takes seriously.

Many missions have a moral conduct policy, but many of the policies were written before the Internet became a major force; and some policies, such as TEAM's, may not be mission-wide. This is an area that numerous mission agencies probably need to revisit.

Procedures or practical steps to follow in cases of need are also crucial for a mission's strategy. For example, what does a wife do when she discovers that her husband has been involved in Internet pornography? What does a missionary do when he finds he has a problem? Does the information technology staff know whom to go to if they discover evidence of Internet pornography on a machine? What steps does a leader take in handling the revelation of a problem in this area?

TEAM provides an example of one way this can work. As a mission, TEAM has a global member care network that provides a number of options for help. These options include senior leaders, country leaders, supervisors, the counseling or medical office in Wheaton, regional member care coordinators (trained counselors), member care facilitators in each country, volunteer lay counselors called Timothy Networkers who visit missionaries, and growth partners. Any missionary in TEAM can go to one of these people and be confident that they will know what to do or whom to call for counsel.

Some of these options in TEAM are more formal, such as contacting senior administrative leaders or country leaders who have the power to make decisions. Some are more informal, such as meeting with growth plan partners or Timothy Network volunteers. The key is that the formal and informal options work together for the good of the missionary and the organization. Procedures in other mission organizations do not need to look like those of TEAM, but mission agencies need to ask themselves: What are the options for our members? What procedures are in place? Are the procedures well known and familiar to field missionaries?

Building an Organizational Strategy: Response

The next step addresses how a mission agency should respond when a report is received that one of its missionaries has a problem with Internet pornography. What options are available for providing help? How can mission leaders know whether the problem is serious? Developing and implementing a plan for responding to persons who report a problem with Internet pornography is the third major domain in a comprehensive strategy for dealing with this issue.[12]

The first step in any response is, necessarily, to take stock of the situation. Before making decisions about action steps, it is important to know the scope and seriousness of the problem. For example: Is this a long term pattern or a recent development? What exactly was or is involved? How has it affected those around the missionary such as spouse, children, and teammates? How has it affected the missionary's ministry? How has it impacted those to whom and among whom the missionary ministers?

An appraisal of the situation will indicate whether the problem at hand is an addiction or some less vicious struggle. When it comes to the reasons people use Internet pornography, one size does not fit all. Pornography use falls on a continuum. At one end is lust (a normal human struggle); at the other end is addiction (a pattern of compulsive use). Some people do not like the word "addiction." They would rather see all problems in this area as problems of lust or as a temporary aberration. Unfortunately, such an approach is counterproductive for both the mission and the missionary. To treat chest pain as merely a muscle strain without undergoing diagnosis by qualified medical personnel could lead to a life-ending heart attack. People do not mind if they learn that their pain was merely due to muscle strain and not a blocked artery, but if it is a blocked artery they are glad to have caught it. Responding to addiction is more involved and substantially different from dealing with a problem of lust.

Sexual addiction, including addiction to Internet pornography, is a reality for some people. Like cocaine, Internet pornography is highly addictive, which is why Patrick Carnes calls it "the crack cocaine of the twenty-first century." Even persons with no previous exposure sexually can become addicted very quickly. Advances in neuroscience help us to understand why, for they indicate that viewing Internet pornography produces a powerful change in brain chemistry that can lead to addiction. It is important to note that identifying a problem as an addiction does not mean that the addicted person is powerless, but that powerful compulsions will need to be identified and addressed during the healing process. It also means that the time and processes for healing and restoration will be longer and will need to reach deeper.

The work of appraisal needs to be done by a knowledgeable person with training and experience in dealing with persons who have a problem with sexual temptation. As mentioned earlier, for Christians shame is a big factor in admitting sexual sin. Experts who work in this area point out that people often shade the truth when it comes to admitting the extent of a problem with sexual sin. As a result details come out slowly over time. An expert counselor will know how to draw out the full extent of the problem.

Once the extent of the problem being dealt with is clear, it will be possible to move to the next step, which is restoration. At TEAM the goal is restoration whether the issue is addiction or a lesser problem. Galatians 6:1 says, "If someone is caught in a sin, you who are spiritual restore them gently." The word for "restore" is the same word used for the disciples' "mending" their nets. It can also mean "setting a bone." Internet pornography is a sin. Sin is always the result of immaturity in some area of our lives. To "mend the net" we must deal with the immaturity as well as the sinful behavior. Sinful behavior is the fish getting out through a hole in the net or the limp of someone with a broken leg. The hole in the net that lets the fish out or the break in the bone that causes the limp is the deeper problem, whether it be immaturity or pride or some other underlying problem.

Stopping sinful behavior alone is not the goal of restoration. Healing is. The deeper issues of immaturity and pride must be healed if we are to restore a brother or sister. Restoration includes identifying, challenging, and changing those underlying attitudes and beliefs as well as altering behavior. Ultimately restoration is about the creation of new habits with lifestyle changes that will prevent a return to the sinful behavior.

TEAM has set up a number of successful restoration programs, each with a specific outline tailored to it. Depending on the nature of the problem, restoration can take place overseas or in the passport country. For addiction to Internet pornography, the restoration program requires leaving ministry and returning to the care of the sending church in the passport country. Other cases may be cared for while remaining in ministry on the field. In either case, two things are necessary for restoration: a care plan and a restoration team.

A care plan sets out clear goals for the restoration. It should also outline concrete steps or actions to be taken. For example, the first step could be to meet with a counselor weekly. The second might be to find a growth plan partner to meet with weekly. A third step could be to get involved in a men's small group, and so forth.[13] Notice that the steps are very specific. This is essential if the plan is to be successful. Care plans should also include estimated time frames, but with one caution. Missionaries often focus on the time frame as an absolute. For example, "You said this would take a year, so I am done." Time frames are not the issue; restoration is. Only God knows how long it will take. A person who is focused on the time may not understand the goal of restoration and may merely be "jumping through the hoops," something that will not work.

The care plan also needs to include clear accountability, which is why a restoration team is needed. This team is made up of mature, trusted people with the ability to come alongside a person (and family) to help him or her complete the restoration. The restoration team is not a committee that meets once a month to see how things are going. Rather, the person in restoration must be willing to submit his or her life to the oversight of this team for the period of the restoration. For this reason the team should be made up of people in whom the missionary has confidence. The missionary will not choose the team members, but should have input into who is on the team. The restoration team decides when the restoration is complete and the missionary is ready to return to ministry.[14]

When restoration takes place in the passport country, it is done under the leadership of the sending church. When it is done overseas, the restoration team will be chosen differently and should be under the guidance of mission leadership. On-field teams may be smaller and the care plan simpler, but the same principles apply. Restorations are challenging to do, but the benefit to all involved, including the mission, is invaluable.[15]

Conclusion

Are your people worth restoring? How much would it cost your organization to replace a three-term missionary leader who has been successful in overseas ministry? Before answering, remember that you cannot simply send a first-term missionary as a replacement. How long will it take the first-termer to reach the same level of effectiveness as the three-term missionary? Restoration is God's plan, and when followed it benefits all involved.

With the increasing sophistication of the Internet and the accompanying opportunities for missionaries to fall, mission organizations are certain to need to deal with this issue. There is no doubt that missionaries are vulnerable to Internet pornography. We need to be prepared. Organizations need a strategy that is both proactive and reactive. Prevention must be the strategy's first priority. It may require work to create an environment of trust and honesty within an organization. Prevention calls for education of everyone in the organization, beginning at the top. It also means that organizations will need to find creative ways to help their missionaries avoid the things that can trap them.

A prevention strategy can lead to organizational policies that will raise awareness of the importance of the issue and identify boundaries for healthy use of the Internet. Members of the organization need to know how to get help if they are struggling with this issue. Leaders need to know what to do when they receive reports of such struggles.

Finally, an organization needs a strategy for handling cases when a missionary falls. The goal of this part of the strategy needs to be restoration. Missionaries who fall can be restored and go on to productive ministry. Through restoration their life and ministry can be transformed. It would be wonderful if we could guarantee that no member of our organization would ever fall in this area; with a good prevention strategy we can decrease the likelihood of its occurring. The history of Christianity and present realities of the Internet, however, suggest that we or some of our colleagues will fall. May God give us wisdom and grace as we address this issue.

Notes

1. These comments are based on statistics provided by Enough is Enough: Making the Internet Safer for Children and Families (www.enough.org; accessed August 2009). The statistics are updated regularly and archives are also available.
2. I am aware of one doctoral student who is currently doing a survey among missionaries.
3. "The Leadership Survey on Pastors and Internet Pornography," *Christianity Today* (www.christianitytoday.com/le/2001/winter/12.89.html); quoted in "Christians and Sexual Brokenness," Enough Is Enough (www.enough.org/inside.php?tag=statistics#10).
4. Ken Williams, *Sharpening Your Interpersonal Skills*, manual available only to participants in Sharpening Your Interpersonal Skills Workshops (Colorado Springs: International Training Partners [http://itpartners.org], 2002), 188.
5. Archibald Hart, "Teams That Thrive and Not Just Survive, Time to Get a Life," *The Cutting Edge* 5, no. 2 (Spring 2001).
6. Patrick Carnes, "Understanding Multiple Addictions," seminar at Summit for Clinical Excellence, Chicago Marriott O'Hare, April 12, 2008.
7. Williams, *Sharpening Your Interpersonal Skills*, 188.
8. Hart, "Teams That Thrive."
9. Williams, *Sharpening Your Interpersonal Skills*, 188.

10. To promote self-control, self-discipline, and personal accountability, Covenant Eyes (www.covenanteyes.com) tracks every Web site visit and sends an e-mail report to an accountability partner. See also PC Tattletale (www.pctattletale.com; monitoring software), Safe Eyes (www.internetsafety.com; content control, program control, time control), Bsecure (www.bsecure.com; filtering software), and XXXChurch (www.xxxchurch.com or www.x3pure.com; accountability software, online workshops).
11. Bob Hodge, TEAM board member, personal e-mail, July 2009.
12. A number of books offer help to persons burdened by sexual addiction. See, for instance, *Hope and Recovery: A Twelve Step Guide for Healing from Compulsive Sexual Behavior* (Center City, Minn.: Hazelden Educational Materials, 1994); Stephen Arterburn, Fred Stoeker, and Mike Yorke, *Every Man's Battle: Winning the War on Sexual Temptation: One Victory at a Time* and *Every Young Man's Battle: Strategies for Victory in the Real World of Sexual Temptation* (Colorado Springs: WaterBrook Press, 2000 and 2002); three books by Patrick Carnes, *Out of the Shadows: Understanding Sexual Addiction* (Minneapolis: CompCare Publications, 1983), *Don't Call It Love: Recovery from Sexual Addiction* (New York: Bantam, 1991), and *Facing the Shadow: Starting Sexual and Relationship Recovery: A Gentle Path to Beginning Recovery from Sex Addiction* (Carefree, Ariz.: Gentle Path Press, 2005); Patrick Carnes et al., *In the Shadows of the Net: Breaking Free from Compulsive Online Sexual Behavior* (Center City, Minn.: Hazelden, 2001); Steve Gallagher, *At the Altar of Sexual Idolatry* (Dry Ridge, Ky.: Pure Life Ministries, 2000); Debra Laaser, *Shattered Vows: Hope and Healing for Women Who Have Been Sexually Betrayed* (Grand Rapids: Zondervan, 2008); Mark R. Laaser, *Faithful and True: Sexual Integrity in a Fallen World* and *Healing the Wounds of Sexual Addiction* (Grand Rapids: Zondervan, 1996 and 2004); Nate Larkin, *Samson and the Pirate Monks: Calling Men to Authentic Brotherhood* (Nashville, Tenn.: W Pub. Group, 2007); Marsha Means, *Living with Your Husband's Secret Wars* (Grand Rapids: Revell, 1999); Bill Perkins, *When Good Men Are Tempted*, 2nd ed. (Grand Rapids:

Zondervan, 2007); Harry W. Schaumburg, *False Intimacy: Understanding the Struggle of Sexual Addiction* (Colorado Springs: NavPress, 1997).

13. A number of therapy resources and workshops are available, e.g., American Family Association (www.afa.net), Bethesda Workshops (www.bethesdaworkshops.org), Faithful and True Ministries (www.faithfulandtrueministries.com), Heart to Heart Counseling (www.sexaddict.com), Operation Integrity (www.operationintegrity.org), Pine Grove Behavioral Health (www.pinegrovetreatment.com), Pure Desire Ministries (www.puredesire.org), Pure Life Ministries (www.purelifeministries.org), Pure Warrior Ministries (www.purewarrior.org), Samson Society (www.samsonsociety.org), Stone Gate Resources (www.stonegateresources.org), and Twelve Step Recovery Programs.

14. Earl D. Wilson et al., *Restoring the Fallen* (Downers Grove, Ill.: InterVarsity Press, 1997), provide an excellent model of a restoration team.

15. For further information on how to do church-based restoration, see Steven G. Edlin, "Elements of a Healing and Restoration Plan" (unpublished paper, 2008). For a copy of the paper, contact me at sedlin@teamworld.org.

6

The Dynamic Relationship Between Ethical Compromise and Ministry Effectiveness

JON FREEMAN

While in college I worked with juvenile delinquent boys aged twelve to seventeen. Staff training prepared us for physical confrontation, and we had clear plans in place for handling aggressive situations. I was able to face physical conflicts, but one night I was confronted by another type of conflict for which I was not at all prepared. One of my coworkers lost his temper with a teenage boy and hit him unnecessarily in the face. Protocol required that any physical confrontation be written up, and my coworker wrote it up as though his actions had been done in self-defense, expecting me to corroborate his account. His action caught me off guard and thrust me into an ethical dilemma for which I was completely unprepared. I was being asked to cover for my friend who had helped me in the past, but doing so required me to sign a statement that I knew to be false. I did not like it, I was not prepared for it, and it caused a great deal of internal stress in my life until I could come to a resolution.

Ethical tension does not arise when a bad option is compared to a good option. If my five-year-old son were asked whether he would rather eat McDonalds chicken nuggets or asparagus, he would have no internal tension or struggle. When I am asked, however, if I will betray my friend or betray my conscience, I have plenty of tension. Prolonged exposure to such tension produces stress that leads to negative physical and emotional consequences. Prolonged exposure to such tensions on the mission field can result in ineffectiveness in ministry. It is imperative that missionaries, churches, and mission agencies recognize the serious nature of stress due to perceived ethical conflict on the mission field.

Carrying out the missionary task is no longer as straightforward as it was even a generation ago. We are reminded of the difficult sacrifices made by brave missionaries in times past who packed their belongings in a coffin in order literally to give their lives to reach peoples who had never heard the Gospel in places afflicted by disease, conflict, and other dangers. Ralph Winter gives perspective on the level of physical sacrifice required of early missionaries, writing, "As I have reflected on this measure of devotion I have been humbled to tears, for I wonder—if I or my people today could or would match that record. Can you imagine our Urbana students today going out into missionary work if they knew that for decade after decade 19 out of 20 of those before them had died almost on arrival on the field?"[1] In some ways, those times and those contexts were simple, demanding physical sacrifice as missionaries counted the cost and were willing to give their temporal bodies in exchange for the opportunity for the Gospel to be proclaimed in locations where the name of Christ had never been preached. By comparison many mission fields today are complex, at times demanding less physical sacrifice while expecting more emotional and mental sacrifice as missionaries are seemingly pressured to compromise deeply held convictions for the sake of ministry and the spread of the Gospel.

Today, missionaries often live and work in contexts which seem to force them to compromise their personal ethical standards to varying degrees. The sacrifice required for a missionary to function effectively today may seem minimal in comparison to the physical sacrifices faced formerly. Significantly, however, missionaries today are unprepared to face the ethical dilemmas they meet, because they have not counted the cost ahead of time. Churches and mission agencies regularly send missionaries to challenging fields while seemingly unaware of this dynamic. The *World Vision Security Manual*, which serves as a field guide for their personnel, does not mention this type of stress, let alone deal with it as part of World Vision's preparedness training.[2] A survey of various Web sites, mission agency publications, and even mission journals yields little in the way of original research on this topic that has significant bearing on screening and training of missionaries.

For this discussion it may be helpful to clarify the concept of ethical compromise. Ethical compromise or pressure toward ethical compromise arises from situations in which one's personal convictions of right and wrong are seen as being in conflict with demands imposed by a particular situation. Thus the missionary perceives that he or she must compromise personal ethical standards in some way in order to live or minister effectively in a particular context. For example, an ethical dilemma exists when a personal conviction of the obligation to share the good news of salvation with sinners comes into conflict with a personal conviction that physical abuse in all its forms is wrong. In such situations missionaries are forced to prioritize, either fostering a relationship with an unbeliever who abuses his spouse or pressuring the unbeliever to stop abusing his spouse, knowing that the latter action will likely drive a wedge between them, weakening the relationship. Perceived ethical compromise occurs when one set of convictions must be ignored or acted against in favor of another set of convictions; in the case just given, this might include a missionary's prioritizing, with misgivings, the relationship with the unbeliever above rescuing the abused woman.

Certainly, standing firm on deeply held convictions and not compromising on core truths, principles, and beliefs is imperative for a missionary in order to maintain personal integrity. Willingness to suffer the consequences of evangelism and discipleship for the sake of Christ was the hallmark of the early church, and it continues to be so today in countries closed to the Gospel. Scripture must be the standard for evaluating moral and ethical principles as well as personal conscience. It is beyond the scope of this chapter to assess the ethicality or morality of particular activities; rather, the focus here is on the fact of perceived ethical compromise and its impact on missionary health and effectiveness.

The following pages seek to clarify the nature and consequences of perceived ethical compromise. Biblical examples and instructions will be examined to discover patterns and principles from which missionaries can obtain help in recognizing the scope of the issue and receive guidance for their own behavior. Finally, the principle of *shalom* in the heart and soul will be examined to determine how a person can or should legitimately deal with ethical ambiguity or compromise, and some practical steps will be suggested that mission agencies can take to assist missionaries working in challenging ethical contexts.

6—*Jon Freeman*

The Reality of Ethical Compromise in Missions

Several years ago I was helping to care for approximately 125 children in an orphanage in Guatemala. At that time, the orphanage could afford to have meat served at only one meal a day. The other two meals were limited primarily to beans, rice, and tortillas, because those items could be secured inexpensively in abundance. The orphanage had expanded, having agreed to care for children from a variety of abusive and unhealthy situations, but constant tension existed between helping more children and providing adequately for those already living in the home. For example, forty girls had to make do with one bathroom. In the midst of difficult times, God was providing, but we were painfully aware of the limits of our ability to meet the vast need that existed among children in Guatemala.

One day I was driving on a main highway heading out of Guatemala City in a van owned by the orphanage. I was carrying the equivalent of US$3,000 in local currency, as I was on my way to purchase items for the orphanage, and I was under strict orders to guard that money carefully, as the orphanage was on a tight budget. The local police pulled me over and told me in Spanish that I must pay a special tax (one that I knew did not exist) for leaving the city on this particular highway. It did not take a professional interculturalist to recognize this as an attempt on their part to secure money from a vulnerable foreigner. Immediately I felt the ethical tension between obeying the governing authorities (in this case corrupt policemen looking for easy money) and being a responsible steward of the money that had been entrusted to me which would purchase food and other essentials for the children living in the orphanage.

Ethical challenges exist in virtually every missionary context in one form or another. In the case above, I chose to feign ignorance of the Spanish language, and I was allowed to continue on my way after showing the policemen a wallet with a couple of dollars in local currency. But had they chosen to search me, they would no doubt have found the money and I could have been in significant trouble. In the midst of this tension there were very real potential consequences whichever course I chose. Similarly, missionaries face a variety of ethical dilemmas that add to the stress inherent in missionary work and cross-cultural interaction, something that they may or may not have taken into consideration before going to the field.[3]

Some missionaries serve in creative access countries where they are forced to be less than forthright about their ministry intentions. For those who hold to a scrupulously high view of honesty, in which withholding part of the truth is tantamount to lying, living and ministering in a country closed to missionaries may seem to demand continual compromise of their ethical standards as they repeatedly withhold their ministry intentions from peers, government officials, neighbors, and friends.[4] I have been with short-term mission teams multiple times for whom this point became an issue. Western organizations often send church members into countries not readily open to missionaries to work alongside local believers in hope of advancing what God is doing there. Ninety-nine percent of the time, the short-term team members are doing activities that are consistent with a tourist visa, including visiting with missionaries or church members, assisting with activities of a church, putting on a training camp to equip believers, training pastors in Bible or theology, and hosting events which are optimal for conversational or relational evangelism. Many people, however, have felt like my friend "Rachel" who struggled with my instructions to put "tourist" in the "reason for visit" box on an immigration form. From her perspective she had signed up for a mission trip at her church and she was, therefore, a missionary. She was very uncomfortable "lying" on her visa application, because for her, doing so compromised her personal integrity.

"Bribery" is a distasteful aspect of everyday life for some missionaries, with many officials actually refusing to perform their responsibilities without additional compensation. Handling this situation can be very difficult for missionaries who view bribery in any form as being morally wrong and fostering corruption within the host country. Though many missionaries are comfortable with the cultural norm of offering additional compensation in exchange for services, others view compromise on this point to be a violation of scriptural imperatives concerning obedience to governing authorities. Unfortunately for them, the persons demanding a bribe are frequently the good officials.

When considering ministry in or moving to a land that is filled with danger, some missionaries become conflicted about the ethicality of taking a spouse or children there. Those from highly individualistic Western cultures face an ethical dilemma in thinking of relocating children to a locality where they may potentially suffer harm without having been given the option to dissent. Missionaries who work in countries where conversion to Christianity means the likelihood of significant persecution or even death are faced with similar ethical dilemmas about sharing the Gospel in those contexts. Typically, being the occasion or cause of another person's suffering is considered morally and ethically wrong, but missionaries working in especially hostile fields inherently put others in harm's way through their missionary actions and activities. For other missionaries, to leave a sick or elderly parent so as to return to their county of service makes them feel as though they are abandoning their parents in their time of need, and so staying on the mission field can also result in ethical tension. If missionaries are not absolutely convinced that their course of action is right because it is what God has called them to do, they will be subject to internal conflict and will feel forced to compromise on what they hold to be virtuous.

Some missionaries find it challenging to participate in activities with or work alongside Christians who advocate doctrines or philosophies of ministry with which they strongly disagree. They may feel that they are compromising their ethical standards if they do so. For example, a missionary who holds to the eternal security of a believer may see it as a compromise of the Gospel to work with a pastor who believes that people can lose their salvation. Missionaries who have always believed that only males should be pastors and elders may find themselves working for an extended period alongside a national church with a female pastor. For some, compromise on this issue is tantamount to rejecting the authority structure that God established for humankind. Once I was attending a church service in Moscow, and the communion cup was passed around. One of my fellow short-term team members discovered that communion wine was being served instead of grape juice, and he demonstratively rejected the communion cup when it came to him, much to the embarrassment of our team. For him, to drink alcohol in any form was sinful, and he chose to be offensive rather than to compromise his personal conviction. On a short-term trip the ramifications are minimal, but for a long-term missionary prolonged compromise on theological and philosophical issues has the potential to produce a high level of stress. Perhaps unease with even potential compromise is the reason so many missionaries choose to remain fractured along denominational and theological lines rather than to work together.

Missionaries are often forced to readjust or compromise certain aspects of their ethical or moral standards as they enter their field assignments. Such compromise comes with consequences which the missionary may or may not fully understand. Taking children or loved ones to dangerous locations, encouraging people to convert even though this will put them in significant danger, compromising on certain theological or philosophical standards, dealing with bribery, and being less than candid about their intentions in creative access countries are clear examples of ethical or moral dilemmas that may confront missionaries during their ministry, and each raises the potential for internal ethical conflict and its consequences.

Perceived Ethical Compromise in the Book of Acts

The twenty-first century is not the first time that perceived ethical compromise has been encountered. Peter, in Acts 10, saw a vision from God that commanded him to violate his existing ethical and moral standards for the sake of sharing the Gospel. One day around lunchtime while waiting for the meal to be prepared, Peter fell into a trance. Suddenly he saw a sheet with reptiles, birds, and all kinds of animals on it descend from the sky, and he heard a voice commanding him to kill the animals and eat them. The passage makes it clear that unclean animals were included, ones that the Old Testament law strictly prohibited Jews from eating. God's challenge to Peter was to reevaluate his previously held ethical standards, based on Old Testament Scripture, for the sake of preaching the Gospel.

We today, with a Western mindset, are hard pressed to understand the ethical turmoil that must have filled Peter's mind as he pondered the sacrifice he was going to have to make in order for the Gospel to go forth to the Gentiles. Believers from Muslim and Hindu backgrounds, coming from strong religious and cultural traditions with similar convictions against the eating of certain meats, might more readily identify with Peter's dilemma. Peter had never eaten an unclean animal in his entire life. He had always considered such behavior to be ethically and morally wrong, and contrary to God's purposes and plan. His resistance was perhaps as strong as our Western revulsion to cannibalism. Peter might possibly have chosen death itself before eating unclean meat had not God called on him directly to partake.

But God called for Peter to compromise or sacrifice certain ethical and moral convictions for the sake of the Gospel, something that was no less significant than if he had called on Peter to sacrifice his physical life for the sake of the Gospel. Had Peter not been willing to reevaluate his ethical convictions, he might have responded as did the apostles and believers in Jerusalem who were uncomfortable with the actions he took and wondered whether God's holy demands were being watered down. Within the early church, the issue of ethical compromise was a source of significant, ongoing tension and turmoil between Jews and Gentiles.

Since it was God who called for Peter to compromise by taking an action that was clearly in violation of Old Testament Scripture, he made his blessing of Peter's decision abundantly clear. Not only did God give Peter the vision, but he also affirmed it through the Holy Spirit within Peter and confirmed it by bestowing the gift of tongues when Cornelius and his house believed. Today many missionaries indicate assurance of having received a personal call from God to see a particular mission field reached with the Gospel. This divine intervention and blessing often provides mental permission for them to set aside or to violate certain lesser convictions, thereby enabling them to maintain internal mental and emotional peace. In Peter's case, God knew how formidable the challenge was for him due to the Mosaic dietary laws; before he would be able willingly to enter the home of a Gentile and eat with him, God provided compelling evidence to support Peter in overcoming his ethical reservations.

What if Peter had refused to compromise in this area? He would have missed out on the opportunity to see Gentiles reached with the Gospel. What if Peter had not come to a place of *shalom* in his heart about the nature of his compromise? What if Peter had not become convinced of the rightness of his decision to present the Gospel to a person who was outside the covenant with Israel? Certainly his effectiveness in presenting the Gospel to these Gentiles would have been hindered. He would have experienced internal disequilibrium and his conscience would have been uneasy. Had Peter not displayed faith and courage by following the Lord into territory that challenged his assumptions about himself, God, and salvation, he would have missed the opportunity to see God work through him to expand God's kingdom in radical ways.

Just as in Peter's time, Scripture should be the normative guide for establishing ethical parameters. As God calls particular missionaries to specific mission fields, they need to realize that "becoming all things to all men" often requires some degree of elasticity in their ethical categories, particularly in the world's more restrictive and challenging countries. The call of God is a potent basis for inner peace in the midst of uncertainty when ethical dilemmas and perceived ethical compromises arise. Mission agencies report a strong correlation between missionaries' sense of call—or lack of call—and missionary attrition. Most agencies rate "expressing a clear call to missionary service" as being extremely important in their missionary selection process even though what is thought to define a call varies greatly from missionary to missionary.[5] When missionaries possess a clear sense of God's providential direction in prayer and the study of Scripture, they are prepared to wrestle with the tensions ethical compromise presents, knowing that God may stretch their categories just as he stretched Peter's so that the Gospel can be proclaimed to the ends of the earth.

Acts 15 describes another ethical dilemma that faced the early church. The occasion was a sharp dispute between those who strongly believed circumcision to be crucial for salvation and those who strongly believed that circumcision was not essential. It is difficult for us as Gentiles in the twenty-first century to comprehend that anyone would think of circumcision as being salvific, but Jewish believers in the first century had never considered salvation apart from Judaism. For Jewish believers, setting circumcision aside from the salvation process undoubtedly felt like a serious compromise of their core beliefs. Conversely, Paul and Barnabas believed that not imposing circumcision was crucial for the spread of the Gospel. Here the threat of spreading two distinct Gospels was real, and the ethical tension needed to be resolved in order for the Gospel to move forward effectively.

Some issues are not ambiguous at all, but rather very clear, and on them missionaries cannot compromise. In Acts 15 each side believed its view to be foundational to the Gospel and the argument that ensued caused so much strife that it threatened the unity of the church as well as of the missionary work in Antioch. The tension was so great that ministry effectiveness was being undercut. The response to the conflict by the church leaders at the Jerusalem council is helpful for our discussion, because the record shows that they were able to persist in working through the issue until both sides could embrace the ethical parameters of their situation and thus pave the way for ministry effectiveness.

Two observations may be made on this passage. First, some issues merit taking a stand. Had Paul and Barnabas compromised on this important issue and acquiesced to the view that circumcision is required for salvation, the church's understanding of grace and salvation would have been distorted, and an unnecessary barrier to the Gospel would have been created. At times our mission or message is rendered ineffective through compromise of our ethical or doctrinal standards. Conversely, however, this passage is a warning that even some of our most deeply held convictions can be a product of our cultural perspective and may be in error. As missionaries continue to work in ministry teams with representatives from a variety of cultural backgrounds, the potential is great for issues to arise that threaten the spread of the Gospel and the effectiveness of the team. When they do, missionaries must unitedly come to a place of resolution in a God-honoring way so that nothing will hinder the advancement of the church of Christ.

The second observation from Acts 15 is that when this seemingly irreconcilable dispute arose, the church resolved it in the context of community in consultation with spiritual leaders. Today also times may arise when it will be necessary for missionaries to seek counsel from a wider group of spiritually mature believers in order to resolve ethical tensions. The church in Antioch appealed to the church in Jerusalem, which was recognized as being led by the most spiritually mature believers, to gain perspective. The church in Jerusalem set up a council which carefully and deliberately weighed the issues, prayed together, and sought evidence of what God was doing in the mission context of Gentile Antioch. As the Jerusalem council came to a decision—that circumcision was not necessary for salvation—missionaries and church leaders from both sides of the conflict came to a point of resolution; there was confidence that God had spoken through spiritual leaders and spiritual authority structures.

Today Western perspectives emphasize personal convictions and individual responsibility; it is easy to overlook the spiritual authority structures that God has instituted which bear responsibility for leading the body of Christ. Missionaries who face ethical dilemmas should willingly embrace the fact that God has placed over them in positions of leadership men and women who can provide perspective and guidance to help resolve ethical tensions, including spiritual leaders from their sending church and sending agency. Similarly, missionaries should work their way through ethical issues in community with other men and women indwelt by the Holy Spirit. Doing so can facilitate arriving at a God-honoring resolution so that the Gospel might be advanced. Paul Hiebert rightly sums up the issue: "Whether we like it or not, young theologians around the world are reading Scripture and interpreting it for their own cultures. To claim that only the missionaries' theology is correct leads to breaks in the relationships between Western missions and the churches they have planted around the world. It also denies the priesthood of all believers and the work of the Holy Spirit in non-Western Christians."[6] Thus, community and authority are two primary safeguards which aid missionaries in resolving ethical tensions and ministering effectively.

Examination of Acts 10 and 15 provides several insights that help us to understand the dynamic relationship between ethical compromise and ministry effectiveness. Missionaries face practices and situations that cause ethical tension, and resolution is required. Some missionaries are tempted to see the world in black and white, and they are inclined to shy away from ministry if the situation does not conform exactly to their preconceived ethical parameters just as Peter shied away from the idea of eating with a Gentile. But, as Duane Elmer asserts, "bringing a cultural practice under the authority of Scripture is not Westerners' exclusive responsibility. All of us are prone to interpret the Bible through our cultural lenses and to mingle our own cultural preferences with biblical teaching. Christians from various cultures would serve one another and the cause of biblical interpretation by joining in prayer and discussion on these matters."[7] Through community, deference to spiritual authority, and sensitivity to the Holy Spirit's leading, missionaries are empowered to evaluate their ethical parameters and come to a place of resolution that enables the Gospel to advance.

Responding to Perceived Ethical Dilemmas

Missionaries, mission agencies, and churches need to recognize the dynamic relationship between perceived ethical compromise and ministry effectiveness. Missionaries may see varying degrees of ethical and moral compromise as a reasonable sacrifice to make for the sake of accomplishing their primary objective, but such sacrifices are far more subtle than physical sacrifice. Suffering hardship or the lack of conveniences, enduring pain or at worst death is difficult, but missionaries are often mentally and spiritually prepared for such possibilities. They are encouraged to persevere in spite of physical setbacks. The extra challenge posed by perceived ethical and moral compromise comes from missionaries' lack of preparation for them. Unfortunately, churches and mission organizations are not equipped to prepare missionaries to face the stress that issues surrounding moral compromise will raise on the mission field. The question, however, is not whether missionaries will be faced with ethical dilemmas, but rather how they will respond to those dilemmas.

To give an example: In living at times among non-Western peoples, I have on occasion encountered high levels of spousal abuse in places where it is culturally acceptable for husbands to physically punish or even beat their wives. In some places even Christian leaders are at times guilty of abuse, something that appears to be a huge blind spot within the church. From my American perspective, spousal abuse is an issue that requires immediate intervention and quick resolution. In situations such as this, a tension exists between, on the one hand, loving or even respecting those who are, according to biblical standards, abusers and, on the other hand, actively seeking to protect their victims. I do not like injustice, but neither do I want to see conformity to a set of moral standards be required of people who are slaves to sin as a prerequisite for them to receive the Gospel. Whatever should be said about spousal abuse, it highlights the reality of ethical dilemmas for missionaries. Would we be able to "overlook," at least for a time, behavior we find repulsive or even evil for the sake of gaining a hearing for the Gospel?[8]

All of us view ethics and morality through the lenses of our customary standards and values. Some of our standards are based on biblical imperatives which must not be compromised; others are based on culturally defined values which are open to readjustment and about which we must be flexible. Many of our values and standards fall somewhere between these two poles. Issues in these gray areas demand much work and discipline if we are to come to a sense of *shalom*, or peace, about the rightness of our decisions. As noted, some people seem to be predisposed toward seeing the world in black and white; such people often suffer the most internal stress on the mission field because they find it difficult to make adjustments without feeling that they are compromising their convictions. Others are predisposed to see the whole world as being an undifferentiated gray. Having themselves no moral compass that helps to guide their decisions leaves them unable to help anyone else.

Certain cultures and mission fields require greater ethical adjustments on the part of Western missionaries than do others in order for them to function well. The fact that adjustments will be needed can be known in advance and be part of missionary preparation and training. But which adjustments will be needed by which missionary must be learned by experience in the field. Until missionaries are confronted with real life situations in another culture that cause internal ethical dilemmas, they are unlikely to recognize their own cultural or ethical biases. As with other aspects of culture and worldview, missionaries' unquestioned assumptions about ethics and morality will inevitably come into conflict with the unquestioned assumptions concerning the same issues held by their national partners in ministry. Internal stress and feelings of disequilibrium are inevitable and must be dealt with if missionaries are to come to internal harmony.

When an ethical dilemma does arise, we feel compelled to seek resolution so as to overcome our sense of moral disequilibrium. When things seem to be falling apart or we are faced with perceived ethical compromise, often the first step missionaries should take is to consider the issues carefully and to explore solutions offered by alternative ethical standards. Next the missionary must come to peace with the new standard by either accepting or rejecting it as an option. All ethical decisions entail ethical consequences, and missionaries must be prepared to accept the consequences of their decisions.[9] Resolution of internal conflict is key to personal well-being, longevity as a missionary, and effectiveness in ministry, because without resolution the missionary will be forever wavering between incompatible courses of action, paralyzed by stress, and unable to function.

In short, perceived ethical compromise, to one degree or another, will unavoidably be part of missionaries' experience. Missionaries may see themselves as challenged to capitulate on some of their moral or ethical standards for the sake of their ministry, but leaving these challenges unresolved is not an option if they are to be effective in ministry. The pressure of ethical challenges and compromise of internal standards can lead to subtle or acute internal stress. Unlike physical sacrifice and stress, ethical sacrifice and stress are not well attested in research literature. Missionaries, churches, and mission agencies, however, should be aware of this subtle dynamic and proactively help missionaries prepare to address the reality of ethical readjustment, if not compromise, on the mission field.

The Importance of Inner Shalom

To function well, missionaries must be able, amid the turbulence of life and the demands pressing in upon them, to arrive at a place of peace within their souls. Though they undergo stress due to ethical choices that are imposed upon them from without, they must also achieve peace internally, in their hearts and minds, about the rightness of their decisions. If they cannot, they risk living with stress caused by internal discontinuity as well. The concept of shalom found in the Old Testament and in

Near Eastern cultures supplies an important model for the way missionaries should strive for peace in all areas of their lives. Those whose way to a place of shalom is barred by perceived ethical compromise will suffer emotional stress. Ultimately their effectiveness as ministers of the Gospel to a lost world will be diminished.

As previously mentioned, a clear sense of calling is necessary for missionaries to be able to maintain inner shalom. Their calling provides the moral framework or divine mandate for them as they enter into ethically ambiguous circumstances. As emphasized in the ReMAP II study, a clear sense of calling is important for missionaries who are considering entry into difficult fields. According to the study, mission agencies have found missionaries' sense of calling to be extremely significant in missionary retention.[10] A strong sense of call, however, is not necessarily sufficient on its own to enable missionaries to overcome all the hurdles associated with ethical ambiguity and compromise. Therefore, it is helpful to explore additional factors which may indicate their potential for arriving at shalom in a particular setting or field.

An interesting finding of the ReMAP II study was that while mission agencies do not highly value psychological tests, these assessments show themselves to be strong indicators when it comes to missionary attrition. The study found that mission agencies, particularly those based in new sending countries, often downplay the significance of missionaries' ability to cope with stress as shown by psychological evaluations. Though psychological assessments have been used for many years in other arenas, mission agencies have only recently begun to utilize them to evaluate missionary candidates.[11] Thomas Hale writes about special risk factors for which mission agencies should be alert, including "inflexibility, dogmatism, unwillingness to submit to authority . . . and uncertainty in the call and motivation of the wife."[12] Standardized psychological evaluations can be helpful in flagging such general personal tendencies, but they are not completely adequate for assessing an individual missionary's fit for a particular field.

Tolerance for ambiguity—or allowing for the presence of shades of gray—is important for arriving at or maintaining inner shalom. The term "tolerance for ambiguity" comes from personality theory. It is used to describe the capacity that a person has for both addressing and dealing with conflicting emotions as well as conflicting value judgments.[13] In essence, a person's tolerance for ambiguity indicates how comfortable she or he is with ethical dilemmas and areas where compromise is required. Persons with a high tolerance for ambiguity quotient more easily survive and even thrive in situations where ethical compromise is prevalent.[14] Missionaries heading to difficult fields where ethical compromise is commonplace will find it difficult to adjust if they view ethical issues and morality as being rigidly black and white. Duane Elmer asserts that Westerners typically do not function well in ambiguous situations and therefore jump to conclusions, often erroneous, whenever there is "confusion."[15] For such reasons, use of psychological testing in order to determine missionary candidates' fit for particular fields can be helpful both for ensuring that they are deployed to suitable locations and for missionary retention.

In a different arena, that of medicine, Rebecca Craik articulates the need for students to acquire a high tolerance for ambiguity. Many health professionals, she states, are frustrated with gray, preferring to see the world in black and white. She calls for her colleagues to embrace the fact that life is not as certain or as constant as we would like it to be, summing up, "Rather than bemoaning the ambiguity in clinical decision making, let's recognize that the choices are unclear and enjoy the process of gathering data to clarify those choices. This process requires each of us to determine whether what he 'holds dear' is based on tradition or evidence, to abandon unsupported methods, to try something new or different, and to communicate new information with peers."[16] Her comments can be helpful for us as missionaries required to make decisions in the midst of ethical dilemmas.

Interestingly, tolerance for ambiguity is associated with creativity and the ability to take risks, characteristics that are needed when working in difficult mission fields. It also seems to be correlated with job effectiveness in challenging cross-cultural circumstances, and the concept is making its way into the corporate world with studies being done concerning leadership and followership in ambiguous circumstances. In *The Ambiguity Advantage*, David Wilkinson shows that ability to handle ambiguous circumstances has a direct bearing on long-term performance.[17] Some people are better at innovating in the midst of chaos and ambiguity and thrive on complexity, whereas others wither under the same circumstances. If mission agencies and churches assign missionaries who are highly intolerant of ambiguity to fields that are by nature highly ambiguous, they are potentially setting them up for internal turmoil and ineffectiveness. Sending agencies and churches will do well to be attentive to missionary applicants' tolerance for ambiguity as shown by psychological evaluations as they assess the candidates' fit for a particular field. (This presupposes that the mission agencies and sending churches have properly assessed the level of ambiguity likely to be present in a given field.) Proper assessment will reduce the number of missionaries suffering undue stress from perceived ethical compromise.

Please note carefully that I am not calling for missionaries to adopt a philosophy of "the end justifies the means" or situational ethics. Scripture, God's revealed Word, should serve as the ultimate and final authority for the missionary. Missionaries should, however, have a flexible filtering system that allows them to consider alternative possibilities when it comes to ethical issues and cultural practices. Such flexibility will allow them to declare with Paul, "I have become all things to all men so that by all possible means I might save some" (1 Cor. 9:22 NIV).

Missionaries must come to a place of shalom in their soul. Otherwise they will suffer mental and relational challenges that may threaten their health as well as their missionary effectiveness. In taking the Gospel to sinful people, who may seem unethical, and in working alongside Christians, who are far from perfect, missionaries will inevitably experience internal conflict caused by ethical and moral dilemmas. Tolerance for ambiguity allows for elasticity in missionaries' ethical parameters so that they can be creative and innovative and can thrive in the midst of compromising circumstances. Mission agencies and sending churches need to recognize the reality of missionary attrition and properly prepare candidates when deploying personnel to difficult fields. Missionaries should be screened in order to determine their predisposition toward risk, ambiguity, and ethical compromise, and strong consideration should be given to guiding candidates to other fields of service if there is a high probability that they will experience stress that is beyond their capacity. Missionaries are, as the title for the volume containing the results of REMAP II declares, "worth keeping."

Conclusion: Living in Shalom as a Missionary

Ethical compromise is by no means the only trauma missionaries experience. Other studies have focused on attrition among missionaries who have suffered physical trauma. Ron Brown examines several steps taken by mission agencies that have helped their missionaries to be prepared for times of testing and that contributed to missionary resiliency after significant physical and emotional trauma. The following observations draw upon his work, but they are applied here to missionaries who face emotional trauma because of stress arising from perceived ethical compromise in a particular ministry context.[18]

As a matter of first importance mission agencies should ensure that networks of relationships are in place as support for missionaries heading into challenging mission fields. These networks are foundational. They provide the opportunity for missionaries to encourage one another as peers. They also create an environment in which missionary coaches, directors, and supervisors can earn the trust of field missionaries as well as monitor their emotional health and well-being. To function as a safety net, this relational foundation must be established before a crisis occurs. The presence of a well-established relational foundation has proven to be a key factor in retaining missionaries who have undergone trauma, and building relational networks that include both peers and supervisors should be a high priority for agencies and churches intending to send missionary personnel into settings with a strong potential for causing emotional trauma. Further, mission agencies and sending churches need to ensure that missionaries are given advance philosophical and theological preparation for coping with emotional distress caused by ethical compromise.

Even with a strong relational network in place and a proper philosophical and theological foundation, missionaries will still experience the pressure of perceived ethical compromise. To help them cope, and even better, thrive, mission agency leaders should be proactive, first acknowledging the fact of stress and then finding opportunities to speak words of encouragement and counsel. For persons facing unfamiliar feelings and emotions, strong and supportive leadership is invaluable. It can make all the difference between a hard pressed missionary's remaining on the field or returning home.

Missionaries often serve in contexts that require them to make ethical or moral compromises for the sake of advancing their ministry. Those who cannot deal with ethical dilemmas suffer from stress that can have traumatic emotional and even physical consequences. Ultimately the stress caused by ethical dilemmas can lead to a missionary's returning home or becoming ineffective in accomplishing his or her missional goals. Psychological and educational research have identified "tolerance for ambiguity" as being salient to this issue. Mission agencies and churches can do more in the way of screening potential missionaries to identify their tolerance for ambiguity, but beyond that they can prepare missionary candidates mentally and emotionally for the stress and trauma they are likely to encounter. In addition, agencies and churches can help missionaries to understand the significance of their divine calling in order to establish a clear moral foundation for their inner shalom. Accepting and embracing the ethical parameters of a given ministry situation are essential prerequisites for long-term well-being and effectiveness on the mission field.

Notes

1. Ralph D. Winter, "Four Men, Three Eras, Two Transitions: Modern Missions," in *Perspectives on the World Christian Movement*, 3rd ed., ed. Ralph D. Winter and Steven C. Hawthorne (Pasadena, Calif: William Carey Library, 1999), 255.
2. Charles Rogers and Brian Sytsma, *World Vision Security Manual: Safety Aids for Aid Workers* (Geneva: World Vision, 1999), 138. The manual states that the list of stressors given is not exhaustive.
3. Tom Steffen and Lois McKinney Douglas, *Encountering Missionary Life and Work* (Grand Rapids: Baker Academic, 2008), 217.
4. The ethicality of conducting missionary work in closed access countries is laid out in the article "Secret Missionaries Draw New Scrutiny," *Christian Century* (May 17, 2003), 12–13.
5. Rob Hay, Valerie Lim, Detlef Blocher, Jaap Ketelaar, and Sarah Hay, *Worth Keeping: Global Perspectives on Best Practice in Missionary Retention* (Pasadena, Calif.: William Carey Library, 2007), 93–95.
6. Paul G. Hiebert, *Anthropological Reflections on Missiological Issues* (Grand Rapids: Baker, 1994), 47.
7. Duane Elmer, *Cross-Cultural Conflict: Building Relationships for Effective Ministry* (Downers Grove: InterVarsity Press, 1993), 133.
8. Eleanor Doumato writes of the challenges missionaries faced in situations where slavery was ongoing and the ethical dilemma that existed for doctors who were called upon to evaluate the health of a prospective slave. See "An 'Extra Legible Illustration' of the Christian Faith: Medicine, Medical Ethics, and Missionaries in the Arabian Gulf," *Islam and Christian-Muslim Relations* 13 (4) (2002): 385–88.
9. Adapted from David Hesselgrave, *Planting Churches Cross-Culturally: North America and Beyond* (Grand Rapids: Baker, 2000), 176–80.
10. Rob Hay et al., *Worth Keeping*, 69–74.
11. Rob Hay et al., *Worth Keeping*, 82.

12. Thomas Hale, *On Being a Missionary* (Pasadena, Calif.: William Carey Library, 1995), 327.
13. Albert N. B. Nedd and Nicholas Marsh, "A Cross-Cultural Test of the Personality Integration Hypothesis," *Journal of Personality* 48 (September 1980): 296.
14. For many years it has been the practice of the United States government to screen workers it assigns to difficult foreign fields for their "tolerance for ambiguity."
15. Elmer, *Cross-Cultural Conflict*, 20.
16. Rebecca L. Craik, "A Tolerance for Ambiguity," *Physical Therapy* 81 (July 2001): 1294.
17. David Wilkinson, *The Ambiguity Advantage: What Great Leaders Are Great At* (London: Palgrave Macmillan, 2006), discusses four levels of leadership. Level 1 leaders are technical leaders whereas level 4 leaders are generative leaders.
18. Ron Brown, "Resilience in Ministry Despite Trauma," in *Worth Keeping*, ed. Rob Hay et al., 315–18.

Part III:

Integrity in Institutional Practice

7

"Deleadered": Ethical Removal of Leaders in Mission Organizations

DAVID BROUCEK

Even the most enlightened forms of leadership involve "meddling around in the lives of others."
—Max De Pree

As with many research and writing projects, the writing of this essay was provoked by dissonance. In my ministry career I have repeatedly observed the removal of leaders from their positions of leadership. In some cases the removal involved a reassignment of responsibilities, in others a termination of employment. Always the removal was disequilibrating to individuals and organizations.[1]

Since disequilibrium is an opportunity for growth, I decided not to turn away from the dissonance but to explore it. By taking a deeper look, I hope to surface insights that may be helpful not only to myself but also to others in the North American mission community. In this chapter I am intentionally limiting my examination to the North American context. If the scope were to be broadened, many more cultural variables such as "power distance," "patron-client relationships," "honor and shame," "face," "achieved and ascribed status," and "direct versus indirect communication styles" would need to be addressed.

My reading as well as conversations with peers convince me that an exploration of this topic is needed at this time. When I started this project, the art of removing leaders seemed to be a "black hole" in the leadership literature. There are hundreds of books and articles that tell you how to become a leader and how to be a leader. Precious few tell you how to graciously cease being a leader when you have been "deleadered," or tell you how to "deleader" someone else graciously when it is your responsibility to do so.[2]

First, some observations.

Mission organizations have long regarded themselves as "family." Nevertheless, while heartwarming in its intent and application, the "mission agency as family" metaphor creates tension when we have to take the business-like actions of removing members from a leadership role or of terminating their employment. After all, you do not dismiss members of your family. A more accurate description of mission agencies was provided by George Murray when he was executive director of TEAM. He described the mission agency as "a cause, a corporation, and a community." This three-fold description is useful as we contemplate the ramifications of removing and replacing leaders.

It is my impression that removing and replacing leaders in mission organizations is taking place at a greater rate today than in previous generations. Replacing leaders and restructuring leadership teams are part of a larger move to create cultural change in mission agencies, particularly in the venerable, older

7—David Broucek

agencies that are retooling to meet the challenges of the twenty-first century.

The influence of business books like *Good to Great: Why Some Companies Make the Leap . . . and Others Don't* and *Good to Great and the Social Sectors: Why Business Thinking Is Not the Answer*—with Jim Collins's emphasis on getting the right people on the bus, the right people in the right seats, and the wrong people off the bus—is another factor that intensifies the drive to replace leaders.[3]

One more stimulus to leadership change is the influx of business professionals into mission organizations. Second-career professionals, moving "from success to significance," bring considerable marketplace expertise into the nonprofit world of mission agencies. Their career-long adherence to the discipline of the bottom line brings an enhanced perspective on performance, productivity, and accountability. The mission movement in North America stands to gain from the energy and vision and passion that new leadership can bring—but only if we do not damage ourselves in the process.

The Pain of Being Deleadered

I have observed no pain-free deleaderings. I sat in the office of a friend whose leadership position had been taken away from him. He had been part of the senior leadership team of a mission organization but had recently been told that the senior leadership team was being redefined and restructured and that he would not be part of the new team. With slumped shoulders and slow, flat voice he told me, "I'm so demoralized and demotivated." His words tore my heart.

Whether intended or not, the message often perceived by those removed from their leadership position is "You're not the right person anymore. You don't have the right stuff." Whether the superiors imply it or the employee infers it, the deleadered leader often struggles with the question, "What's wrong with me?"

Think with me. What do you lose when you are removed from leadership? Here are some losses; you might think of others.

- access to information
- ability to influence
- decision-making authority
- respect
- resources
- relationships
- in the worst case scenario, employment

No wonder being removed from leadership is disequilibrating.

I have come to believe that being deleadered is one of the most difficult aspects of the leadership journey. The experience is much more stressful than achieving a leadership role in the first place. For one thing, attaining a leadership position entails excitement and gain; leaving it entails loss. For another, being put into leadership and being removed from leadership are asymmetrical. When you are offered a leadership role, you have a choice. You can say to those who are offering you the position, "When do you need to know? I'll make it a matter of prayer." When you are removed from a leadership role, you are not given a choice. You do not have the option of saying, "Well, I'll pray about it and give you an answer next week." There is a difference in the power equation.

I believe that power is neutral. How power is exercised, and the ends it seeks to achieve make power ethical or unethical. But we need to avoid binary choices. Often it is not a case of right versus wrong but of a better way versus a more hurtful way.

The Pain of the One Who Has to Make the Decision

So far it may seem as if I am implying that leaders who have to make difficult personnel decisions are the bad guys. They are not. In my experience, leaders in mission organizations who make leadership changes are selfless individuals who are motivated by a sincere desire to advance the cause of the kingdom of God through their organizations. They experience pain when they make decisions that they know will hurt others.

Randy Rowland, lead pastor of Sanctuary, a church in Seattle, Washington, poignantly expresses the emotional toll of making difficult leadership decisions: "Nearly 20 years ago, I found myself in a difficult situation with a work colleague whom I treasured. I had to exclude this person from a project. I knew this action would wound terribly, but I had to do what was right rather than what would feel best. I found this situation pushing me to an emotional and spiritual breaking point."[4]

Even leaders who are not squeamish about getting rid of people, such as Steven Sample, president of the University of Southern California, acknowledge the pain. He writes, "I would cheerfully fire one or more of [my senior officers] if they were consistently unable to resolve their differences among themselves." Yet in spite of his "cheerfully fire" bravado, Sample admits that "one of the most painful aspects of leadership [is] firing lieutenants." He compares it to a farmer shooting his own horse.[5]

Carly Fiorina, former high profile CEO and chairman of Hewlett-Packard, wisely stated, "Sometimes bosses forget to see employees as people, but sometimes it's just as hard to see the person in the boss."⁶ It is important to recognize that everyone is human in these situations—both the subject and the object of the action.

Gary Corwin was right when he asserted, "You can only exercise and sustain personal leadership to the extent that you can bear pain."⁷ I do believe, though, that the frequently quoted statement, "Leaders don't inflict pain, they bear pain," is not quite accurate.⁸ If the examples above are correct, leaders sometimes cause pain as well as bear pain.

The Difference Between Pain and Harm

The first rule of medicine is said to be "*Primum non nocere*" (First, do no harm). I would suggest that the same principle is the first rule of leadership. Just as doctors though well-intentioned can cause harm, so can leaders. But there is a difference between pain and harm. Pain, if caused by skillful intervention, leads to recovery and wholeness. Though hard to bear while it occurs, the memory of pain is often mitigated upon recovery.⁹ You can recover from harm, too, but it's harder. Harm leads to deterioration and brokenness, often for a long, long time.

Organizationally, harm means decreased commitment and loyalty. Harm means hard feelings and severed relationships. Harm can be done both by those who do the deleadering and by those who are deleadered. Among the former, harm is caused by hasty action, lack of transparency, and smugness. Among the latter, harm is caused by undermining, gossip, and grudges.

Ethical Principles

How we handle leadership transitions has a moral component. As Ted Ward succinctly put it, "Any value that affects the well being of even one other person is a moral value."[10] More specifically, as David Ardagh and Rob Macklin state, to be ethical an action must have three characteristics:

- Ethics is concerned with how persons should treat each other with respect to well-being/harm, i.e. what type of actions are right, obligatory, commendable, permissible, prohibited, etc.
- Ethics is concerned with people's motive, intent and good character (virtue), not just their external behavior.
- When we appeal to ethical considerations, we appeal to norms that we hold bind others as well as ourselves.[11]

Note that good intentions are not enough, nor are correct actions with wrong motives, nor are norms that we apply to others but not to ourselves.

In light of the characteristics of ethical actions, I offer here nine principles that can mitigate both the pain and potential harm—and that might even result in better than expected results—when removing someone from leadership or when being removed from leadership. Underlying each principle is the fact that head and heart go together. Highly cognitive people may forget that emotions are important, but Daniel Goleman, Richard Boyatzis, and Annie McKee well state that "no matter what leaders set out to do—whether it's creating strategy or mobilizing teams to action—their success depends on *how* they do it. Even if they get everything else just right, if leaders fail in this primal task of driving emotions in the right direction, nothing they do will work as well as it could or should."[12] Further, as a caution against leaderly hubris, they call attention to "one of the biggest mistakes leaders can make: ignoring the realities of team ground rules and the collective emotions in the tribe and assuming that the force of their leadership alone is enough to drive people's behavior.[13]

"Speak the truth in love" (Eph. 4:15 NLT). This principle is fundamental. Be honest. Be loving. When we combine these two qualities, we imitate Jesus who was "full of grace and truth" (John 1:14 NIV).

The Greek word "grace" (χαρις) in the New Testament is not just a theological term. It also includes something of the meaning of our English word "graciousness"—pleasantness, courtesy in speech and behavior.

Let me venture an approach to lovingly honest communication in situations of deleadering. Here are some sample statements:

> I appreciate you for your godly character and your dedication to the Lord.
> I admire your gifting and experience.
> I love and respect you. I want you to know this.
> I value the gifts and qualities I see in you. (Name the gifts and qualities.)
> I also want to tell you that I have come to the conviction that I need to change this role in a way that draws on a somewhat different gift-mix. (Perhaps name the new gift-mix.)
> I would like to reassign you to another role which will significantly bless the organization and further our cause. (Describe both the role and the blessings and benefits expected.)
> I realize that this is a big change that will affect not only you but also many others.
> Let's talk about this.

Whether or not these words fit your particular mode of expression, I do believe that a combination of sincere affirmation and expression of love combined with candor is better than less forthright alternatives. One key to acceptance will be the sincerity and humility of the one conveying the news.

If rather than reassigning the leader you are actually dismissing her or him, you still need to treat persons with dignity and truthfulness. Tell them the reasons. In most mission organizations we are employed "at will," which means that we do not have contracts and can be terminated for any reason at any time; yet when we are terminated, we still deserve to be told why. Attorney Stephen P. Chawga says, "If an employee has not performed up to standard, you should do a quick review of recorded deficiencies and efforts to correct them. This should take the element of surprise out of the decision to terminate."[14] Michael Zigarelli, associate professor of management at the Regent University Graduate School of Business, advises, "Your criticisms should be honest and factual, avoiding subjective or unsupportable conclusions. Calmly explain your rationale for the decision and avoid arguing with the employee.[15] What this advice means is that the person who says, "What troubles me is that I do not know why I was let go," has a legitimate complaint. You cannot just say, "Well, we're restructuring." The person who is not given information that would help him or her do better in the next position is not being treated fairly.

Deciding what to tell others in the organization can also be a challenge, especially in sensitive cases. On the one hand, we have an obligation to protect employees from public embarrassment. Privacy laws, not to mention compassion, constrain disclosure of details that may be unfavorable to the employee. On the other hand, if leaders who are well-liked and perceived by their peers to be doing a good job are summarily dismissed, the leaders who do the dismissing cannot simply gloss over it. "A decent respect to the opinions of mankind requires that they should declare the causes which impel them to the separation."[16] Leaders must keep faith with all employees. Truthfulness with the rest of the organization is crucial to trust.

One tempting tactic that destroys trust is to use budget-related downsizings to dismiss leaders who need to be replaced for other reasons. Recently the Southwestern Baptist Theological Seminary was publically accused of planning to lay off certain professors over theological issues but using the budget as an excuse. The accusations forced the president to assert that "he would not hide behind a screen of economic problems" if he thought a professor needed to be removed for other reasons.[17] I witnessed one downsizing in which the organization's director told the staff that though most of the terminations were necessary because of a budget shortfall, a small number were for "performance reasons" and that in these cases the employees were fully informed of the reasons. It was sobering to staff to learn that some were let go for failing to do their jobs properly, yet the statement was confidence-building because we felt that the senior leaders were honest with us and with the employees they had dismissed. I witnessed another downsizing in which the leaders were less candid, giving the appearance that the budget was being used as an excuse to replace certain leaders. Perceptions are powerful forces in organizations. To use the terminology of the Sharpening Your Interpersonal Skills workshop (www.itpartners.org), in these two cases the former was an example of "trust-building" communication; the latter was "trust-busting."

I believe that most of us can handle the truth better than we can handle silence or innuendo. We are resilient if we have the truth.

Try to understand the other person; exercise empathy. Sometimes visionary, highly committed leaders wound people in their organizations. John Perkins, founder of Voice of Calvary Ministries, was more candid than most when he wrote:

> My strengths as a leader are in the areas of motivation and vision, causing people to believe in themselves and in what they're doing. But I'm not a counselor. I don't have patience. As a result, I sometimes run over people, and that's a weakness.... I put the good of the vision over the good of any particular person. I admit that. That's a part of myself I don't always like. Sometimes that causes pain–to others, but also to me. As someone once told me, "If a person gets caught going against your philosophy, you chew him up and spit him out." That may be putting it too strongly, but I confess I have had to fire people and make unpopular decisions because individuals were not in line with the vision. Some of these people have been hurt. I really wish I could restore those individuals I've wounded.[18]

There seems to be evidence that top leaders view their companies or organizations differently than do those lower in the hierarchy. In one experiment, researchers put thirty-five situations before human resource managers (HRMs) and chief executive officers (CEOs). Respondents were asked to indicate whether the situations would pose a problem for them. Then the researchers compared the responses of HRMs and CEOs. Here is an example: You have to choose between two "change interventions." "One intervention will result in greater productivity increases but more hardship in terms of lost jobs and employee stress than the other

165

intervention." Of the HRMs, 65.8 percent said that making this choice would pose a problem for them. Less than half of the CEOs (42.0 percent) said that this decision would pose a problem for them. The researchers concluded, "We would infer from this table that HRMs are more concerned about individual's needs and about questions of justice than CEOs."[19]

Does this mean that CEOs do not care about people's needs? No. The explanation the researchers offer is this: "We would argue that the significant differences can be explained by the likelihood that HRMs are more embroiled on a day-to-day basis with actual human activity in organizations than CEOs." If the researchers' interpretation is correct, high level leaders will benefit from trusted "lieutenants" (to borrow Steven Sample's term) who *are* in touch regularly with all employees.

One way for a strong leader to develop empathy is to imagine himself or herself in the other's shoes. Randy Rowland, when he had to dismiss someone, tried this activity. "I . . . found myself pondering times I had been excluded and how that felt. I realized I could not love my friend by excluding him unless I came to grips with my own experiences of rejection."[20]

For some leaders, Rowland's exercise may not be sufficient. If you are the type who does not need much affirmation or emotional support, you may assume that others do not need much either. If this is your case, try applying the "altered version of the Golden Rule" offered by Bill Robinson: "Do unto others as they would like you to do unto them."[21]

The shoe must also be placed on the other foot; trying to understand the other's point of view works both ways. Those who lose their jobs or lose the position to which they were attached may not know how hard it is for their supervisors to make tough calls. Herman Melville captured something of this dynamic in

Billy Budd: "Little ween [imagine] the snug card-players in the cabin of the responsibilities of the sleepless man on the bridge." Those who carry executive authority will tell you from experience about the tremendous burden borne by "people at the top."

It may help to remember that you do not usually know all that the leader knows about the situation. Lem Tucker, John Perkins's successor at Voice of Calvary, makes the point well. "Occasionally I have to make a difficult decision about personnel. Someone's job must be changed, even terminated. When that happens, coworkers normally murmur, divide into factions, and chew on whatever the rumor mill produces. I've often wished I could tell everyone all the factors that went into the decision, but in many cases, some of the information must remain private."[22]

If you knew what the decision-maker knows, you might realize that the decision made was truly for the good of the cause *and* for the good of the individual. This thought leads to another principle.

Give the leader the benefit of the doubt. Do your best to trust him or her. Trust means that you believe your leaders are in place by God's providence. Their motives are sincere. They have thoroughly analyzed the needs of the organization and the placement of the team members and have exercised their best judgment.

Lem Tucker expressed his deep appreciation for people who gave him the benefit of the doubt. "They know the difference between agreement and loyalty. They don't always agree with the decision I've made, but they're willing to stick with me anyway. They're 'on my side' not because we always think alike, but because we've walked enough paths together that they know my commitment and motivation, and they're willing to give me the benefit of the doubt."[23]

SERVING JESUS WITH INTEGRITY

In my own experience I remember a missionary's response to staff turmoil over certain leadership changes. The missionary responded that the director surely had good reasons for the changes and had no doubt acted on the basis of wise counsel for the good of all concerned. The sentiment expressed in his note was quite rare in those days. It is the kind of sentiment any leader longs for from followers.

The principle of giving the benefit of the doubt may be difficult for the one who is experiencing a sense of pain, rejection, and loss to apply. It is *hard* to think pleasant thoughts about the person who removed you from a place of significance and influence. But a major question to ask is: "What is the underlying motivation of the leader who made this decision?" If you can honestly answer that the leader understands the organization's purpose and is committed to doing whatever is necessary for that purpose to be fulfilled and at the same time desires for all personnel to be lovingly treated in the process (even if this is imperfectly carried out), then, even if you cannot fully agree with the action taken, you can come to terms more easily with the consequences and move on from your hurt.[24]

Provide member care for those who are deleadered. A news article highlighted the admirable way in which the Billy Graham Evangelistic Association treated fifty-five staff whom it had to lay off. These fifty-five constituted ten percent of the workforce. The BGEA announced that "full-time employees who are laid off get a month's notice, a severance package, and 'outplacement' and spiritual counseling."[25]

In contrast, I observed one distressing deleadering incident in which a mission agency laid off two leaders, one with more than a decade of service and the other with twenty-five years of service with the agency. There was no advance notice. The leaders were informed of their termination on one day, were given the next day to clean out their desks and say goodbye to immediate colleagues, and then they were gone. There was no time for preparation, no public recognition of their contributions to the organization, no official thank you, no chance for them to say goodbye to overseas colleagues who were not present, and no provision for transitional services, though a severance package was provided. Surely we can do better than this!

There is a better way. In "Landing on Your Feet: Assisting International Workers When They Return Home," Dennis Robert (pseudonym) describes how his mission agency helps missionaries whose services are not being renewed. Using the Clifton-Gallup "Strengths Finder," Myers-Briggs Type Indicator, DISC, and other instruments, the agency helps the missionaries understand their strengths. They talk with missionaries about their skills that are transferrable to the marketplace and which sector of the workplace they might be best suited for. They inform them where job search information can be found in their geographical region. They help them write a professional resume. If counseling is needed, the agency sees that it is provided.[26]

The Psalmist declares, "Happy are those who deal justly with others and always do what is right" (Ps. 106:3 NLT). While the agency just mentioned provides services upon termination of employment, it should not be difficult to go further and provide similar services, particularly strengths assessment and counseling, for leaders who are kept in service but given other assignments.

Use the occasion for self-examination. If you have been deleadered, you may need help in doing self-examination, for as Eugene

Peterson notes, "the kingdom of self is heavily defended territory."[27] Your tendency will be to find fault with those who hurt you rather than to ask yourself, "Why am I wounded?" Nevertheless, educators Richard Ackerman and Pat Maslin-Ostrowski tell us:

> This question [why am I wounded?] asks the leader to look inward and deeply at his wound and at the life that led to it. The question encourages the leader to get acquainted with what is going on within and to become open to all elements of the leadership experience. Tackling this question is a lifelong process, not some static achievement. The challenge is to be able to stay there in the leadership questions, to inquire further, and to unlock one's leadership: What are the parts of myself as a leader that I fail to know or see? What parts of myself can't I let others see or know? What if all of me showed up?[28]

Counseling, that is, the help of an objective outsider, can be invaluable as you walk through this process. This is why exit help such as that provided by the BGEA and the agency just described is so valuable.

Not only can you do self-examination, but you can also think of the opportunity before you. Why not? As one of my longtime friends reminded me recently, "There's energy and excitement in starting a new chapter."[29]

Self-examination applies to both sides. Leaders who have had to remove others from leadership should consider to what extent the difficulty is with their own leadership and management behaviors. For example, did you provide regular formative evaluation along the way? To deleader someone is a summary judgment. My former colleague Lee Hotchkiss used to say in his Servant

Leadership and Management Skills workshop: "To do summative evaluation without formative evaluation is immoral."

Avoid counterproductive behaviors and attitudes. One harmful response is to "quit and stay"—to quit mentally and emotionally, yet remain physically present. This response is counterproductive for you and for your organization.

Another harmful response is to view yourself as a "victim." You have to get beyond this imagery.

Another is to stay and perpetually criticize the leaders. This becomes a trial to them and a demotivator to you.

Another is to hold a grudge. "You don't hold a grudge—a grudge holds you."[30] As satisfying as it may feel, you are not doing yourself or anyone else a favor by holding on to your resentment. If you dwell on the loss and the perceived injustice of it all and entertain hostile thoughts about the person who caused the loss, you will never recover.

This list could be extended indefinitely, but I will name one more counterproductive attitude: envy. Envy is a feeling no one wants to admit even to himself.[31] The fact is you may be sorely tempted to be jealous of the leader who replaces you, especially if he or she is promoted while you are demoted or moved laterally. Jealousy is rooted in two powerful emotions that we try to keep at bay—inferiority and insecurity. "The life of the Spirit . . . means we will not compare ourselves with each other as if one of us were better and another worse. We have far more interesting things to do with our lives. Each of us is an original" (Gal. 5:25–26 *The Message*). The key to freedom is to turn off your compulsion to compare yourself to others, and turn on your discovery of the unique person God created you to be.

If you have been deleadered, accept the benefit of your isolation. Those who study leadership patterns testify that most leaders have "wilderness" or "isolation" experiences, as Shelley Trebesch calls them. Her book *Isolation: A Place of Transformation in the Life of a Leader* provides wise guidance for embracing the "inward transformation, spiritual transformation and ministerial transformation" that God brings in the wilderness.[32] She describes the causes, processes, inner workings, and fruitful results of isolation experiences. Make use of this time!

David Osborn, director of the doctor of ministry program at Denver Seminary, has written, "Too often we try to use God to change our circumstances while He is using our circumstances to change us."[33] Even if you feel your removal was unjust and you cannot muster trust in the wisdom of the leader, place your trust in God. If the leader was right, you have learning and growing to do. If the leader was wrong, trust God anyway. Human fallibility does not stop God from operating for the good of his children.

Do not pay too much attention to the hurt. It can lead to greater usefulness than ever before. As A. W. Tozer said, "It is doubtful that God can use any man greatly until he's hurt him deeply."[34]

For all of us, hold our positions loosely. We do not "own" our positions, God does. If we recognize this fact, we can more easily change roles and positions.

In a radio interview Brady Boyd, former senior associate pastor of Gateway Church, Southlake, Texas, and now pastor of New Life Church, Colorado Springs, Colorado, extolled members who are willing to "change seats" for the good of the ministry. "What I would tell the staff is, 'Are you willing to change seats if it's for the benefit of the organization?' . . . We were fortunate to find people with those kind of kingdom attitudes. People who just wanted to build the church and grow the church and weren't concerned necessarily about where they were on the bus. They were just glad to be there. They were happy to change seats if they needed to, if it was best for the church."[35]

Do not be smug. Sometimes you hear leaders refer to underperforming workers as "deadwood." This is a dehumanizing term. Be careful of your language. Even those who irritate you are to be treated as persons of dignity and worth.

You also sometimes hear leaders refer to others as "resistant to change." Jerry B. Harvey, professor of management science at George Washington University, astutely observes that the term "resistant to change" is used by those who do not expect to suffer from a change they want to introduce. The term becomes "a scientifically justified and subtly sophisticated approach to blaming the victim."[36] For instance, someone who fancies himself as a "change agent" might stoutly contend that "Joan is fighting my reengineered organizational structure [that will cause her to lose her job, give up many of her friends and colleagues, abandon the standard of living to which she is accustomed, and quit using a cherished skill that has taken her years to develop]. She clearly is resistant to change."[37]

Using disparaging language weakens the bonds of trust and respect that leaders should have for their followers.

Conclusion

It is my conviction that in God's economy (using "economy" in the original sense of "managing a household") there is no ultimate contradiction between the good of the individual and the good of the cause.

After even painful deleaderings, I have seen good. One friend who is thriving in a new ministry after being removed from high level leadership in a previous organization told me, "I can look [the person who "deleadered" me] in the eye and feel no bitterness." Another who is also thriving in a new ministry after a long stint in leadership elsewhere said, "God meant it for good." That he did not quote the first part of Genesis 50:20 (RSV), "you meant it for evil," but only the second part, showed me that he harbored no bitterness against the one who occasioned his leaving his previous leadership role.

These examples convince me that positive outcomes are possible after a deleadering. My hope is that the principles I have touched on here will help some to manage the deleadering process less traumatically and more effectively. This chapter is not the last word on this subject. It is a first word. Others more capable, experienced, and wise are urged to develop these principles further.

Questions for Discussion

1. Discuss the tensions associated with deleadering individuals by Christian organizations. What are the trade-offs between exercise of pastoral concern for personal growth and maturity versus seeking to foster organizational efficiency and the achievement of an organization's underlying objectives?
2. Given the emotional turmoil associated with having to deleader someone, how might a mission organization provide both emotional and organizational support to the person or persons who have to make that decision?
3. Inasmuch as most individuals who are deleadered will believe they are being unjustly or unfairly treated, what guide-

lines might you want to suggest to someone who has been deleadered?
4. What does it mean to speak the truth in love, especially in light of the qualities of love found in I Corinthians 13?

Notes

1. The epigraph comes from Robert Banks and Bernice M. Ledbetter, *Reviewing Leadership: A Christian Evaluation of Current Approaches* (Grand Rapids: Baker Academic, 2004), 122.
2. I have borrowed the term "deleader" from Brent Lindquist, president of LinkCare Center, Fresno, California. In an e-mail to the author, June 3, 2007, he wrote: "There is not a lot out there regarding helping leaders transition when they have been deleadered, nor about helping leaders get more sensitive."
3. Jim Collins's books were published by HarperBusiness in 2001 and 2005.
4. Randy Rowland, "When You're the Firing Squad. Are You Making Those Tough Decisions for the Right Reason?" www.christianitytoday.com/le/currenttrendscolumns/leadershipweekly/cln50328.html.
5. Steven Sample, *The Contrarian's Guide to Leadership* (San Francisco: Jossey-Bass, 2002), 138, 135.
6. Carly Fiorina, *Tough Choices: A Memoir* (New York: Penguin, 2006), 57.
7. Gary Corwin, "Second Look: Leadership as Pain-Bearing," *Evangelical Missions Quarterly* (January 1998); www.emisdirect.com/emq/issue-130/499.
8. David Hubbard, quoted by Max De Pree, "The Leader's Legacy: A Conversation with Max De Pree," *Leader to Leader Journal*, no. 6 (Fall 1997); www.leadertoleader.org/knowledgecenter/journal.aspx?ArticleID=149.

9. A member of our adult community at church provides an example. She shattered her femur and had surgery to place a long rod in her leg, followed by days and nights of disorientation and pain. After recovery she wrote, "God in mercy has erased the memory of those terrible days" (circular e-mail to the International Perspectives class, College Church, Wheaton, Ill., March 25, 2009).
10. Ted Ward, *Values Begin at Home* (Wheaton, Ill.: Victor Books, 1979), 18.
11. David Ardagh and Rob Macklin, "Ethics and the Human Resource Manager," *Business and Professional Ethics Journal* 17, no. 4 (1998): 62.
12. Daniel Goleman, Richard Boyatzis, and Annie McKee, *Primal Leadership: Realizing the Power of Emotional Intelligence* (Boston: Harvard Business School Press, 2002), 3; italics theirs.
13. Ibid., 176.
14. Stephen P. Chawaga, "How to Take the Backfire Out of Firing," www.christianitytoday.com/yc/1999/julaug/9y4054.html; originally published in *Your Church Magazine* 45, no. 4 (July/August 1999): 54.
15. Michael Zigarelli, "A Christian Approach to Firing Employees," www.christianitytoday.com/workplace/articles/issue8-firing.html.
16. From the first sentence of the Declaration of Independence of the United States of America.
17. Jim Jones, "Tiptoeing Through TULIP: Layoff Allegations Reveal Calvinism Tensions at Baptist Seminary," *Christianity Today* (April 13, 2009), 13; www.christianitytoday.com/ct/2009/april/3.13.html.
18. John Perkins, "We'll All Be Replaced Someday," *Leadership Journal.Net*, posted October 1, 1987; www.christianitytoday.com/le/1987/fall/87l4068.html, then scroll down.
19. Ardagh and Macklin, "Ethics and the Human Resource Manager," 66.
20. Randy Rowland, "When You're the Firing Squad. Are You Making Those Tough Decisions for the Right Reason?" *Leadership Journal.Net*, posted March 28, 2005; www.christianitytoday.com/le/currenttrendscolumns/leadershipweekly/cln50328.html.

21. William P. Robinson, *Leading People from the Middle: The Universal Mission of Heart and Mind* (Provo, Utah: Executive Excellence Publishing, 2002), 189. Robinson is president of Whitworth University, Spokane, Washington. Too few leaders are aware of his book. It is personal, humorous, wise, and grounded in both academic research on leadership and decades of successful leadership experience.
22. Lem Tucker with Bill Chickering, "Following a beloved predecessor," *Leadership Journal.Net*, October 1, 1987; www.christianitytoday.com/le/1987/fall/8714068.html.
23. Ibid.
24. In a most helpful e-mail exchange George Murray has challenged my thinking on these ideas. I am grateful for his insights though I have applied the ideas in my own way; personal e-mail to the author, December 1, 2008.
25. Michael Ireland, "Billy Graham Organization Laying Off Workers," ASSIST News Service, February 25, 2009; www.goodnewsdaily.net/modules/news/article.php?storyid=10850.
26. Dennis Robert, "Landing on Your Feet: Assisting International Workers When They Return Home," *Evangelical Missions Quarterly* 45 (January 2009): 100–3.
27. Janice Stubbs Peterson, ed., *Living the Message: Daily Reflections with Eugene H. Peterson* (San Francisco: HarperSanFrancisco, 1996), entry for July 21.
28. Richard H. Ackerman and Pat Maslin-Ostrowski, *The Wounded Leader: How Real Leadership Emerges in Times of Crisis* (San Francisco: Jossey-Bass, 2002), 22–23.
29. Barry Olson, personal phone call to author, March 12, 2009.
30. Ron Hutchcraft, "Poison in Your Soul," transcript of a radio talk, posted February 7, 2005; www.hutchcraft.com/a-word-with-you/your-most-important-relationship/poison-in-your-soul-4716.

31. Quoting Herman Melville's *Billy Budd* again: "Well, though many an arraigned mortal has in hopes of mitigated penalty pleaded guilty to horrible actions, did anybody seriously confess to envy?"
32. Shelley Trebesch, *Isolation: A Place of Transformation in the Life of a Leader* (Altadena, Calif.: Barnabas Publishers, 1997). Her book is another gem that deserves wider recognition.
33. L. Lee McDowell, "Embracing Change," *Women of the Harvest* Online emagazine, January/February 2006; www.womenoftheharvest.com/emag/jan06a.asp 1 (membership is required to access this secure Web site).
34. Quoted by Marshall Shelley, "Surviving a Power Play," *Leadership* 6 (winter 1985): 57.
35. H. B. London, Jr., "Transitions in a Pastor's Life," interview with Brady Boyd, Wade Brown, Dan Chaverin, Pastor to Pastor podcast; www.parsonage.org/p2p/A000001847.cfm.
36. Jerry B. Harvey, *How Come Every Time I Get Stabbed in the Back My Fingerprints Are on the Knife? And Other Meditations on Management* (San Francisco: Jossey-Bass, 1999), 133.
37. Ibid.

8

Seven Stealth Ethical Issues Flying Under the Radar of Many Mission Agencies

GARY R. CORWIN

Many of the ethical challenges facing the mission community have their roots in the nature of cross-cultural ministry itself. These are crucial and are rightly the primary focus of missiologists' attention. But there are also ethical issues that have their roots in the operational ethos and culture of the agencies that engage with the missional task. This chapter examines seven important examples from the latter group that are often overlooked and, where possible, suggests ways by which they might be handled well.

Maintaining Board Balance

How do agencies insure that their boards maintain appropriate accountability in their public and fiduciary systems, by having enough outsiders involved, and at the same time maintain their commitment to their core values through the presence of enough insiders? How is drift in organizational mission to be avoided?

The issue raised here is at the same time both quite simple and quite complex. Simple because it boils down to acknowledging the need to maintain such balance and to make a commitment to pursue it, and complex because self-perpetuating boards have a tendency to drift over time. Board members instinctively seek to appoint additional board members who share their background and think the way they themselves do. Particularly influential or persuasive board members can change the complexion of a board over time unless equally vigorous efforts are made to maintain balance. Complexity ratchets up exponentially if the task is to try to restore balance once it has been lost.

To complicate matters still further, a divide exists over whether balance is even possible and over whether maintaining faithful adherence to core values (primarily through insider board membership) or maintaining accountability to supporting constituencies (primarily through outsider board membership) is the chief function of the board.

Ralph Winter was a strong advocate of adherence to core values, while also acknowledging any board's responsibility to the State to take "necessary action to remove a leader who is corrupt or deranged."[1] The Evangelical Council for Financial Accountability (ECFA) has probably been the most outspoken proponent of boards' responsibility to maintain accountability to supporting constituencies, emphasizing the necessity of having a majority of board members be outsiders. This emphasis is understandable given ECFA's primary mandate to insure financial accountability, but its standards are closely mirrored by one of the two major North American evangelical associations of mission agencies, CrossGlobal Link.[2] While representatives of neither of these views would argue that the concern expressed by the other side is unimportant, each would argue that that concern is secondary to its own emphasis and that the concern highlighted by the opposing viewpoint can, in any case, be handled quite adequately by a board constituted in its preferred manner. It may be observed, however, that too rigid an adherence to either point of view is unhelpful. Both emphases are essential and they are best maintained through diligent efforts to maintain board balance.

Practical steps for maintaining balance include bylaws that set quotas for types of members, inclusion of members-at-large to supplement internal office holders, and the scheduling of periodic reviews of board membership to determine whether criteria related to insider-outsider balance are being observed. The logistics for insuring balance are not complicated, but they do require regular attention, and that probably requires constitutional mandate.

Maintaining Operational Consensus

What are appropriate guidelines in a consensus-driven mission agency for maintaining institutional integrity vis-à-vis its stakeholders, while allowing maximum freedom to members and employees? How has this been complicated by recent advances in communication technology?

The operational ethos characteristic of many venerable mission agencies through the years may be described as the consensus principle. As they are voluntary organizations, after all, consensus is the glue that holds them together.[3]

In the past this principle has acted as a rarely articulated but generally understood outworking of the way members believed things ought to function. As much as anything it has reflected a global understanding of what it means to be an evangelical follower of Jesus Christ and of how to work well together as his followers. But understandings of consensus have also been formalized in policy at various times when agency leadership has concluded that the issues in contention were serious enough to threaten unity and effectiveness.

Most simply, the principle may be defined as "keeping the main thing the main thing" and not becoming sidetracked by secondary matters. That includes granting colleagues liberty and respect concerning secondary matters over which there may be disagreement, but it also includes agreeing not to promote sincerely held views on secondary matters if doing so would disrupt unity and effectiveness in achieving shared primary goals.

Fifty years ago the matters that most threatened unity and effectiveness in mission agencies were theological. They included issues such as speaking in tongues, modes and timing of baptism, and forms of church government. Ethical questions surrounding such things as the use of alcohol and tobacco also existed, but these were most often seen as cultural issues that needed to be handled by the sending and receiving offices on a case-by-case basis.

Today the most common challenges tend to be ethical, although some critically important theological questions have also emerged. It is also true that these categories often overlap. Ethical issues confronting mission agencies are as varied as the multitude of cultures their membership represents, including such matters as the sanctity of life, biblical standards for appropriate marriage and divorce, gender roles, the showing of appropriate respect for parents, adequate care for the poor, and sexual purity. The more recent theological flashpoints often revisit matters of ancient orthodoxy—such as understandings concerning the eternal destiny of the lost or the fate of those who have never heard the Gospel. The complex challenges posed by both theological and ethical issues are compounded by being overlaid with the larger than usual generational divide that correlates significantly with modern versus postmodern ways of viewing the world, our relationships, and the outworking of our faith. All in all, challenges to organizational unity seem greater today than ever.

How should mission agencies respond to these challenges? At least three primary steps seem essential. First, there must be a reaffirmation of what is non-negotiable—"the main thing." Second, agencies must update and clarify those areas that they do not consider part of the main thing, however important they may be to the personal and individual commitments of stakeholders. Third, they must articulate clearly the guiding principles and practical steps that will be pursued in order both to keep the main thing the main thing and to live and work together respectfully with regard to secondary matters of belief and practice.

The Bible and the history of evangelical faith provide the substance of what ought to be the main thing for any agency that wants to be called evangelical. This is not to say that evangelical mission agencies are carbon copies. Differences in doctrine and practice distinguish them from one another, but they also share a core body of evangelical tenets and practices. Put most simply, the core includes belief in salvation by grace through faith in the finished work of Christ, and adherence to the Bible as the very Word of God and the final authority in all matters of faith and practice. Additional traits characteristic of evangelical missions, both in the past and now, include holding to values of courage, certainty, clarity, and a compulsion to preach the Gospel.

The next two areas pose great challenges. How can an agency know with certainty which ethical or other issues will be divisive? How can it mold its own managerial approach so as to, all at the same time, achieve its core purposes, maximize entrepreneurial freedom on the part of its members, maintain unity, and minimize confusion on the part of all the ministry stakeholders involved? Answers to these questions are not easy.

Real answers to these important questions need to be both concrete and agency specific. First, agencies need to define with some clarity what the flashpoints for divisiveness are, taking into account both their cultural setting or settings and their organizational ethos. Doing so will require attentive listening and survey work. Second, agencies must articulate clearly what constitutes the main thing and strengthen resolve in their screening processes, so that the most egregious departures from expectations are weeded out early before major disruptions occur. Third, they must articulate the ground rules for communication regarding potentially divisive matters so that things over which sincere believers may honestly disagree do not become sources of serious contention between them. Handling of this third point is particularly tricky in an era when so many avenues of communication are so widely available and operate at such high velocity. When newspapers and periodicals were among the few avenues accessible to average citizens for sharing opinions (and that not without difficulty), it was fairly easy to monitor communication with a simple directive to run written drafts by a supervisor before submitting them for publication. Today communication is virtually instant and the power to disseminate information or a viewpoint is available to everyone. With vehicles for Internet-based communication rapidly multiplying, each with varying degrees of possible control over content or over who has access, the challenge of potential miscommunication facing agencies has greatly increased. But it a challenge that must be met, primarily through provision in advance of reasonable but clear guidelines concerning what communication and what form or means of communication are or are not appropriate.

Limiting Fiduciary Risk

What is an appropriate standard for agencies regarding investing cash flow and longer-term designated assets? Why might there be a higher standard for agencies in limiting risk than there is for individuals? Under what circumstances is it appropriate or inappropriate for agencies to invest in the stock market?

While this may seem to be an extremely specialized question, it has risen to prominence on board agendas for a number of mission agencies because of the financial upheavals of recent decades. The bursting of the tech bubble at the close of the twentieth century and especially the bursting of the housing bubble in 2008 have caused considerable financial pain. That pain in turn has generated greater circumspection on the part of board finance committees.

Circumspection has become necessary primarily because numerous agencies, in the expectation of higher returns with which to finance worthy projects and to meet ever-rising operational costs, abandoned the extremely conservative cash flow policies that had been their norm for multiplied decades. For a number of years those expectations were fulfilled, and benefits were reaped easily and quickly. But the risks were largely forgotten. The question can reasonably be asked, "Were the risks taken simply the result of generational amnesia, or was there confusion over the difference between risk-taking that is appropriate at the personal level but inappropriate at the institutional level, especially when institutions are the recipients of charitable gifts?" The possibility of the latter scenario makes this question an ethical one.

It is arguable that with the exception of designated monies set aside for long-term obligations, such as retirement subsidies or pensions, it is neither proper nor prudent for mission agencies ever to invest in the stock market or long-term bonds. Even in the context of such long-term situations, prudence would dictate stock market investment of a very modest percentage. Even short-term and intermediate-term notes should be avoided unless they are of a very high investment grade.

The reason is one of propriety. Almost all of the monies of which mission agencies are stewards come directly or indirectly from the hands of God's people. There is an obligation that they be used to further God's kingdom through the ministries of those agencies. Risking such monies for other than direct ministry purposes, or risking any more than is absolutely necessary, is surely a breach of that implicit contract even when explicit law may permit taking the risk.

From the point of view of prudence, history has shown irrefutably that markets go up and they go down, often at unexpected times and in unexpected ways. It is never wise to invest money that will be needed in the near future (i.e., cash flow) in instruments that do not provide a guaranteed short-term return. Return *of* investment, rather than return *on* investment, must be the highest priority. The stock market, though normally liquid enough to meet the criterion of access, offers no guarantee of the value of an investment at any particular point in time. If money is needed, therefore, at a particular time in the near or intermediate-term future, it is most unwise to tie it up in stocks. Doing so provides no opportunity to wait out down cycles in the stock market.

While it is understandable that board finance committees would want to maximize investment income to permit maximum ministry engagement, doing so in the stock market is equivalent to playing Russian roulette. There is always the potential for loss—sometimes dramatic loss.

Reducing Recruitment Risk and Enhancing Missionary Retention

The mission "industry" is the only one in the world that normally prospers financially by increasing the number of its "employees" rather than by increasing its productivity and "sales." That being the case, how do agencies avoid a bias toward accepting candidates who should be rejected or keeping members who really should be dismissed?

Whether a mission agency has fifty field personnel or 5,000, certain fixed or nearly fixed costs must be met in order to function, let alone to prosper. Home office functions such as receipting, accounting, recruiting, fund-raising, screening, training, and member care, must be carried out by every agency, whatever its size. The implications of this fact for financial viability are enormous, since most mission funding for such activities comes as a percentage of the overall support raised by individual missionaries.

It is obvious that the larger the missionary membership providing such support, the smaller the burden that will fall on each member—or, conversely, the more robustly the home office will be underwritten. From an ethical standpoint the challenge is in combating the natural bias to accept recruits who probably should be rejected and to keep members who should probably be let go. It is hard to imagine that the decisions of mission personnel offices could be uninfluenced by such subtle pressures.

Solutions to this challenge are far less obvious, although simply setting a high standard and committing the agency to uphold it for the sake of the Gospel no matter what, is not really that hard to understand. It is just very hard to do and very easy to rationalize away in the name of mercy and grace.

The problem is made doubly difficult when strong desires to keep the agency not only financially viable but also independent are involved. A desire to keep an agency financially afloat is understandable, though it possibly does not value the wisdom of divine leadership enough in setting the boundaries of an agency's life span, just as God does for each individual. A drive to keep an agency independent whatever the cost is less easy to excuse. When held too tenaciously the desire for independence probably has as much to do with ego and pride as it does with kingdom purposes and quickly becomes a symptom of personal kingdom building, a topic discussed further below.

Avoiding Hype

How do agencies keep their "marketing" concerns from undercutting the integrity of their communication? How do agencies insure that stakeholders receive what they need to hear and not only what they want to hear (and will respond to) or what the agencies want them to hear?

The presence of too many examples to cite of exaggeration and truth shading by leaders of mission organizations has troubled me for years. The hubris evident in the predictions and pronouncements concerning the year 2000, for example, was breathtaking. We should know better and do better.

"Evangelistically speaking" has been a euphemism for exaggeration of ministry results for as long as I can remember. So the problem is not new. But it is something of which we should be ashamed, rather than something we laugh about. Our words and our claims should have the ring of truth all the time.

Abuse of the truth takes many forms, but two of the most common forms evident in mission circles consist, first, in what is not said (even though what is not said is often of vital importance) and second, in false impressions that the communicator intentionally seeks to leave with the reader or listener. Both forms can be used without actually stating anything false, just leaving the impression that something false is true. Sad as these phenomena are, there is no getting around their existence.

We should not have to cringe when we hear of mission groups launching new marketing plans, expanding public relations departments, or engaging in "branding" exercises. Each of these steps may have its place (no blanket condemnation is intended), but we do well to be on guard, for each of these and similar activities are also breeding grounds for the professionalization of falsehood. Would we lose a great deal if we just focused on being faithful to our values? The most important thing is to speak the truth—in love, yes, but also in fact.

But public relations activities and marketing hype are not the only places where shaded truth emerges in the mission enterprise. From rank and file missionary prayer letters to the most articulately argued missiology the danger is also present.

It will be too discouraging to our donors, we surmise, to burden them with the real struggles that we may be facing. Things like loneliness, uncertainty about what to do next, and feelings of depression are not the stuff of missionary heroes. Besides, our partners support us in order to see certain things accomplished, and they want to hear how those are happening, not the hindrances that we are facing. Particularly is this so, we may conclude, when those hindrances possibly reflect personal or professional inadequacy on our part. But in shading the facts, are we not declaring how unimportant we really think prayer is?

At the other end of the spectrum, missiologists sometimes advance theories as facts and simply assert that God is doing a new thing. Or they set up straw man arguments to bolster their case in realms in which they are not confident that they can win the argument on its merits. A prime case in point is the debate in recent years about contextualization in Muslim contexts. Some have asserted or implied that watershed differences exist over cultural issues, when in fact those differences are primarily theological in nature.

Widespread agreement exists among evangelicals that a Muslim who becomes a follower of Christ should not have to cease being a good cultural Algerian, Nigerian, or Indonesian of whatever her or his ethnicity by birth. Followers of Christ do not have to be "extracted" from their roots or claim the title "Christian" in the cultural sense in which the term is often equated with perverted Western lifestyles. They can continue to honor their family and heritage, and to do the things that members of their society do, up to a point. And that point is reached when something one does or does not do communicates falsehood about who Jesus is and what faith in him means.

Falsehood is hyped when this issue is treated as if there are only two choices—extraction or remaining a good Muslim, Hindu, or Buddhist. The issue is complex. While there is an almost universal commitment about avoiding extraction and keeping new believers functioning in their home societies, there is a continuum of understanding as to where lines must be drawn in order to maintain faithfulness to Christ and the Gospel. To paint the issue as other than that is to engage in a misleading reductionism, an effort that has at least the appearance of intentional obfuscation in order to gain acquiescence to one's views where otherwise acceptance would not be granted.

How often has this kind of reductionism been carried out in mission and church circles? More often than any of us would like to acknowledge. To be ethical we must do better.

Kingdom Building

When does a stubborn commitment to maintaining organizational independence betray God's kingdom in favor of ours? What factors might make the case for maintaining organizational independence an overwhelming one?

Stripped down to its most basic elements, the issue of "whose kingdom?" is in essence the sin of our first parents in the Garden, as well as the temptation that Christ faced at the hands of Satan in the wilderness. The temptation to sin in each case is essentially a temptation to pride of position and autonomy, to be in a Godlike position of independent authority and action. This analogy may seem extreme when applied to the desire to maintain an agency's independent existence despite obvious and compelling reasons to amalgamate or merge. But if we are truly oriented to God's kingdom, will not the question as to whose kingdom it is be seen in this light?

Instincts that cause us to want to maintain distinctive and focused agency goals and imperatives, and the independent authority to pursue them, are normal and upright. They can be an appropriate response to duty. But when such desires are allowed to become paramount, at the expense of both efficiency and effectiveness, at the risk of economic default, and even at the risk of members' health, then things have gone too far and the wrong kingdom is being served.

Hudson Taylor expressed it eloquently: "God's work done in God's way will never lack God's supply." But the converse is also likely to be true: "Work not done in God's way, and lacking God's supply, may have ceased really to be God's work." When that is the case, being ethical means being willing to change.

Unity and Diversity

What factors can turn a commitment to unity into an excuse for unethical exclusivity? When does a commitment to diversity become an equally unethical dilution of vision and purpose?

In most modern social and organizational contexts, diversity and its related concepts, multiculturalism and pluralism, have risen to the level of ideals. Sameness is considered unhealthy, a mark of narrow partisanship and bigotry, something that is to be avoided at all costs. Yet there are circumstances and contexts in which unity (or sameness as a byproduct of shared ideology) is absolutely essential. Whenever common ends and means are being pursued, the importance of unity is hard to overstate.

But achieving diversity, too, is a wonderful social state. It reflects the character and history of God's creation and of his interaction with the world. Whether one thinks of flowers, insects, or peoples, our God manifests a love of diversity and displays his commitment to it in practically all that he does.

While it is possible to hold both ends of the spectrum appropriately in balance, problems arise when one end is overemphasized or the other is anemically pursued. Also, when any concept, even if perfectly good in itself, rises to the level of a politically correct mantra, it tends to overthrow all semblance of balance. Such is the challenge the unity/diversity spectrum poses for evangelical mission, not to mention evangelical church life in general. Rather than *e pluribus unum* (out of many one), the result too often is disunity, division, and chaos.

Can diversity be achieved while maintaining unity, so that both goals can be honored and the work be more effective? As evangelical mission agencies take up this challenge, the following five guidelines offer a starting point.

Acknowledge that diversity and unity are about different things. On the one hand, diversity is about getting beyond the "givens," such as race, gender, and ethnicity, that historically have served as walls that divide humankind. These are things that people do not choose for themselves. They are also dividing walls that the Gospel is specifically designed to break down (Gal. 3:28). Unity, on the other hand, is about shared purposes and values, and it requires intellectual assent and commitment of the will. It is a prerequisite for harmonious joint labor. With Amos (3:3 21st Century KJV) we can ask, "Can two walk together, unless they be agreed?"

Celebrate diversity but cherish unity. An unfortunate part of the heritage of evangelical missions is that we have not always valued and celebrated diversity. We rejoice that this attitude seems to be changing, particularly with regard to race, gender, and ethnicity. At the same time as focus has shifted toward a proper revaluation of diversity, however, cherishing unity may be suffering a devaluation. No doubt our culture's idolization of individualism and mavericks plays a part in leading us instinctively to question the necessity and value of organizations as well as the high value institutions, if they are to function at all, must place on unity. Though we may finally be improving our posture with regard to diversity, we are faced with the danger of losing our grip on the necessity for unity. Both are essential and need intentional cultivation.

Recognize that unity is grounded in shared commitments, but nurtured in relationship. Diversity gets the right people into the room, but conscious pursuit of unity through regular mutual affirmation and relationship building provides the energy that moves things forward. Commitment to common values, goals, and means for achieving them makes unity possible; but relationships are the sinews of an effectively functioning organization. The community of faith, the church and those involved in its mission, must show by their mutual love that unity and diversity are not opposites but the faithful partners of a holy marriage.

Resist diversity as a goal, but embrace it as a means. Diversity is not an end in itself, but it is a significant part of the answer to the question, "How are we going to do this?" We shortchange ourselves if we ignore the diverse abundance of resources God has provided for a particular task, but we have set our goals much too low if diversity itself becomes our primary focus. God has larger issues he wants us to address, but he wants us to work in the same way he does things, by celebrating and benefiting from the diverse and uniquely valuable resources he has provided.

Base commitments to both unity and diversity on the nature and commands of the God we serve, not on the dictates of groupthink or political correctness. The latter will fade like the late afternoon sun; the former will last forever. While the latter changes with a new day's headlines, the former have stood, and will stand, the test of time. One Lord. One faith. One baptism. One God and Father of our Lord Jesus Christ. And yet around the throne stands a multitude from every tribe, tongue, nation, and people. What a great God we serve!

Questions for Discussion

1. How might this chapter be turned into a helpful guideline for new missionary candidates in choosing a responsible mission agency?
2. How might this chapter be used by mission leaders to do their own internal examination in order to promote healthy and ethical guidelines?
3. What standards and skills ought to be required when choosing members for a mission board?
4. What strategies ought to be followed in order to keep a mission board focused on its stated mission and distinctives in respect to its leadership, its members, and its supporters?

Notes

1. "The Principle of a Sodality" (unpublished manuscript, January 27, 1994; rev. September 1, 2006), 1; available from the U. S. Center for World Mission, Pasadena, California. See also Ralph D. Winter, "How to Run a Mission Society," in *Perspectives on the World Christian Movement—Study Guide*, Steven C. Hawthorne, revised by Ralph D. Winter (Pasadena, Calif.: William Carey Library, 1992), C-1–C-9.
2. See CrossGlobal Link (www.crossgloballink.org/Standards) and the Evangelical Council for Financial Accountability (www.ecfa.org/Content/ECFABestPractices.aspx).

3. Some of the materials in this and the following sections are adapted from Gary Corwin, "The Consensus Principle," *Evangelical Missions Quarterly* (July 2009): 270–71; "Evangelical Mission Values," *EMQ* (July 2008): 278–79; "The Audacity of Hype... and Humility," *EMQ* (January 2009): 6–7; and "Doing Diversity Well," *EMQ* (October 2008): 416–17.

9

Organizational Justice: Perceptions of Being Fairly Treated

DAVID R. DUNAETZ

Missionaries live in a world of organizations. They are members of sending organizations from their home countries. They form organizations among themselves on the field. Their goal is often to create organizations for the people whom they serve, such as churches or training centers. At other times they wish to serve existing organizations run by national leaders. Many are accountable to and dependent upon another set of organizations in their sending countries, the local churches that support them.

Although the Bible gives far more information concerning the way individuals should act than the way organizations should act, the actions of organizations immensely influence missionaries and the people whom they serve. How these actions are perceived by individuals within the organization is the subject of a relatively young field within the behavioral sciences known as *organizational justice*, the systematic study of the causes and effects of the perception of fairness and unfairness within an organization (Colquitt et al. 2001; Folger 1977; Lind and Tyler 1988).

Organizational justice is both similar to and different from God's justice or righteousness. Both deal with what is believed to be right, fair, and just. God's justice, however, examined from a theological point of view, is defined by God, has its source in him, and is revealed by him. It is immutable and is a trustworthy measure for judging the value of our own behavior. We are called to be righteous (Matt. 5:48), but inevitably fall short (Rom. 3:23). Through faith in Jesus Christ and because of his work on the cross, the righteousness of God is imputed to us (Rom. 3:21–22). This righteousness is very different from what is meant by organizational justice, which is defined from a psychological point of view. Organizational justice measures the degree to which an individual perceives an action within an organization (by a hierarchical superior, a peer, or "the system") to be fair or unfair. Whether the action is actually fair or unfair (which from a Christian point of view would be defined by God's righteousness) is not what is being examined, however important that may be. What is examined is the perception of fairness or unfairness, the cause of this perception, and the effect of the perception.

Compared to God's justice, organizational justice may seem trivial. Good reasons exist, however, for systematically studying it. First and perhaps foremost is that we can actually measure organizational justice (the perceived fairness of the behavior of individuals) and its effects. Neither theologians nor psychologists would attempt to measure empirically the degree to which individuals in an organization behave in accordance with God's righteousness and measure the consequences. Justice by God's standard is internal to an individual (Matt. 15:18–20) and is not easily measured by an outside observer. How would you feel if your mission announced that it was going to measure the righteousness of each of its missionaries? Closer to home, how many of us would think that we ourselves are good judges of how we personally measure up to God's justice? If others cannot measure how just we are, could we do it ourselves, say on a scale ranging from "filthy rags" (Isa. 64:6) to "holy and faithful" (Col. 1:2)? We rejoice that this is an issue that God has dealt with by sending his Son. But organizational justice is another question. We can very easily ask people, "On a scale of 1 to 10, where 1 means very unfair and 10 means perfectly fair, how fair do you think that such and such a decision was?" They may be completely wrong in their judgment, due to biases, misperceptions, and a lack of information, but their feelings are real, and those feelings have real causes and consequences.

For example, empirical research has shown that when the perception of organizational justice is high, people are more willing to serve in the organization and to strive to accomplish its goals (Brockner and Wiesenfeld 1996). This willingness becomes especially apparent when negative events occur within an organization, such as interpersonal conflict, a failed program, or a loss of financial resources (all of which occur fairly regularly in missionary efforts). When perceptions of organizational justice are high, members are much more likely to take negative events in stride. But when organizational justice is perceived to be lacking, negative events are likely to evoke strongly negative reactions, sometimes leading to attrition of members. My purpose in this chapter is to describe the various dimensions of organizational justice that have been discovered, to present the results of empirical studies indicating what consequences can be expected when organizational justice is not present, and to suggest ways that mission organizations can make sure that their ministry is characterized by a high level of organizational justice.

The Difficulty of Seeing Missionary Injustices

By God's grace, instances of egregious organizational injustice within mission agencies are not overly common. Most of the time mission organizations make good decisions that promote the spread of the Gospel, the well-being of their members, and the well-being of the people whom they serve. By and large missionaries and their organizations strive to be fair in their dealings with one another and with others. But occasionally things can go wrong, horribly wrong. Situations arise in which missionaries are perceived by the people with whom they work to be incredibly unfair. National workers may feel abused by their missionary employers when they compare their salaries to what other missions pay. A missionary may feel unfairly treated if asked to resign and no meaningful reason is provided. Loss of funding for a project for which missionaries have sacrificed a good part of their lives may lead to accusations that those cutting the funding are unfair, which in turn may cause contributors of funds to feel unappreciated and unfairly treated by the missionaries.

These problems are compounded by the fact that as humans we tend to be biased in our perceptions of fairness. We can recognize unfairness very quickly in others, but it is difficult to recognize it in ourselves. A study of fifty-four nations (Park, Peterson, and Seligman 2004, 2006) indicates that throughout the world most people see themselves as being very fair; on a scale of 1 to 5, most people rate themselves at around 4.0. For most countries 4.0 is a higher score than people give themselves for honesty, love, humor, or social skills. Since we see ourselves as being fair in our outlook and dealings, a lack of fairness tends to be a problem that we see, not in ourselves, but in others.

Part of the reason we believe ourselves to be so fair is due to our biases. One of our most common biases is known as the *fundamental attribution error* (Ross 1977). When we see something go wrong, we tend to attribute the difficulty to a cause. Research has shown that people tend to be biased when making this attribution. When we see things go wrong in the life of someone else, we tend to attribute the problems primarily to the person's personality or character traits or to choices that the person has made. If something goes wrong in our own lives, however, we tend to attribute the problem to circumstances around us that have made the situation inevitable. For example, if someone is late for an appointment with us, we might come to the conclusion that the person is lazy, disorganized, or uncaring. But if we are late for an appointment, we tend to believe that it is because of traffic problems, some important issue that came up, or any of a myriad of other possible hindrances. Therefore, when someone does an injustice to us, we easily come to the conclusion that the person is unfair. If we do an injustice to someone else, however, we tell ourselves that we did not really have any choice due to the circumstances or that the person deserved it because of his or her own actions. Even though we tend to see unfairness on the part of others as an expression of their character, we do not view ourselves as intrinsically unfair, because we tend to see the reasons for the problem as being exterior to ourselves.

Our biases may prevent us from seeing what other people perceive as being unjust. Wikipedia, under "List of Cognitive Biases" (http://en.wikipedia.org/wiki/List_of_cognitive_biases), offers descriptions of a number of such biases, such as confirmation bias, status quo bias, the false consensus effect, and the Lake

Wobegon effect. Each can prevent us from recognizing our own acts of unfairness or from seeing why others might perceive what we do as unfair. Fortunately, though our acts of unfairness are difficult for us to see, with God's grace we may be able to learn to recognize them and even to rectify them.

Four Types of Organizational Justice

A typology of injustices will be helpful for understanding perceptions of fairness or unfairness in organizational settings such as missions, churches, and parachurch agencies. Organizational scientists use four categories of organizational justice—distributive, procedural, interpersonal, and informational—to classify perceptions regarding the fairness or unfairness of various actions taken within organizations (Colquitt 2001; Colquitt et al. 2001). Not only do these classifications allow us to understand why some actions are considered unfair, but empirical studies also indicate what type of reaction can likely be expected when one or another of the types of organizational justice is perceived to be low. As will be seen, a lack of organizational justice has many negative consequences.

Distributive Justice

James 5:1–6 condemns rich, unfair employers who do not pay their employees what they deserve. Such stinginess is an example of a lack of distributive justice arising from a perceived—and in this case real—lack of fairness in how the outcomes of invested labor are distributed. Employees expect to receive the wage for which they have a contract either in writing or by convention. When they work and do not reap the expected benefits, they feel cheated. But questions of distributive justice are not always so clear cut.

What should missionaries receive in return for their work? God will certainly grant them heavenly rewards, but in the meantime most would probably like to eat regularly and maybe even send their children to college. In the missionary setting, distributive justice is a complicated issue, and it becomes even more so if we ask to what degree faith missions are responsible for missionary salaries. In determining what constitutes fair outcomes for the work that employees or agents provide an organization, three allocation rules come into play. Unlike most organizations, missions tend to use a combination of all three.

The first allocation rule is *equality*, whereby all members of an organization receive the same amount. To a certain degree, many missions follow the rule of equality in setting salaries. There may be differences due to seniority rules, cost of living adjustments, or bonuses for being on administrative staff, but the salary range in most mission agencies is far narrower than in the great majority of other organizations, both Christian and, especially, secular.

The second rule focuses on *needs*. Missionaries tend to have a salary that is high enough to carry on a ministry in both the United States and their country of service, but lower than what they could make in their home culture in a secular job. Their salary level ensures that they have enough to live on; it also ensures that getting rich is not a motivating factor in deciding to become a missionary. Missionaries who work in countries with a high cost of living or who have more children needing health insurance and bedrooms have greater needs; therefore, they may receive a higher salary and more benefits than others who do not have such needs.

The third allocation rule, the one followed by most Christian and secular organizations but less by faith missions, is called *equity*. This rule says that what one receives should be in proportion to what one contributes. For example, an engineer is expected to contribute more to the success of an organization than a file clerk, so the engineer will receive a higher salary. Although never stated publicly, especially in promotional materials, this rule probably comes into play in the lives of most missionaries, but only in the context of fund-raising. Missionaries who have a very successful ministry leading people to Christ, starting churches, building hospitals, feeding the poor, or doing whatever their ministry consists of will probably find raising funds easier and will be more likely to receive full support than will missionaries who encounter one failure after another. If that is so, the missionaries' salaries will be somewhat proportional to what they contribute to the organization. Similarly, missionaries who are good fund-raisers (e.g., those who are able to turn even their failures into appealing and exciting prayer letters) will probably be more likely to be fully supported than those who are not similarly gifted. These examples show how a skill that is useful to an organization, in this case, a mission agency, is rewarded proportionately to its level.

But salary is not the only reward that missionaries receive for their services. There are also intangible rewards, even beyond the heavenly rewards promised by God. Perhaps the most influential of these for most missionaries is the internal sense of well-being that comes from doing what they believe God has called them to do. Another intangible reward is the appreciation or esteem that they receive from other Christians. Rightly or wrongly, missionaries and their families are held up as examples of what it means to be committed to Christ and to serve God. Other people may feel good about themselves because of material goods they possess or because they drive a Lexus or BMW; missionaries can feel good about themselves because people in their sending churches remind them that they are doing the right thing, although they may be driving a car that most of their supporters would not be able to identify. Other rewards include the support and encouragement of colleagues and mission administrators. Missionary work thus offers both tangible and intangible rewards.

When the "needs" and "equity" rules do not appear to be followed, a feeling of a lack of distributive justice occurs. Certainly, if people do not receive what they believe they need so as to live at a minimally sufficient level, they will feel that their organization is being unfair. Needs are basic and must be met. But lack of equity will also cause a sense of injustice. If a missionary makes what he or she considers to be a significant contribution to the organization but does not receive adequate rewards (such as support and encouragement from colleagues or administrators), she or he will feel unappreciated and may experience a sense of injustice. Many studies show what occurs when people suffer a lack of distributive justice, especially when there is a lack of equity. The results are described by *equity theory* (Adams, 1965), which states that a perceived mismatch between inputs and outputs will lead to changes in people's inputs or in their perceptions so as to bring about equity. People who contribute more than what they believe their rewards are worth tend to contribute less over time. For example, suppose a widget factory pays its best worker (who makes ten widgets per day) the same as its pays average workers (who make five widgets per day). Very likely the best worker will feel undervalued and treated unfairly. This worker is also likely to reduce his level of effort and eventually to make fewer widgets per day. If, however, the worst workers (who are currently making two widgets per day) are paid the same as the average workers, they are likely either to feel guilty about not contributing enough to the organization (and to try to produce more widgets) or to change their perceptions about their work and to justify their high salary by telling themselves that they merit it for one reason or another (their widgets are higher quality, they contribute to the work atmosphere, they encourage others, and so on). In any case, the feelings evoked by being underpaid tend to be much stronger than those for being overpaid.

On a practical level, studies of employees who believe they are suffering distributive injustice (Colquitt et al. 2001) indicate that they are, in general, less satisfied with their job, more likely to call in sick, more likely to steal from their employer (believing that this balances out the injustice), and more likely to leave the organization. In addition, the quality of their work goes down. For missions, this means that it is important for missionaries to receive sufficient support and salary. Although it might seem "spiritual" for missionaries to say that they do not need to be fully supported, it is in the interest of both the mission and the missionaries to require a minimum level of support that meets the missionaries' needs and that ensures that they feel they are being treated fairly. But salary is not the only remuneration that a mission can give missionaries. The support and encouragement of administrators and colleagues can counterbalance a salary that is considered to be low for the work provided. Support and encouragement do not come naturally when everybody has an individual agenda and a personal set of priorities. For this reason, mission leaders must consciously structure their priorities to include support and encouragement of missionary staff and colleagues. It may be easier to criticize than to affirm and encourage, but criticism of those who feel under rewarded and insufficiently appreciated is quite likely to lead to attrition rather than improvement.

Procedural Justice

When King Solomon commanded that a baby be cut in two, the true mother responded in outrage (1 Kings 3:16–28). From a distributive justice point of view, such a decision might be considered just (but most likely not). The process by which the decision was made, however, was inherently unfair. The true mother (and the baby) would suffer an irreparable and unbearable loss, and thus responded in outrage to the mere thought of it. Solomon recognized this outrage as coming from a sense of injustice and was thus able to identify the true mother. In much the same way, organizations need to be sensitive to cries of outrage coming from their members. Not all complaints are justified, but even so, they need to be given a fair hearing. Whenever a decision is made in an organization, people can be expected to respond negatively if they think the process of decision making was biased or unfair. Perceptions of favoritism during budget setting, perceptions of unwillingness to hear another missionary's point of view, or perceptions that not all the available information has been taken into consideration in decision making—all such situations are likely to be interpreted as lacking in procedural justice.

Suppose that missionary John Dutiful has begun attending a church started by a young national church planter. His intent is to provide stability and support to the new congregation and to encourage the church planter. But missionary Dutiful does not really enjoy the church. He does not live near it, he and his wife are not significantly integrated into the community, and they have to get up early to get there on Sunday morning.

The national church planter is a gifted pastoral leader, which means that many of Dutiful's gifts cannot be used. Nevertheless Dutiful continues to attend because he feels it to be his duty. Now, Dutiful also happens to be on the committee that places new missionaries in ministries. About a year ago a young, single missionary, Jack Young, came to the field, integrated into a church with other people his age, and learned the language remarkably quickly. Somehow Dutiful gets the idea that it would be a good idea for Young to replace him at the church plant he and his wife have been attending. This idea might be coming from God–or maybe not. Such a decision needs to be examined carefully and with sensitivity to all parties involved. Dutiful might be able to convince the placement committee that the assignment is a good idea, but if Young is against it (perhaps he feels God is calling him to stay at his present ministry because he has developed solid relationships), he will likely perceive any decision to redeploy him to the new church as unjust. If, however, Young and Dutiful meet together (perhaps along with the placement committee), discuss all the issues involved (even the delicate ones), and make sure that they understand each other's point of view, whatever decision is made will likely be accepted more willingly, even if one of the missionaries would have preferred another outcome.

Studies of procedural justice have shown six elements to be essential for a decision to be perceived as just, especially when at least one party is adversely affected by the consequences of the decision (Colquitt et al. 2001; Leventhal 1976). If any one of these six elements is missing, decisions that adversely affect a member of an organization quite possibly will be perceived as being unjust.

Decisions must take into account the opinions of all parties involved. Even if I do not like the outcome of a decision, if I know that my point of view has been heard and understood, I will be more likely to accept the decision. This is called the "voice effect." If missionaries, national employees, short-term workers, and church members are able to express their point of view on an issue, and know that they have been heard, it is much more likely that they will perceive the final decision as just. But if they do not have a voice in the decision, even if the final decision is thought to be in their best interest, they will be more susceptible to feeling that an injustice has been done. This underlines the importance of making sure that all personnel associated with a mission have the chance to express their opinions to the decision makers, who must set apart time not only to listen but also to give feedback to interested parties in a way that allows these parties to feel that they have been heard.

Procedures used to make decisions must be consistent across people and across time. If members of an organization feel that some people are treated with favoritism or that the rules for obtaining what one wants are shifting, they will harbor perceptions of procedural injustice. James 2:1–4 describes an obvious case of favoritism concerning the rich and the poor. In missions we are more likely to show favoritism to people who are more like us in terms of age, values, personality, culture, or interests. James 2:4 describes the motives behind such favoritism as evil.

Similarly, we expect policies and decisions to be applied consistently, day after day, month after month. If older missionaries see that policies that once cost them dearly (such as rules concerning length of home assignment) are now ignored by others with impunity, they are likely to see the discrepancy as unfair.

This fact does not mean that policies should never change, but it does imply that much careful communication needs to accompany changes. Leaders implementing change need to take into consideration the voices and feelings of all concerned. Once decisions are made, the changes need to be communicated clearly (perhaps using multiple means to communicate them) so that they do not come as a surprise when someone finds out that the old policies are no longer being applied.

Decisions must be made using accurate information. If one missionary accuses another missionary of wrongdoing, any decision or action by a third party against the accused missionary will be considered unjust if the accused missionary believes that the information on which the judgment was based is inaccurate. Mission leaders (or any third party involved in solving a problem) need to make sure that all parties believe the leaders have accurate and complete information. If accuser and accused have different beliefs about what is true, any intervening party needs to be sure that he or she fully understands both points of view. Moreover, it is essential that the missionaries themselves believe that the third party understands their points of view and has all relevant information in hand. This process is often time-consuming and emotionally draining, but God has called us to live in truth and love, regardless of the cost.

An incorrect or flawed decision must be correctable. A church-planting couple apparently angered someone in their mission's leadership. They received a letter saying they were to resign from the mission within a week. When they asked why, the mission leader said he would not explain, because they would not agree. When they asked if they could appeal the decision, he said no.

The couple felt they had no choice but to resign. All attempts at reconciliation were rejected by the mission leadership. Not only did the mission lose a successful church-planting couple, but also relationships were damaged in a way that probably did not please the Lord. Part of the problem was that the mission did not have in place a policy that could correct potentially flawed decisions. Whenever decisions are imposed on a less powerful party by fiat with no possibility of appeal, such as bringing in a mediator, they are likely to be perceived as unjust.

Decisions must be unbiased. If a national employee feels that she or he is being underpaid compared to employees of other missions, a decision that the pay level is correct, if made by the hiring mission, may well be seen as biased. If it is in the hiring mission's interest to pay less (which is most likely the case due to such things as chronic under support of missionaries), mission decision makers are quite likely to give greater weight to information that says that a lower wage is just and less weight to information that says that a higher wage is just. Undoubtedlythe mission leaders will believe that they are acting free of bias, but that is not likely to be the perception of the employee who feels underpaid. A decision to maintain or change the employee's salary will be much better accepted if it is seen as coming from an unbiased third party, fully trusted—and this is essential—by both the mission and the employee.

Decisions must be made on the basis of prevailing ethical standards. In secular organizations the issue of prevailing standards can be slippery. In Christian organizations, by contrast, the Bible is the usual standard for questions of ethics, and decisions must be made in light of biblical principles of goodness and justice.

Most of the time in a Christian organization, this result is exactly what both parties want. Occasionally, though, disputes become so emotionally entangled that one or both parties do not want to discuss the issues, even if the Bible has something to say about them. In one situation a field leader would not meet with a missionary for over a year to discuss problems because emotions were so high. The situation could have been improved quickly if the two had been able to calm down, discuss the issues, and understand what the other was perceiving. They could then have committed themselves to working through the issues using biblical principles.

When any of these six elements is missing, a mission will be perceived as lacking procedural justice. When the level of procedural justice is low, members of the organization tend to be highly unsatisfied with both the organization and its leadership (Colquitt et al. 2001). Trust deteriorates, attrition goes up, and people tend to respond to stressful situations in destructive ways. Instead of exchanging information in order to solve problems, members tend to withdraw or even sabotage the organization, making coordination of efforts to accomplish the organization's mission difficult. We harbor the hope that Christians would not normally be mean-spirited, but we must acknowledge that the negative effects mentioned can also infect Christian organizations. If missionaries are serious about reaching the world for Christ, they must coordinate their efforts, at the very least within their own organizations. Such coordination cannot occur unless all members believe that the decisions being made are characterized by procedural justice.

Both distributive justice and procedural justice are necessary for an organization to be perceived as just. But other less obvious forms of justice must also be in place. Interpersonal justice and informational justice focus on the ways two parties interact, regardless of the decisions that are made.

Interpersonal Justice

Even when an organization's members feel adequately rewarded and are satisfied with the procedures used in making decisions, if they are treated poorly by others, especially by those in leadership, they will believe that they are being treated unfairly (Greenberg 1993). Interpersonal justice is the perception that leaders treat members with politeness, dignity, and respect. Leaders also need to show emotional support; that is, they must be sensitive to what others are feeling and they must recognize the legitimacy of those feelings. Any signs of intimidation, threat, condescension, or manipulation will be interpreted as violations of interpersonal justice.

Some people, especially women, are more naturally gifted than others at demonstrating interpersonal justice. This is one of the most difficult areas of growth for leaders. If we have authority, we tend to believe that we are to use it. Respect, emotional support, and persuasion are costly in terms of time and effort, and we can easily conclude that they are just too costly if we are to work efficiently. But perhaps these types of interaction are what Jesus had in mind when he said, "Those who are regarded as rulers of the Gentiles lord it over them. . . . Not so with you. Instead, whoever wants to become great among you must be your servant" (Mark 10:42–43 NIV). One characteristic of servant leadership is a strong regard for those being led, seeking their good and being sensitive to what they are feeling and experiencing. Intimidation, threats, and ultimatums do not seem to be appropriate tools for servant leaders.

Interpersonal justice can have a major impact on the members and the esprit de corps of an organization, especially when the organization runs into difficulty. Jerald Greenberg, a professor at Ohio State University, studied nurses who were suffering injustice: their salaries were cut but they were expected to carry out the same amount of work (Greenberg 2006). Both right before and soon after the pay cut, he measured the stress reaction (the amount of reported insomnia) to this injustice among several groups of nurses. The amount of reported insomnia increased significantly after the pay cut. He then provided training in interpersonal justice to about half the supervisors of the nurses. The training included information on how to treat subordinates with politeness, dignity, and respect, as well as how to demonstrate emotional support and avoid intimidation. The supervisors were also instructed to approach any of their subordinates whom they thought might feel that they had been treated unjustly by their supervisor and to do what they could to make the relationship right. During the first two weeks after the training, the nurses whose supervisors were trained in interpersonal justice suffered significantly less insomnia than those whose supervisors had not received the training. The beneficial effect continued for at least another six months. This study is an excellent example of how higher levels of interpersonal justice can dramatically improve people's lives, even when other forms of justice are absent.

Besides reducing insomnia, increased interpersonal justice has been shown both to reduce negative emotional reactions to a perceived lack of distributive justice and to increase "organizational citizenship behaviors" (Colquitt et al. 2001; Folger and Cropanzano 1998). Organizational citizenship behaviors are voluntary behaviors which are not included in one's job description but which help the organization achieve its goals, such as voluntarily helping other members of the organization with their responsibilities, keeping up on company policies, working to do an especially good job on the tasks one is assigned, and tolerating inconveniences without complaining (Greenberg 2005). The perception of interpersonal justice also predicts a favorable attitude toward one's supervisor, something that is especially important in mission organizations since missionaries need to trust one another in order to function as a team.

Examples of problems of interpersonal justice in missionary contexts include missionaries' refusing to communicate with each other, destructive accusations made against one another, and missionaries' being unwilling to work out complex interpersonal relationship problems between themselves. Justifying these behaviors with "spiritual" reasons, such as "I'm doing God's will and that other missionary is getting in my way," may be easy and tempting, but such behavior is not what God is calling us to, even if it gives us more time to work on what we believe to be our primary mission. Love, joy, peace, patience, kindness, and the rest of the fruit of the Spirit (Gal. 5:22–23) are far more in line with what a God-directed ministry would look like. Even from a secular perspective, the qualities, emotions, and values described as the fruit of the Spirit are far more beneficial to an organization than are those that characterize a lack of interpersonal justice.

Informational Justice

The final type of organizational justice, which is to some degree independent of the others, is informational justice. It consists of clear communication concerning the reasons behind decisions that have been made (Folger and Cropanzano 1998; Greenberg 1993). If inadequate information is provided, especially concerning decisions that have a negative outcome for some members of the organization, those giving (or withholding) information will be viewed as unfair.

To be considered fair, information concerning unfavorable decisions must first of all be perceived as *true*. If information that a decision maker provides appears to be false, there clearly will be perceptions of injustice. Second, the information must provide *sufficient justification* for the decision. If the decision is unfavorable to some, the reason why they are expected to suffer personally needs to be justified by the benefit that the change brings to the organization. For their decisions to be accepted as fair, leaders must allow their decisions to be questioned, and they must fully engage stakeholders who wish to provide a different point of view or want more complete information. Third, the information communicated must be *reasonable*, that is, logically consistent, showing that the decision takes all the available information into consideration. Fourth, it must be *timely*, available to the organization's members when they want it. If information is not made available when the persons affected want it, leaders will appear to be trying to hide something. Finally, communication must be *specific*. Vague generalities will not satisfy those who want to understand exactly why a decision was made. Vague communication will, again, be interpreted as an attempt to hide information.

In missions, communication characterized by informational justice can be costly. Under any conditions such communication requires time and emotional energy. But in mission contexts, geographic distances often make face-to-face communication difficult. When "context rich media" such as face-to-face or video conferencing are not possible, the next best solution is extended telephone conversations, an option that with the advent of Internet technology, such as Skype, has become extremely inexpensive (Daft and Lengel 1986; Dunaetz forthcoming). Telephone and video conferences may lessen the time commitment required, but such conversations can still be draining emotionally. They are necessary, however, for maintaining and building trust within an organization. If at all possible, information that risks provoking negative emotions should not be communicated through "context poor media" such as e-mail or printed documents. Emotionally negative information requires circumstances in which a maximum amount of information can be shared, explained, interpreted, re-explained, reinterpreted, and understood by both parties simultaneously.

Practical Applications

With the four dimensions of organizational justice, their causes, and their effects firmly in view, what can missions do on a practical level to become organizations that are more just? Following are two ideas that can be applied within home offices, on the field among missionaries, and within national organizations associated with missions and missionaries.

Training in organizational justice. One of the most immediate and practical steps is to provide training for all members in positions of leadership. Leaders include home staff, regional supervisors, and missionaries who provide oversight on the field, whether of other missionaries or of nationals.

Training in organizational justice is typically spread over several weeks or months and consists of a number of sessions, perhaps four half-day sessions (Skarlicki and Latham 1996, 1997). The program could consist of teaching about the various dimensions of organizational justice, discussion among the participants concerning the relevance of organizational justice to their sphere of influence, case studies, role playing, and developing strategies for increasing the perception of justice within the organization. An important aspect of organizational justice training consists of assignments that the participants carry out between the sessions. They are required to talk with at least one subordinate or colleague who might have perceived something the participant had done as being unfair. This assignment gives them a real life opportunity to put into practice what they have learned by detecting, understanding, and correcting a perceived injustice. At the following session they share their experiences within a small group. Frequently stories of reconciliation and restored relationships that are brought about while carrying out these assignments become a highlight of the training experience.

The establishing of a conflict management system. Even with missionaries well trained in organizational justice, conflicts will occur. Among passionate and strong willed missionaries, such conflicts often surpass their ability to resolve them on their own. Mission organizations need to have a conflict management system in place that all who wish to can access (Costantino and Merchant 1996). The system needs to include the availability of mediation for any who desire it (typically it is the person in the less powerful position who wants mediation, while the more powerful person resists it). The organization must ensure the availability of a mediator who is willing and able to invest large periods of time in understanding the conflict, building a trust relationship with the parties involved, and helping them to understand each other before any constructive solution can be found. For this reason, mission agencies should designate a person as mediator who is able to travel as needs arise, or they should provide funds to hire local mediators who can intervene where conflict occurs.

Conclusion

Organizational justice is not a subject about which most Christian leaders want to think. It is far easier to think that our pure motives, our wise decisions, and our love for individuals will be clearly seen and understood by those for whom we have responsibility and over whom we have influence. Unfortunately, that is not always the case. Occasionally we are not as pure, wise, or loving as we think we are. Even more often, our actions are misinterpreted by those who observe us. This means that there are undoubtedly instances when those around us perceive our actions or decisions to be unjust.

We can be motivated to increase organizational justice simply because it will enable our organization to function better. But for the Christian, organizational justice is not just a means by which members can be motivated to work toward the organization's goals. Organizational justice is part of our responsibility to live in a Christ-pleasing and biblical manner, loving others as God has loved us.

Discussion Questions

1. What are some of the self-serving biases that we have as human beings that prevent us from correctly evaluating the fairness of our decisions?
2. How is organizational justice similar to the biblical concept of justice? How are they different? Why would we want to measure organizational justice?

3. What is the difference between the principles of equality and equity? When would one be more appropriate than the other?
4. What is procedural justice? How does it differ from other forms of justice? Why is it so important?
5. What is informational justice? Why is it so hard to achieve? For whom is this type of justice most important?
6. What can mission organizations do to make sure their missionaries feel that they are being treated fairly?

References

Adams, John Stacey. 1965. Inequity in social exchange. *Advances in Experimental Social Psychology* 2:267–99.

Brockner, Joel, and Batia M. Wiesenfeld. 1996. The interactive impact of procedural fairness and outcome favorability: The effect of what you do depends on how you do it. *Psychological Bulletin* 120:189–208.

Colquitt, Jason A. 2001. On the dimensionality of organizational justice: A construct validation of a measure. *Journal of Applied Psychology* 86:386–400.

Colquitt, Jason A., Donald E. Conlon, Michael J. Wesson, Christopher O. L. H. Porter, and K. Yee Ng. 2001. Justice at the millennium: A meta-analytic review of 25 years of organizational justice research. *Journal of Applied Psychology* 86:425–45.

Costantino, Cathy A., and Christina Sickles Merchant. 1996. *Designing conflict management systems.* San Francisco: Jossey-Bass.

Daft, Richard L., and Robert H. Lengel. 1986. Organizational information requirements, media richness and structural design. *Management Science* 32:554–71.

Dunaetz, David R. Forthcoming. Long distance managerial intervention in overseas conflicts: Helping missionaries reframe conflict along multiple dimensions.

Folger, Robert. 1977. Distributive and procedural justice: Combined impact of "voice" and improvement on experienced inequity. *Journal of Personality and Social Psychology* 35:108–19.

Folger, Robert, and Russell Cropanzano. 1998. *Organizational justice and human resource management.* Thousand Oaks, Calif.: Sage Publications.

Greenberg, Jerald. 1993. The social side of fairness: Interpersonal and informational classes of organizational justice. In *Justice in the workplace: Approaching fairness in human resource management*, ed. Russell Cropanzano, 79–103. Hillsdale, N.J.: Erlbaum.

———. 2005. *Managing behavior in organizations.* 4th ed. Upper Saddle River, N.J.: Prentice Hall.

———. 2006. Losing sleep over organizational injustice: Attenuating insomniac reactions to underpayment inequity with supervisory training in interactional justice. *Journal of Applied Psychology* 91:58–69.

Leventhal, Gerald S. 1976. The distribution of rewards and resources in groups and organizations. In *Advances in Experimental Social Psychology* 9:91–131.

Lind, E. Allan, and Tom R. Tyler. 1988. *The social psychology of procedural justice.* New York: Plenum.

Park, Nansoon, Christopher Peterson, and Martin E. P. Seligman. 2004. Strengths of character and well-being. *Journal of Social and Clinical Psychology* 23:603–19.

———. 2006. Character strengths in fifty-four nations and the fifty US states. *Journal of Positive Psychology* 1:118–29.

Ross, Lee. 1978. The intuitive psychologist and his shortcomings: Distortions in the attribution process. In *Cognitive theories in social psychology: Papers from advances in experimental social psychology*, ed. Leonard Berkowitz, 173–220. New York: Academic Press.

Skarlicki, Daniel P., and Gary P. Latham. 1996. Increasing citizenship behavior within a labor union: A test of organizational justice theory. *Journal of Applied Psychology* 81:161–69.

———. 1997. Leadership training in organizational justice to increase citizenship behavior within a labor union: A replication. *Personnel Psychology* 50:617–33.

Part IV:

Integrity in the Field

10

Ethical Guidelines for Church Planters: A Suggested Proposal

J. D. PAYNE

It is rare to hear the words "church planting" and "ethics" used in the same sentence. I cannot recall a single conversation with church planters over the past decade in which anyone mentioned ethics while discussing missionary activity. This lack of discussion does not imply that church planters are a group of intentionally unprincipled barbarians. The hundreds of church planters I have encountered love God and love others and manifest godly lifestyles.

Discussion of ethics and church planting in relation to missionary practices, however, is long overdue. The proposals offered in this chapter are based on years of experience as a church planting missionary as well as of teaching courses on church planting and evangelism. Though some of what I write may be provocative, challenging well-established contemporary philosophical and methodological paradigms, I do not write to create unhealthy discord. Rather, I write with hope for healthy change.

The ethical guidelines for church planters proposed here attempt to hold missionaries to a level of theological and missiological accountability that is conducive to the multiplication of disciples, leaders, and churches across the globe. The discussion addresses a number of ethical problems that arise when missionary practices deviate from a kingdom ethic, while following kingdom ethics fosters the birth and multiplication of healthy churches.

The Kingdom Ethic

Life in the kingdom of God is life lived by a kingdom ethic that transcends the ethic of this world. For example, in the kingdom, lust is equated with adultery and hatred with murder (Matt. 5:21–22, 27–28). The first is last (Mark 9:35), and the servant is the greatest of all (Mark 10:44). Our Lord stated, "If you love me, you will keep my commandments" (John 14:15 NRSV). The calling to be a kingdom citizen is a calling to walk as Jesus walked (Col. 2:6). Indeed, the apostle Paul called on the new believers in the newly planted churches to imitate him as he imitated Christ (1 Cor. 11:1).

In essence, the kingdom ethic tells kingdom citizens how to live in relation to God (Matt. 22:37), to other kingdom citizens (John 13:35, 15:12; cf. Matt 22:39), and to those outside the kingdom (Matt. 22:39). Missionary practices are *not* outside the jurisdiction of the kingdom, for the kingdom ethic applies to all of life, including what the church has come to describe as ministerial life. For missionaries, this ethic also addresses church planting paradigms.

Failure to follow the kingdom ethic is a failure to be faithful to the King from whom the kingdom ethic extends. The kingdom ethic is a way of life for the kingdom citizen that, according to the grace of God, enables one to accomplish good works (Eph. 2:10) and bear much fruit (John 15:1–11) for the glory of the King. By the King's grace, the kingdom citizen is one who loves Jesus and keeps his commandments (John 14:15). The way of life is the way of Jesus. Just as kingdom citizens received him, they must continue to walk as Jesus did (Col. 2:6). Since life in the kingdom consists of being a slave (Matt. 25:14–30), being a good steward of the King's resources (Luke 12:35–48), making the most of time and opportunities (Col. 4:5; Eph. 5:16), and walking in wisdom (Eph. 5:15), *freedom with regard to missionary practices should be permitted only to the extent that proper stewardship, faithfulness, and wisdom are not compromised for a lesser good.*

Missionary practices are ethical reflections of biblical foundations. Orthopraxy must be driven by orthodoxy. Poor missionary practices are not simply poor practices; rather, they show a lack of integrity and a neglect of the moral duty and stewardship proper to kingdom citizens.

The Matters of Concern

Two matters of concern in particular have influenced me to suggest the need for church planting teams to develop a contextualized set of ethical guidelines. First, church planting is a very difficult ministry. The spiritual warfare is intense. The challenges in seeking to start something from nothing are numerous. Second, because the ministry of church planting is so challenging, church planters are subject to many temptations to shortcut the work of the Spirit in the birth, growth, and multiplication of churches.

Beset by great spiritual opposition and multitudinous ministerial challenges, church planters often face the temptation to accomplish something *good* for the kingdom at the sacrifice of accomplishing something *great* for the kingdom. When funding resources diminish over time, the people lack receptivity to the Gospel, or pressure to start a public worship service and reach a certain number in attendance at a worship gathering mounts (whether the pressure comes from external factors such as supervisors and partnering churches or from internal factors such as personal insecurity, desire for acceptance, fear, or the need to prove something), many times missionaries are led down a path that deviates from biblically based church multiplication strategies. The guidelines that follow are intended to aid missionaries in staying properly focused and engaged when challenges come.

A standard of ethical practice must keep both the welfare of the church planters *and* of the new churches in mind. First, a standard is a means to assist church planters in their walk with the Lord. It is an aid in the church planters' own sanctification by keeping a kingdom ethic before them to which they can align their ministries, especially before days of difficulty arrive when temptation to make compromises will also come. Second, a standard of ethical practice must assist church planters in planting churches that are healthy from their birth and assist them in presenting everyone fully mature in Christ (Col. 1:28).

The eleven points of action outlined below can serve as a starting point for a code of ethics. The matters covered are not exhaustive, but they can help missionaries to start a conversation on these issues. I do believe that the following points allow missionaries to maintain the necessary philosophical and methodological freedom in which to fulfill their calling, while simultaneously establishing healthy biblical and missiological parameters in light of the kingdom ethic. A code of ethics should not be restrictive, but liberating, assisting church planters to guard against substituting good missionary practices for the best missionary practices. All guidelines and codes of ethics should be contextualized, that is, adapted to the context and circumstances of the ministry team.

Setting Priorities

Since the global need for the Gospel is so great, unless God reveals otherwise, *we will begin our ministry among people with the greatest need and with a high level of receptivity to the Gospel.*

It is an unethical practice to begin laboring in areas where there is little need for additional evangelical witness and where the level of receptivity is low while there are four billion people in the world who are not believers and have little or no access to the Gospel. Knowing that church planters are called first of all to make disciples and *not* to plant churches, all church planters must have the world as their parish (Matt. 28:18–20). Church planters must think both locally and globally as they develop strategies for church multiplication. Failure to integrate local strategies with global strategies is a matter of poor stewardship.

The Gospel travels faster and farther and produces fruit more rapidly among peoples who are more receptive to the message than among those who are more resistant. *Unless there is a strong calling of God to labor elsewhere,* the proper approach should be for church planters to labor where the Spirit is working with those who desire to know more about Jesus (*remember: sometimes the most receptive peoples are those with little previous access to the Gospel*).

Donald McGavran once noted that receptivity to the Gospel is similar to the ocean tides. He wrote, "One thing is clear, receptivity wanes as often as it waxes. Like the tide, it comes in and goes out. Unlike the tide, no one can guarantee when it goes out that it will soon come back again."[1] It is unethical to neglect those asking the question of the Philippian jailer (Acts 16:30) when others are cursing the name of Christ.

Though we know that no one comes to the Father except through the work of the Spirit (John 3:8, 6:36), we do not know when the regenerative act will occur. For example, a man may be receptive to the Gospel over a period of several months; he may later become resistant to the Gospel for the next twenty years, only to become more receptive once again near the end of his life. Someone in the kingdom shares the Gospel with him and the man decides to follow Jesus, but only after years of debauchery have elapsed since the first time he was receptive to the truth. What if the Gospel had been presented to him twenty years earlier when he was initially receptive? He might have come to faith and had twenty years of kingdom service, including preaching of the Gospel across his circles of influence. Unless the Lord leads church planters to a hard soil area, the ethically appropriate direction in service is to give priority to labor among the most receptive and most evangelically needy.

Reproducible Methods

Since the world contains four billion unbelievers, with two billion who have never heard the Gospel, our strategy will involve the use of highly reproducible church planting methods.

An ecclesiology and missionary practices that are paternalistic hinder the birth and multiplication of contextualized churches and do not take the global aspect of the Great Commission with utmost seriousness. It is unethical for missionaries to model before new believers and churches the idea that church planting requires complex and highly technical methods, for such methods are generally difficult to reproduce. Charles Brock is correct when he notes, "In an age when perhaps more than four billion people do not know Christ in a personal way, it borders on immorality for a planter to plant a church without considering reproducibility."[2] For church planters to push the time when new churches will be capable of carrying out the task of church planting off into the distant future, because such activities are thought to be too complicated for new churches to carry out, reveals a conviction that is not derived from the kingdom ethic.

Conversion, Not Transfer

Since biblical church planting is evangelism that results in new churches, we will not prioritize transfer growth over conversion growth by designing ministries that will primarily attract believers.

Biblical church planting is evangelism that results in new churches. Church planters are missionaries, following after the apostolic paradigm modeled by Jesus and the apostolic church. Though not all transfer growth is bad (e.g., someone moves into a new city due to a job transfer and desires to become part of a church), it should not be the primary or even secondary concern for church planters. In fact, the church planting team should not even desire transfer growth. Church planting is about making disciples, impacting the kingdom of darkness, and seeing people become kingdom citizens who live according to the kingdom ethic as a part of local churches. Church planters are to have the desire expressed by the apostle Paul: not to build upon another person's foundation (Rom. 15:20).

Church planting is not about attracting a crowd or launching a worship service, but rather it is about the advancement of the kingdom as unbelievers become followers of the living God through local expressions of the body of Christ. Though crowd attraction and starting a new worship service are not necessarily bad things, their manifestations do not necessarily mean the kingdom has advanced. In many cases, the persons such events actually attract are largely already kingdom citizens. For church planters to settle for an abundance of transfer growth is not the way of the apostolic church.

Unity in Witness

Since unity among churches in a geographical area is a powerful witness to the Gospel, we will be concerned with other evangelical pastors laboring in the same area as our team and will take the initiative to meet with them to share our calling, vision, and ethic.

Jesus prayed that his church would be unified (John 17:11, 23) and noted that the world would know his disciples by their love for each other (John 13:35). A spirit of division, competition, resentment, or hostility between believers hinders sanctification in the body of Christ and kingdom expansion. Therefore, whenever church planters enter new areas where other evangelical churches are present, they need to take the initiative to meet and share their calling with the pastors of those churches.

During an informal study I conducted a few years ago of 190 church planters in North America, I discovered that one of the five most critical issues they faced was the issue of "turfism"— the attitude on the part of established churches that a particular geographical area was theirs and that church planters moving into their area were a threat. Though some pastors are insecure in their position in Christ and will see a church planting team as a threat regardless of any attempt to alleviate their fears, at least the team will have made a good faith effort to live at peace with everyone (Rom. 12:18; Heb. 12:14).

In meeting with local evangelical pastors at least three matters should be addressed. First, a copy of the church planting team's ethical guidelines should be provided to the local church leaders. This document will allow pastors to see the ethical parameters within which the church planters intend to work in seeking kingdom expansion. Second, church planters should communicate that they subscribe to a biblical definition of church planting (i.e., evangelism that results in new churches). Third, the church planting team needs to share that it does not want to compete with existing churches for members and that a specific protocol will be followed if any of the established churches' members attempt to become a part of the new church.

Protocol on Transfers

Since we desire to respect other evangelical pastors in the area, desire biblical church planting practices, and desire sanctification in the lives of any transfers from local churches, we will have a systematic plan for responding to transfers who want to become part of the new church.

It is important that a church planting team have a plan in place to address the issue of transfer growth. Even church planters who are doing everything possible to discourage transfer growth will encounter it. Especially in the North American context, members of other churches will be interested in the new work. Some of these brothers and sisters will have a genuine desire to serve in a new work. Others, however, will be dominated by the prevalent consumerist outlook, seeking out the most novel thing in town. These "new-experience Christians" will remain as long as their desires are met. Like parasites, they will participate to take until they get their fill or until something "better" comes along to attract them. Rather than understanding who they are in Christ and their place in the work of the ministry (Eph. 4:12), they reduce following Christ to an individualistic, self-gratifying, desire-fulfilling experience that is void of biblical *koinonia*. Regardless of local church members' motivation in wanting to be part of the new work, it is unethical for a church planting team (and the new churches) to receive them as members without regard for the local church family in which they are presently involved in a covenant relationship.

What protocol could a team follow in relation to persons who seek to transfer to the new church? First, the church planting team could find out the evangelical church in the community of which the person is a member and why the person desires to leave that fellowship. The person desiring to transfer needs to be informed that his or her pastor or pastors need to be consulted on the matter. Second, the team could contact the pastors of the church with the name of the member, inquiring as to why he or she would desire to leave the fellowship of the church. Third, the person could be allowed to become a part of the new work only if all three of the parties (the individual, the church, and the church planting team) believe that the prompting for such a move is from the Lord.[3]

Calling and Finances

Since our calling to this ministry, people, and location is from God and is not based on money, we will not end our church planting ministry in an area simply because our financial support ends, but rather we will make appropriate plans for the future of our personal finances.

Knowing that commitments of funding are quickly running out, many church planters who began well decide to shortcut the work of the ministry due to lack of funds. Models of successful growth (albeit with much transfer growth) from other parts of the country are held up by many as the norm, with the expectation that all church planters must do likewise. Thinking by analogy to an investment in a flourishing company, ministry supporters and supervisors sometimes believe their investments must always produce the desired results in the desired time. The ethic of the kingdom, however, transcends the ethic of this world's economy. Remember that the widow's two mites were worth more than all of the large sums of money from the wealthy (Mark 12:42–43). What may appear insignificant in the eyes of man is great in the kingdom of God.

When the work is not progressing at the desired rate, church planters should ask, "What is the Spirit doing among these people?" A second, follow-up question should be, "Is it possible that the work of the Spirit among these people may take longer than we expected?" It is a deviation from kingdom ethics to be guided by someone other than the Spirit.

While missionaries must remember that God's timetable is not based on human expectations and demands, church planters should not be prevented from establishing goals to be accomplished in designated periods of time. It must be remembered, however, that all planning is dependent upon the will of God (James 4:15–16). The apostle Paul made definite plans to take the Gospel into Asia Minor and Bithynia (Acts 16:6–7), but his plans were interrupted by the Spirit. Supervisors and partnering churches can encourage teams to make plans for the new church to have 200 members within the first two years, but God directs the steps (Prov. 16:9, 20:24).

Long before funding ceases, church planting teams must strategize in light of the question, "What if our funding ends?" If the team has only three years of funding, then before they begin their work they must ask, "How will we provide for ourselves and our families in three years?" Avoiding the question with the attitude that "God will provide" may simply be a lack of wisdom masquerading as faith. God will provide, yes; but what if he wants the team members to become tentmakers? Such a change would require substantial adjustments. Are the church planting team and the new church prepared for the shift in schedules and changes in availability that will come after three years of "full time service"?

Church Planting Teams

Since the biblical model for church planting is a team approach and many liabilities come when working as a solo church planter, a team will be developed before the work begins.

Whenever church planters "go at it alone," they fail to follow the model set forth in Scripture of a team approach. A lone ranger approach to mission creates an ethical dilemma that raises the potential for missiological malpractice. Though solo missionaries have doubtless planted many healthy churches over the years, the solo approach is potentially problematic. It sets up the church planter for potential burnout because the labors of ministry cannot be divided up. It sets up the church planter for potential discouragement due to a lack of teammates to provide encouragement. It sets up the missionary for a lack of accountability because there is no one to hold him or her accountable. Since intensive spiritual warfare is to be expected in missionary labors, wise is the church planter who takes every precaution to forestall future problems. Why would anyone, undertaking so great a task related to kingdom expansion, attempt to do otherwise?

Nurturing Family Life

Since one of the most critical issues in missionary circles is stress on the family, we will not neglect our families for the sake of church planting but will begin our work with a strategy in place for nurturing our family life while serving as church planters.

Whether the perception is factually based or merely anecdotal, ministers are notorious for neglecting their families for the sake of the ministry. The anecdotal evidence is sufficient to alert church planters to the problem and for them to prepare accordingly. Of all people serving the body of Christ, church planters may be among the most susceptible to this temptation. As missionaries they have not only the normal pressures of ministry, but also the daunting task of working to create something from nothing.

Paul wrote to the new churches to imitate him as he imitated Christ (1 Cor. 4:16, 11:1). Contemporary church planters must provide a similar model for the new churches they start. A healthy family life is a powerful witness to the power of the Gospel. The church planting family provides an example for new believers and churches to follow. *Members of a church planting family do not have to be next to perfect; they have to be perfect.* While that statement is hyperbolic, the point is that if the family falls due to neglect, the ministry falls even harder. Like the ever-expanding ripples after a rock is tossed into a calm pond, the impact of the collapse of a church planter's family will extend well beyond the church planter's home, beyond the new believers, and beyond the immediate community.

Failure to prepare one's family adequately for missionary labors and failure to maintain a healthy ministry that includes continually shepherding the growth in Christ of one's family is reflective of a person more concerned with accomplishing the ministerial task of planting a church than with living according to a kingdom ethic (1 Tim. 3:4–5).

Personal Walk with Christ

Since we are kingdom citizens, we will not neglect our daily devotional time with the Lord by allowing ourselves to be distracted due to the numerous needs and tasks to be accomplished in the labor of church planting.

The Lord does not need us for his work; he can find someone else if we are unfaithful to him. He desires obedience rather than sacrifice (1 Sam. 15:22). One of the greatest ironies concerning the ministry is that many church planters believe there is so much to do for the Lord that they do not have time to spend with the Lord. They find themselves too busy to pray, to be still, and to maintain daily devotions at the feet of Jesus. Whenever the demands of the church planting ministry detract from church planters' devotional time, an ethical dilemma exists. Whenever church planters begin to substitute building the church for spending time with the One who promised to build his church, the ministry is being built upon sand.

Diligence in Contextualization

Since the task of missionary work involves effective communication, we will work diligently toward contextualization rather than bringing our preferred church traditions to the people.

Contextualization of the Gospel is always challenging, with some situations being more difficult than others. As church planters work to communicate effectively, they may find themselves laboring in an area for some time before they see the first converts and the birth of new churches. For example, it was thirty-three years after missionaries first brought the Gospel to the Ao people of Nagaland before the first church was planted.[4]

A temptation church planters face is to practice paternalism rather than contextualization. Paternalism manifests itself as an attitude of superiority rather than humility. Practically, it takes the form of the church planters' "knowing" the "best" culture for a new church, with that best culture generally reflecting the missionaries' personal preferences. Rather than teaching people how to understand themselves to be the body of Christ in their context and to function appropriately according to the Scriptures, a paternalistic approach elevates the church preferences of the church planters above biblical revelation and leads new believers to rely on the missionaries rather than on the Spirit and the Word.

For example, many church planters begin with a mental picture of a church that has a well-developed organizational superstructure and set of programs. Rather than reaching people from the harvest and teaching them how to be the body of Christ in their local community—thus allowing the structures to develop from the people and grow with the people—many teams attempt to put the cart before the horse. They create the structures and try to make the people fit into them. The people have little or no biblical or missiological foundation for the structures, do not own the structures, cannot financially support them, and are not qualified to provide oversight for them. The possibilities for multiplication are diminished. It is as if someone were to fit a child who is only able to wear a size 4 shoe with a size 15 and then to teach the child that a size 15 approach to "shoe life" is the normal way. Similarly, many times church planters create the structures and culture, communicate to the people that these constitute "normal" church life, and then become frustrated whenever the people do not sustain the organizational apparatus. Such missiological malpractice is unethical, for it substitutes missionary preferences for teaching a biblical ecclesiology.

Pragmatism—the philosophy and methodology of whatever works to accomplish the goal—is another unhealthy approach that often is given priority over contextualization. Though all followers of Jesus should be pragmatic to a degree—we are told to make disciples; therefore, we want to know what works to accomplish this task–taken too far, pragmatism becomes unethical, for it hijacks the normal learning process of the new believers. Church planters who are overly eager to see results many times will do whatever works to get a church "started." Pragmatism tends to result in unhealthy dependence of new churches on the church planters.

Integrity in Reporting

Since integrity and accuracy are important in reporting statistics related to our missionary labors, we will strive to report only numbers and descriptive details that truly reflect what the Holy Spirit is doing in our context.

Intentionally reporting inaccurate numbers related to a team's ministry is unethical. It is deceptive and makes God out to be a liar, by providing reports that bear false witness against his Spirit. Missionaries must speak the truth (Eph. 4:25); the Bible never portrays liars in a favorable light (1 Tim. 1:10, 4:2; Tit. 1:12). Though all statistical reporting must be above reproach, particular care must be exercised in reporting numbers of baptisms and churches planted.

An evangelistic gathering is not a church. A Bible study group is not a church either, even if the group consists of baptized believers. A worship service is not a church, and church planters must not report such groups as churches. They may call them Bible studies, seeker studies, seed groups, community groups, preaching points, worship gatherings, but must not describe them as local churches. Unless the baptized group of believers has agreed (i.e., covenanted) to exist and function as the local expression of the body of Christ, with all the rights and responsibilities appertaining to themselves according to the Scriptures, then they are not a church.

Accuracy in reporting must extend beyond the simple reporting of raw numbers. This matter is especially important in areas that are not highly receptive to the Gospel. Missionaries should provide a "thick description" of what the Holy Spirit is doing among the people. Stories need to be shared. Not that missionary reporting must be akin to writing the next *War and Peace*, but brief accounts from the field need to be communicated regularly and consistently. Such stories, particularly when the numerical growth is slow, will encourage both the missionary teams and those who read and hear their reports.

Conclusion

My hope is that what has been written here will serve as a starting point for contextualized ethical guidelines *and* begin ethical conversation among missionaries. Kingdom citizens are called to live according to a kingdom ethic. This divine ethic is not concerned simply with avoiding acts such as adultery, fornication, lying, and murder. It touches all of life and speaks as well as to matters related to missionary practices, philosophies, and methods.

Notes

1. Donald A. McGavran, *Understanding Church Growth* (Grand Rapids: Eerdmans, 1970), 218.
2. Charles Brock, *Indigenous Church Planting: A Practical Journey* (Neosho, Mo.: Church Growth International, 1994), 25.
3. Often I hear church planters ask, "But what if the person's church isn't a Gospel-preaching church?" If a church is heterodox, then transfer of membership is obviously justified. I strongly believe, however, that heterodoxy is not always the issue; rather, the new work in an area has the allure or "promise" of a better flavor or brand of church, with better music, better preaching (not necessarily more biblical), and better programs—ironically, things that appeal to people with a church background, rather than to unbelievers.
4. Paul Hattaway, *From Headhunters to Church Planters: An Amazing Spiritual Awakening in Nagaland* (Waynesboro, Ga.: Authentic Publishing, 2006), 13–14.

11

Some Ethical Considerations About Short-Term Mission

GORDEN R. DOSS

Short-term mission (STM) has become an important part of American Christianity's continued engagement with what Philip Jenkins (2002) calls the "South." Robert Wuthnow (2009) agrees with Jenkins that the majority of Christians live outside the "North" (largely the United States, Canada, and Europe). He challenges, however, the implication of Jenkins's demographic studies that U.S. engagement and influence with churches of the developing world have diminished (Wuthnow 2009, 42).[1] One evidence of continued strong engagement is STM. Over a million Americans spend $1–2 billion a year on STM trips. Of this number, two-thirds stay fourteen days or less (Priest, Dischinger, Rasmussen, and Brown 2006, 432).

The character of U.S. mission engagement with the world, including STM, has produced what Wuthnow (2009, 8) calls a "huge debate" in leadership and missiological circles. What *is* the nature of that engagement? Is it "a kind of cultural imperialism . . . spreading Western values," such as materialism and consumerism? What will be the missional consequences, both intended and unintended, of STM?[2] In spite of the debate among leaders and missiologists, Wuthnow found that most Americans assume that the consequences of American interaction abroad are wholly beneficial.

In contrast to the "celebratory rhetoric" frequently found in the United States about STM, Gary Corwin (2008, 144) believes that STM's inherent limitations cause it to produce results that "seem to be less than meets the eye." Gene Daniels (2008, 152) observes that the "dark little secret" that missionaries and indigenous people who host STM groups are reluctant to articulate is that "the average short-term missionary takes far more than he or she gives. The time invested to host the person, the resources he or she drains from the church's world mission budget, the problems the person sometimes causes ... all-too-often ... cost more than whatever benefit the visitor brings to the field."

Missiologists, of all people, do not want to be naysayers, because we are convinced that only God knows the ultimate outcomes of various strategies and methods. STM has become a prominent method in mission, and the best approach seems to be to promote best practices for STM. Part of best practices is making sure that STM is done ethically.

I need to disclose my biases and perspective. I grew up with missionary parents in Malawi, served there sixteen years as an adult, and now teach mission in a seminary. My experience and observation lead me to favor STM lasting three months or more. When short-termers stay for several months, fill well-defined roles, and get beyond the honeymoon, tourist, and spectator phases, I have observed them making excellent contributions, even among some less receptive peoples.

In broad terms, I think that doing STM ethically means promoting the wholistic well-being, or *shalom*, of both visitors and hosts so that God is glorified and his kingdom is advanced. From the many potential topics for consideration, I have chosen two: motivation and power imbalance.

The Motivation for Short-Term Mission

What motivates STM, either for guests or hosts? Some potential benefits are similar for tourists and hosts. These could include broadening global perspectives, developing appreciation for other cultures, developing intercultural skills, having good fellowship, developing long-term transcultural relationships, experiencing spiritual renewal, and deepening commitment to Christian mission, among others. Some potential benefits are different for the two groups. The pilgrimage character of STM gives the guests a heightened sense of drama and awareness that can facilitate dramatic learning. Travelers often observe suffering and poverty in a new way. The hosts typically receive material benefits for personal and ministry needs. This list of potential benefits could be expanded.

Unhealthy, mixed motivations are possible for both hosts and guests. For STM travelers, there can be a "naughty little secret" (my term, complementing Daniels's "dark little secret") that involves the good feeling one gets by making a contribution to the STM fund that partially fulfills one's stewardship commitments, counts as an IRS tax deduction, gives one the feeling of "doing real missions," provides an intense spiritual experience, and offers the family an exotic overseas vacation—all in one. The "naughty little secret" can link up with the "trickle-down theory of STM" (my term) which states that any money spent for mission trip expenses is fully justified by contributions made on the trip to the hosts and by the increased support for world missions and humanitarian service that STM generates down the line. Unfortunately, research indicates that STM does not generate the increased support assumed by the "trickle-down theory" (Priest, Dischinger, Rasmussen, and Brown 2006, 435).

STM hosts can also succumb to unhealthy motivations. Believers in developing countries can view visitors as mere money carriers and use them opportunistically in a way that is unhealthy both to themselves as individuals and to the local church. Relationships built on phony, manipulative friendliness are unhealthy. When local congregations become dependent on U.S. donations their long-term congregational development is hindered.

Paul discussed mixed motivations for preaching Christ and concluded that "the important thing is that in every way, whether from false motives or true, Christ is preached" (Philippians 1:18, NIV). The history of Christian mission documents an abundance of mixed motivations. Thus, STM must not be held to a perfectionist standard. Yet seeking good motivation for every type of Christian service is a requirement because growth in Christ includes the purification of motives and because motivation shapes service.

I will not try to parse the multilayered, unhealthy motivations that are possible for everyone involved with STM. Rather, I will address motivation for STM broadly by asking whether the motivation to benefit the traveler or the host should be primary. Many specific issues of motivation will be addressed by answering this question.

The mission pastor of a large church told me that because the outcomes of STM are recognized to be ambiguous for the hosts, his church had decided to be honest and forthright by defining the benefits for the travelers as primary.[3] His goal was to give every member an STM "experience," not at the expense of the hosts, but with the recognition that the visitors might benefit most. A long-term medical missionary reflected the same perspective by telling me that he was a missionary primarily for the blessings he received from the experience. I hasten to add that neither the mission pastor nor the missionary was uncaring about the people worked with. The fact that the mission pastor and the long-term missionary shared a similar view suggests that the question of motivation involves basic theological assumptions.

Is it ethically or theologically acceptable to make the blessings for the one who goes on a mission trip primary? I think not. However blessed the experience of performing any Christian service may be for the one serving, the primary motivation has to be to benefit those served. Surely the whole "divine drama" of God's mission (Moreau, Corwin, and McGee 2004, 28–37), with the incarnation at its center, supports this assertion. Paul's epistles record many joys and pleasures which he experienced along with the hardships. It is unimaginable, however, that having a "good experience" was the primary motivation, either for himself or for his team. Training a missionary team was an important element of Paul's strategy, but his primary focus was on nonbelievers and the believers in the churches he planted.

If, as research suggests, the long-term effects of the STM "good experience" for the visitor are less positive and less long lasting than is often assumed,[4] making the visitor's benefit primary is wrong for pragmatic reasons in addition to ethical and theological ones. Could making a "good experience" for the traveler the primary motivation of STM be the reflection of a narcissistic culture? Wuthnow (2009, 15–16) critiques Christianity in the

United States for its "consumerist mentality" that makes the church member a "religious consumer" of ecclesial products and incentives. Does STM fall under this critique when having an "experience" is the primary motivation?

I submit that the primary motivation for STM must be that "Christ is preached" effectively to the hosts and their community through a variety of contextually appropriate modes of wholistic missionary service. Assessing effectiveness is more challenging than counting people who come forward or are baptized. The valid benefits for the travelers must be seen as secondary gifts of grace, gifts for which thanks is given, much as preachers give thanks when preaching is a blessing to themselves. Attention should be paid to maximizing these secondary gifts in quality and duration through pre-trip training and post-trip debriefing with the STM team and their home church.

Making service to the hosts primary gives STM a biblical focus that can guide decisions about particular issues. A cluster of important questions are implied which STM planners need to ask about the hosts:

- How is God working among and through the people we wish to visit?
- How can we best join and enhance their ministry?
- What needs have been identified by the hosts?
- Which of those needs can our group address, at least in part?
- What human and material resources are available to enhance the hosts' ministry and address their needs?
- How can trip expenditures reflect the primary focus on service to the hosts?
- How many people with what skills are needed to achieve the trip goals for the hosts?

- What training and preparation does the team need in order to fulfill the trip goals for the hosts?
- How can we prepare to initiate (or enhance) a long-term partnership if the hosts want to form such a partnership?

Making benefits for the travelers secondary (though important) implies another set of questions:

- What are the trip goals for the travelers and how can they be achieved?
- What human and material resources are needed to achieve the trip goals for the travelers?
- How can expenditures reflect the secondary focus on the traveling team?
- What training and preparation does the team need so as to fulfill trip goals for themselves?

Some questions for individuals are also brought into focus by making the hosts primary:

- Do I sense an authentic call from God to serve in STM?
- Will my contribution to this trip be greater if I go or if I stay home and give support with an offering?
- If I go, what contribution to the trip goals for the host and the team can I make?
- What do I need to do to prepare myself for effective service to the hosts and my team?
- What do I need to do to facilitate my personal trip goals?

I think that the group and individual reflection suggested above would produce STM teams that were smaller, more focused, and more effective on the field. Sending churches could move away from simply trying to get as many members as possible onto the plane. The logistical burden of hosting STM teams would be decreased. Most of all, trip goals for the hosts and their community would be better defined and more likely to be accomplished.

Dealing with Power Imbalances in Short-Term Mission

Most STM trips bring people who, materially, are relatively wealthy into contact with people who have less material wealth. In this kind of encounter, there are inherent power as well as wealth imbalances. Teenage visitors often have more pocket money than their adult hosts earn in months, to say nothing of adult visitors. American teams, with their good clothing, computers, cameras, iPods, and sound equipment, simply "reek" of riches that local people can only dream about. This makes today's STM travelers susceptible to some of the same mistakes made in the colonial era when missionaries controlled everything and locals sometimes merely went along because of their powerlessness.

Even though partnership is an oft-stated goal and theme for STM, Corwin suggests that it is generally more of a "power trip" than a partnership (Corwin 2008, 144). Edwin Zehner (2006, 512) critiques the "Delta Force" model, and Hunter Farrell (2007, 69) critiques the "Paratrooper Incursion" model, both of which view the STM trip as a military-like operation of spiritual power projection. Oscar Muriu (2009), a pastor in Nairobi, says that Kenyans know when it is summer in the United States because the color of Nairobi's streets changes as STM groups appear in full tourist regalia.

Relationships are unavoidably warped in different ways when there is a wealth and power gap. If you are from the United States (or another wealthy country), put yourself into the picture by visualizing how you would respond if you lived in a declining rural town and Bill Gates came with a group of wealthy friends to spend two weeks working with your church. The more wealthy tend to view themselves and their contributions more favorably than can be justified, and the less wealthy tend to be more agreeable and less critical than can be justified. The valid desire for a new church building can cause a local pastor to support almost any suggestion made by the STM team, while the STM team may think that every idea they express is contextually appropriate because the pastor never disagrees (Koll 2010).

Recently, a multicultural STM group arrived at a Christian university in Africa with plans to hold a week of revival meetings and do some construction. When the university provost asked who was to be the revival speaker, he was shocked to discover that the main speaker was a man with a gold earring and hairdo that were strictly forbidden on his campus and by the local Christian community. Using his best diplomacy, he told the group that no one looking like that could preach on his campus. The group responded that unless "Pastor Earring" was allowed to preach, they would take their donation and themselves back home. Much conflict ensued with frantic calls to denominational executives and board members. In the end, the provost preached the revival sermons himself and the donation was received. Had the provost been weak-kneed, the STM group would have presented a very negative view of Christianity in the local context.

Ethically the reality of relational warping caused by power imbalance places an obligation upon the travelers to be what Jonathan Bonk (2006) calls the "righteous rich" and to practice what Miriam Adeney calls "godly tourism" (Adeney 2006, 464). Human encounters involve the exchange of both material and nonmaterial assets (such as friendship, loyalty, esteem, and reputation), sometimes consciously and other times unconsciously. Ethical encounters bring roughly equal benefits to the parties while unethical encounters exploit one or both parties. Both parties can be exploited when they use each other to achieve material or nonmaterial ends. In a worst case scenario, STM visitors use hosts as ecclesial "Disney employees" to give themselves a spiritual-cultural-missional high, while the hosts say and do almost anything to milk dollars from the visitors.

When Americans visit the developing world, they are usually in a "power-up" position in both material and nonmaterial capital. The material advantage comes from their obvious wealth while the nonmaterial advantage comes from being seen as more modern, sophisticated, educated, and socially or politically powerful. The obligation for Christians on the "power-up" side is to make every possible effort to ensure that those on the "power-down" side receive equitable benefits from the encounter, even if not all of their issues and needs can be resolved.

Adeney has noted that STM involves several kinds of encounter or exchange (Adeney 2006, 464–72). First, there is a physical encounter. Tourists consume local resources and place a burden on the local economy, environment, and infrastructure without necessarily benefitting the local people. An ethical physical encounter will bring at least as much good to the hosts as the visitors receive. "Godly tourists" will intentionally seek to benefit local people by directing spending toward local businesses and minimizing their "footprint" on the local environment and infrastructure as much as possible.

Second, there is a cultural encounter. The temptation to feel culturally superior can be overwhelming for visitors from wealthy, powerful countries. An STM "power trip" can bring a team of task-oriented bulldozers (human and sometimes mechanical) into a community in a way that is culturally disorienting and disruptive. Single-minded focus on completion of the task can eclipse relationship-building activities. One church building team virtually refused to interact with the locals as they sought to complete the task on time. The training for one group of student evangelists included instruction to stay in the hotel room each day studying the evening's sermon instead of associating with the people. Ethical STM tourists will show respect for the local culture for both theological and practical reasons. Theologically, God's "cultural mandate" allows all peoples to create and maintain their own cultures, and ethical visitors will show respect, even if locals may seem "backward" to them. For purely practical reasons, visitors must work cooperatively and respectfully within local cultural norms so that whatever initiatives they launch will be sustainable when they are gone.

Third, STM involves a spiritual encounter. Ethical visitors will respect the fact that the spiritual environment of the hosts may be quite different from their own. Worship, music, and preaching styles may be very different. The utilization of spiritual gifts also differs between cultures. If local patterns are not respected, the character and quality of worship in the host church can be so changed that it bears no relationship to regular life and worship. Visitors should arrive as spiritual seekers and learners, willing to be served spiritually and willing to have their service shaped by the local spiritual environment. Visitors should not be the only ones singing, preaching, and witnessing during the visit.

In encounters where power and wealth are not in balance, it is important that the assessment of the exchange be accurate and that it include both material and nonmaterial assets. Unless care is taken, visitors could make an inaccurate assessment of the net material benefits they bring to their hosts. Visitor travel expense should not be counted as a contribution to the hosts—because it is not. The full cost of hosting the STM team, including hidden costs, needs to be assessed. Muriu (2009) says that his own church often provides a "reverse subsidy" to visiting groups, of which the visitors are oblivious. In other words, hosting STM teams is a net expense for his church. Those of us who have organized any kind of conference know that there are always expenses of which many attendees are unaware. Ethical STM teams will ensure that their hosting organizations do not suffer a net financial loss. This will require tact and diplomacy because accepting hospitality is part of being a good visitor, especially in places such as Africa where showing hospitality is a strong traditional value. Making sure that hosts do not suffer a net loss is the lowest, minimal standard. If benefits for the host are defined as primary, perhaps STM groups should set a higher standard. Is it too radical to suggest that material benefits for the hosts should exceed what the visitors spend on themselves?

Nonmaterial assets must also be included in the assessment of an encounter. One issue for STM visitors from the West is that our culture predisposes us to undervalue the nonmaterial assets that are part of human encounters. When seen in their true scale, the nonmaterial gifts host communities give to their STM guests are to be greatly valued. These gifts can include a warm welcome, personal time and energy needed to facilitate the visit, patience with cultural unfamiliarity, forgiveness for cultural blunders, advocacy with immigration or police authorities or business people, protection from thieves, provision of the general social guidance needed for negotiating an unfamiliar culture, loyal support of visitors' ministries, and openness to consider suggestions they may offer. In Africa, hospitality is such a strong value that hosts often superextend themselves in nonmaterial ways to make visitors welcome.

On the other side of the encounter, the visitors also convey important nonmaterial gifts. The hosts often receive enormous social capital in their communities by receiving American guests, people who are often accorded celebrity status by the local community. Being the intermediaries for the celebrities elevates the status of the hosts. When genuine friendships are established they carry great significance for "power-down" hosts. Such social capital can enhance mission and ministry in the local community.

Understanding the importance of the mutual nonmaterial exchange may be most important for Westerners. The hosts stand to benefit greatly from the fellowship and relational dimensions of STM, which travelers sometimes undervalue because of their task-oriented, materialistic approach. Material gifts have value, but the gift of true friendship and the building of long-term relationships are greatly treasured. The travelers often benefit more than they realize from the generous nonmaterial benevolence of the hosts. Ethical travelers will value and intentionally facilitate a generous and equitable nonmaterial exchange.

Conclusion

I have addressed ethical considerations in two areas related to STM: motivation and power imbalance. There are many other areas deserving careful study. My prayer is that all of us engaged in some aspect of STM will make reflection upon its ethical character a constant exercise to the glory of God and the advancement of his kingdom.

Discussion Questions

1. Which points made in the chapter do you agree or disagree with? Why?
2. What does this chapter imply about the ethical quality of STM trips you have been involved with?
3. What additional topics about STM do you think need ethical reflection?
4. What do you think is the long-term impact of STM on global mission?

Notes

1. Robert Wuthnow spends much of his book discussing research he has conducted that demonstrates the ongoing influence of the American church around the world. He helpfully takes the analysis of the context for today's global mission several steps beyond that of Philip Jenkins.
2. For a concise summary of missiological reservations about STM, see Alex Smith (2008).
3. For example, church buildings can sometimes be built for one-tenth the cost by local people as compared with American teams.
4. See Priest, Dischinger, Rasmussen, and Brown 2006, 435–45, and other articles in *Missiology*, October 2006, for a summary of research findings. See also articles in Priest 2008, especially Ver Beek (475–502), Park (505–28), and Decker (559–89).

References

Adeney, Miriam. 2006. Shalom tourist: Loving your neighbor while using her. *Missiology* 34 (October): 463–76.

Bonk, Jonathan J. 2006. *Missions and money: Affluence as a missionary problem—revisited*. Maryknoll, N.Y.: Orbis Books.

Brown, C. M. 2008. Friendship is forever: Congregation-to-congregation relationships. In *Effective engagement in short-term missions: Doing it right!* Ed. Robert J. Priest, 207–37. Pasadena, Calif.: William Carey Library.

Corwin, Gary. 2008. Of partnerships and power trips. *Evangelical Missions Quarterly* 44 (April): 144–45.

Daniels, Gene. 2008. The character of short term mission. *Evangelical Missions Quarterly* 44 (April): 150–56.

Decker, Murray S. 2008. Student sojourners and spiritual formation: Understanding the intersection of cross-cultural adjustment and spiritual disorientation. In *Effective engagement in short-term missions*, ed. Priest, 559–89.

Farrell, Hunter. 2007. Short term missions: Paratrooper incursion or "Zaccheus encounter"? *Journal of Latin American Theology* 2 (2): 69–83.

Jenkins, Philip. 2002. *The Next Christendom: The Coming of Global Christianity*. Oxford: Oxford Univ. Press.

Johnstone, David M. 2006. Closing the loop: Debriefing and the short-term college missions team. *Missiology* 34 (October): 523–29.

Koll, Karla Ann. 2010. Taking wolves among lambs: Some thoughts on training for short-term mission facilitation. *International Bulletin of Missionary Research* 34 (April): 93–96.

Livermore, David A. 2006. *Serving with eyes wide open: Doing short term mission with cultural intelligence*. Grand Rapids: Baker Books.

Moreau, A. Scott, Gary R. Corwin, and Gary B. McGee. 2004. *Introducing world missions: A biblical, historical, and practical survey*. Grand Rapids: Baker Academic.

Muriu, Oscar. 2009. Short-term mission from a Kenyan pastor's perspective. Paper presented at the conference Being There: Short-Term Mission and Human Need, Trinity Evangelical Divinity School, Deerfield, Ill., July 31.

Noll, Mark A. 2009. *The new shape of world Christianity: How American experience reflects global faith*. Downers Grove, Ill.: IVP Academic.

Park, Kyeong Soon. 2008. Researching short-term missions and paternalism. In *Effective engagement in short-term missions*, ed. Priest, 505–28.

Priest, Robert J., Terry Dischinger, Steve Rasmusen, C. M. Brown. 2006. Researching the short-term mission movement. *Missiology* 34 (October): 431–50.

Priest, Robert J., ed. 2008. *Effective engagement in short-term missions: Doing it right!* Pasadena, Calif.: William Carey Library.

Smith, Alex G. 2008. Evaluating short-term missions: Missiological questions. In *Effective engagement in short-term missions*, ed. Priest, 35–61.

Ver Beek, Kurt Alan. 2008. Lessons from the sapling: Review of quantitative research on short-term missions. In *Effective engagement in short-term missions*, ed. Priest, 475–502.

Wuthnow, Robert. 2009. *Boundless faith: The global outreach of American churches.* Berkeley: Univ. of California Press.

Zehner, Edwin. 2006. Short-term missions: Toward a more field-oriented model. *Missiology* 34 (October): 509–21.

12

Sustainable Missions: Ethical Principles for Holistic Practice in a Broken World

JOHN R. WOOD AND MICHAEL P. FERBER

On January 12, 2010, an earthquake of magnitude 7.0 struck sixteen miles west of Port-au-Prince, Haiti. The quake killed over 200,000 people, injured 300,000, and displaced another 1 million persons. This disaster came on the heels of four major storms in the summer of 2008, tropical storm Fay and hurricanes Gustav, Hanna, and Ike. These natural disasters brought renewed world attention to the plight of Haiti, yet even before they had occurred, Haiti was already being used by Jared Diamond as an example of a nation in crisis and an illustration of what happens to a society when it degrades the environment on which it depends for life.[1] Though Haiti is one-third the size of the Dominican Republic, the country with which it shares the island of Hispaniola, its population is significantly larger, and the country's population density is nearly 1,000 people per square mile. In Haiti the primary source of household fuel is charcoal, but only 1 percent of the original forest remains to be exploited for fuel or to supply timber for building houses. Even more disconcerting, deforestation has caused soil erosion, loss of soil fertility, watershed deterioration, and a reduction of annual rainfall leading to decreased agricultural yields. These issues are further complicated by social dilemmas such as governmental corruption and major health crises including HIV/AIDS. When Diamond visited Haiti while preparing to write his bestselling book, he asked residents what they felt about the country's future. Again and again, he was told that there was no hope for Haiti. The natural resource base necessary to support their population was already exhausted.

Haiti is not the only place where environmental degradation is affecting the fabric of economic and social relationships. In fact, few corners of the earth remain where people's consumption and degradation of critical resources such as water, soil, and forests do not outpace the ability of natural systems to keep up. This disequilibrium is wreaking such havoc in so many locations that few people involved in mission need to be persuaded that ecosystems in their place of ministry are under significant stress. The stress is worsening as human populations increase and resources diminish. We are overfishing the oceans, destroying land habitat, using greater and greater quantities of water, and polluting the water that is left with chemicals and waste. In the words of one evangelical leader, "The earth is dying."[2] Some people find the use of such language problematic; however, agreement is widespread that we are faced by an environmental crisis of a global scale.[3]

In *Earth on the Edge,* a 2006 television special, Bill Moyers interviewed Adrian Forsyth, president and co-founder of the Amazon Conservation Association. Referring to the possibility that in the foreseeable future humans will continue to degrade the environment, Moyers asked, "What will the world look like?" to which Forsyth responded, "I think it will have degraded to the point where it is like a Haiti." The answer surprised Moyers. "When you say [it will] resemble Haiti, what is the picture in your mind?" he asked. The scene Forsyth painted is dismal and frightening:

> A land that is being stripped of its topsoil, where there are no fish in the rivers, where the rivers dry up every season so that water is scarce, where you don't have enough fuel wood to cook, to boil your water, so that your children have intestinal parasites. A land where you have to risk your life and the lives of your family members to get on a raft and sail across the ocean to Florida. Ultimately, when we destroy the natural resource base we have to move on to another place, and what if there is no other place to move on to?[4]

Throughout the era of the modern missionary movement the response to stories like this has been twofold: compassionate concern for the reality of human need, and evangelistic outreach, that is, preaching that emphasizes the role of human sin.[5] The new dimension now emerging is a growing awareness that these two facets of response are not sufficient either for the task we face or for the scope of the Gospel revealed throughout the entirety of Scripture. In what follows we address first what the contours of a holistic mission framework would look like and then offer examples of such a mission in practice.[6] The view of environment and mission for the twenty-first century that we offer is based on the contemporary yet deeply biblical concept of sustainability. To aid consideration of the issues involved, we unfold our discussion on a framework of three types of capital—social, economic, and natural.

Sustainable Missions

For the last thirty years social capital has been advanced as a critical concept for missions, primarily in terms of social justice for the poor.[7] We agree that social capital, most often defined as "meeting basic human needs,"[8] is a vital component of missions, and we advocate continuing to develop approaches that build social connectivity. Churches and mission organizations have a tremendous capacity to build and enhance social capital; indeed, as Robert Putnam writes, "faith communities in which people worship together are arguably the single most important repository of social capital."[9]

Likewise, economic capital holds a position of prestige in mission circles. Economic capital provides the means of doing mission and is what we commonly mean by the term "stewardship." Often simply called "capital," in this classic sense it can be defined as investment of resources in the marketplace with the expectation of an increase in or return on our investment.[10] Examples of using economic capital to enhance missions are numerous, but especially common are approaches that function through microloans and microenterprise development.[11]

While social capital and economic capital will continue to be critical aspects of missionary endeavor, we advocate that a third form of capital is necessary, noting that the other two forms are in fact dependent upon it. This third critical component is natural capital, defined by Steven Hackett as the "components and the structural relationships in the earth's ecosystems. The integrity of the biosphere and the biogeochemical systems within it is essential for life on earth."[12] In mission practice what W. Dayton Roberts in 1994 called "bottom-shelf ecology" was already being modeled by development and mission agencies such as World Vision,

ECHO, Floresta in the United States, and A Rocha International in the United Kingdom, but about two decades ago this third sector within a holistic and sustainable mission began to take conceptual form in academic literature.[13]

The decade of the 1990s saw rapid development on the part of both secular and Christian academics and practitioners of the theoretical and practical foundations for this third form of capital. A number of factors converged to drive this development including the Brundtland Commission (1987), the World Convocation on Justice, Peace, and the Integrity of Creation sponsored by the World Council of Churches (Seoul, 1990),[14] and the U.N. Convention on Biodiversity (1992) in Rio de Janeiro. In early 1993 the Evangelical Environmental Network (EEN) supervised the drafting of *An Evangelical Declaration on the Care of Creation*.[15] This clear statement of the theological basis for creation care, one of the first by evangelicals, maps out primarily the environmental or natural capital sector of sustainability. The term "creation care" (sometimes rendered "caring for creation") was widely adopted after the Global Stewardship Initiative and gives religious expression to deep concern for and valuing of the natural world.[16] At this point an important distinction must be drawn between secular and religious understandings of nature. Natural capital, a term borrowed from the literature of economic sustainability,[17] is commonly defined in terms of usefulness for or value to humans. Yet the real value of nature includes its intrinsic worth. Nature has value in itself apart from its utility for human ends or purposes. On this point the perspective of creation care has made its most salient contributions. Though the fact has been eclipsed by modernity, the natural world does not consist merely of stuff or of materials for humans to exploit. At bottom the created world is, in the words of Fred Van Dyke et al., "both a work of God and a revelation of God." Other created beings are creatures too, and they are part of God's sustaining and redemptive plan. Therefore, when we use the shorthand term "natural capital" to speak of creation, we need to remember that what we are referring to is the independent creation of God. We humans, "as both creatures, made from dust, and stewards, tilling, keeping and naming in God's image are here with purpose, power and dignity,"[18] but we are not the exclusive beneficiaries of God's concern or delight. Seeing the earth in this way is transformational, and we see natural capital as the necessary, though not the exclusive, foundation for the other two forms of capital.

Thinking conceptually about these three forms of capital is valuable, for they are profoundly interrelated and help to illuminate the question of sustainability. Although sustainability has a complex and contested history, it is a flexible concept that is useful for organizing our thinking. Lutheran theologian and ethicist Robert Stivers, in 1976, was one of the earliest to use the word sustainability.[19] In a 1980 discussion on justice and mission, Waldron Scott explored "the triangular relationship between three biblical themes: mission, discipleship, and justice." He pictured this three-way interaction as occurring within a surrounding context consisting of "The World."[20] In secular literature Andres Edwards describes "The Three E's" of economy/employment, equity/equality, and ecology/environment.[21] Many people have attempted to design a graphical representation of the components necessary to achieve sustainability. The dynamic interactions among the three forms of capital, we believe, can be well represented in what we call the Triangle of Sustainable Missions as shown in figure 1.

Figure 1. **Triangle of Sustainable Missions**

Our diagram is an adaptation of Scott Campbell's Planner's Triangle, a concepptual framework he developed to aid urban planners in building cities that would integrate three goals: they would grow economically, offer equal opportunities, and not degrade the environment.[22] Like the Planner's Triangle, the Triangle of Sustainable Missions is a conceptual tool. It enables missionary practitioners to evaluate their work along three axes as they consider the sustainability of their endeavors. Borrowing from the Brundtland Report's definition of sustainable development, sustainable missions are missions that serve the needs of the present without compromising the ability of future generations to serve their own needs. All three axes of the triangle are important individually, but for truly sustainable missionary practice all are essential collectively.[23]

The Triangle of Sustainable Missions emphasizes a new twist on the concept, by now a cliché, of incarnational ministry. John Mackay defines the incarnational principle as the Word becoming flesh,[24] on which Darrell Guder comments, "This means that the witness must identify 'in the closest possible manner' with one's environment."[25] Traditional use of the term "environment" in this way signified the cultural and relational dimensions of mission work. We argue, however, that Christ's taking on flesh and dwelling among us is also profoundly ecological. In the flesh Jesus was just as dependent upon the bountiful provisions of creation as are we, and he was not immune to the effects of its degradation.

The triangle also helps us to guard against a dualistic approach to mission that separates the spiritual from the social, economic, or ecological components of life and ministry. Just as poverty theorists such as Bryant Myers have identified a false duality between spirituality and development work,[26] so we are forced to recognize a tendency to separate serving God by serving people from serving God by serving other aspects of his creation. Both forms of service are required for a biblically balanced and holistic faith.

It is important to note that while the triangle is intended to map holistic missionary practice, it is in no way comprehensive in the sense of presenting a holistic theological representation of the Gospel. Therefore, the triangle of sustainable missions, like all such conceptual devices, has weaknesses. The most prominent problem for our discussion is that it does not address the central concern of the Gospel—the moral and spiritual vacuum that lies at the heart not only of our lack of care for creation, but also of all the tribulations of humanity.[27] But as a conceptual framework, the triangle enables missionary practitioners to evaluate their practice of mission and to achieve a better balance of economic and social approaches with missionary earthkeeping.

Missionary Earthkeeping and Creation Care

Missionary earthkeeping, or what is sometimes called the "greening of mission,"[28] is a robust field with a well-developed theology and praxis. Introduced into the ecological lexicon by the Au Sable Institute for Environmental Studies, the adjective "missionary" in "missionary earthkeeping" has a double meaning, referring both to the expansive spirit of those who care for the earth and to the environmental dimensions of the Christian mission in the world, particularly in developing countries.[29] Although it may still seem counterintuitive to some to suggest that the Gospel has anything to do with the environment, the truth is far different. James Huston put it this way: "The world has forgotten its Creator, and man has fallen in love with his introspective powers instead. We need once more to see the vision of the sanctity of creation, where common things are sacramental."[30] Jonathan Wilson claims that "we have failed to maintain a proper dialectic of creation and redemption,"[31] by which he means that what we know (and believe) about God's work in nature needs to interact with what we believe about the Gospel. The saving grace of Christ, who redeems us, is also made available to the rest of creation (see, e.g., Col. 1:15–16, 19–20; Rom. 8:19). This evangelistic linkage was one of the main reasons for the writing of *An Evangelical Declaration on the Care of Creation*, which emphasizes the scriptural basis for evangelistic outreach through creation care.[32] Yet much of the church in North America seems caught in a "log-jam in evangelical thinking" on this issue, placing social action, evangelistic endeavor, and care for the creation in opposition to each other.[33] In North American churches, let alone the mission field, greater attention to creation care is needed. Randolph Haluza-DeLay's research identifies some of the barriers to environmental awareness present in churches, along with some of the church's organizational and cultural strengths that can make it a force for generating proper respect for God's earth.[34]

For some time the missional priority of stewarding creation has been on the agenda of mainline denominations.[35] Consider, for instance, the Five Marks of Mission endorsed by the Lambeth Conferences of 1988 and 2008.[36] Developed in the Anglican Church, recently this statement has been growing in influence. It provides churches and mission groups with a shared understanding that includes the obligation to "safeguard the integrity of creation, and sustain and renew the life of the earth"—along with the imperatives to proclaim the good news, teach new believers, respond to human need, and transform unjust societal structures.

The church's failure to respond to the environmental crisis is filled with ambiguity. This issue has been explored at length and we will not cover that ground again here, except to say that there appear to be systematic blind spots in our theological discourse on the relationship of humanity, the contemporary creation, and God.[37] Even a great communicator such as Francis Schaeffer could not get traction in the evangelical community with his early and insightful book, *Pollution and the Death of Man*.[38] The book is still in print but it is apparently little read in the context of missions. Still, the past three decades have seen a lively recovery of Trinitarian discourse in relationship to creation.[39] Despite the fact that the challenges facing the development of the Christian mind in North American disciplinary scholarship parallel those in the pew, the theological community seems well positioned for translating these newly recovered insights into a much needed corrective for popular theological understanding.

In a chapter titled "Missions with the World in Mind," Tony Campolo asserts that Christians are in the best position to mitigate the pending ecological crisis. Christians alone, he claims, have "both the resources and the moral imperatives to promote economic practices that can make the difference in the poor and struggling countries of the world. Indigenous Christians linked with their brothers and sisters in wealthy countries could come up with programs that might begin to restore our messed up creation to its original glory."[40]

Creation Care in a Global Context

The most significant developments at the interface of missions and creation care today are happening outside traditional professional channels. The economic and technical forces driving globalization are creating a dynamic and fluid array of opportunities for service. A generation ago in the 1960s "short-term" mission assignments were a new and creative development. Daily jet passenger service around the globe had begun, and television brought Billy Graham's powerful evangelistic message into the First World living rooms of North America and Europe. In 1956 *Life, Look,* and *Reader's Digest* magazines carried the electrifying news of the martyrdom of Nate Saint and his fellow missionaries in Ecuador and, in 1964, of the death of Dr. Paul Carlson in the Belgian Congo, where civil war had broken out. During this period Wycliffe Bible Translators and Missionary Aviation Fellowship were finding their stride by applying technologies developed during the Second World War; overarching twentieth-century superpower politics and nuclear detente set the global context for missions. On college campuses baby boomers lined up for a few months of real missionary service with Operation Mobilization,

Youth With a Mission, or forward-thinking denominations. In the "hot, flat, and crowded world" of today, as described by Thomas Friedman,[41] we are simultaneously and somewhat paradoxically broadly connected and narrowly isolated. Technological, economic, military-political, and cultural forces shape the form and content of contemporary mission,[42] and today short-term missions continue to grow as a mission strategy, though not without controversy.[43]

To illustrate some of the changed realities facing mission today and the global interconnectedness now present, as we write this chapter a missionary colleague of ours flew in the past six days first to Nigeria, then back to Canada when his aging father passed away. He shared timely updates along the route, which included a cell-phone-mediated detour to avoid local violence. He had received word of his father's passing while in the Frankfurt airport; one day before returning to his work in the field he e-mailed pictures of the memorial service to us. Once back in the field he began a writing and translating project designed to be completed during a series of commutes back to Canada. All of this rapidly paced and effective service is made possible in our globalizing world by speed-of-light digital communication technologies. We are only beginning to dimly perceive the depth and extent of the changes through which we are living.[44] The arc of these events, from the 1950s and 1960s when large denominational organizations dominated missions to now, is changing not just missionary practice, but the concept of "mission" itself. The multiple facets of globalization, instantaneous communication, jet transportation, and broadening understandings of mission form the context within which we must look at the rise of sustainable missions.

Serving Jesus with integrity in the twenty-first-century context, characterized as it is by groaning on the part of both humankind and the natural creation, requires openness to new ways of thinking and acting. In the face of global challenges to our supplies of air, soil, water, and food, it is easy to wonder, "What can missionaries do?" Even if the state of the planet and our call to stewardship are fully understood, how are missionary practitioners to set about acting faithfully? Many suggest that we must strive to be simultaneously globally aware and locally faithful in our actions. We find in this expression the paradox of the Gospel. When God intended to transform the world, redeeming it by his Son, he sent Jesus into a small town in a region with a poor reputation in a country that was under siege. Sustainable change—brought about in the economy of God, which includes ecological systems—happens in the context of relationships. It happens today when people know people and the places they live and the creatures and systems—biotic, geologic, hydrologic, economic, educational, political, and social—that sustain their lives in those places. We need to look carefully or we may miss the relational complexities of changes that are occurring right before us.

In August 2009, I (John) enjoyed a worship service "mash-up" at Christ the King Community Church in Coupville, Washington.[45] The service that Sunday was a walking tour around forty acres on the Au Sable Institute Pacific Rim campus. One station displayed colorful string bags and wearable art made by women at a small highlands school in Papua New Guinea. The handiwork is mailed to Carol, a volunteer. She markets the bags locally in Washington, collects yarn donations, and then sends back the proceeds so that the cycle can begin again. This microenterprise has empowered members of the PNG community, including Pastor Bonio and his wife. They can now send their children to high school and a son to university. This is not simply recycling. It is the Gospel of the Sermon on the Mount at work, transforming lives on both sides of the planet.

On another Sunday morning at a church in Zionsville, Indiana, sustainable coffee is being served that is grown in Panama and brought back directly by members of the congregation. Church members combine "coffee flights" with more traditional mission activities of spreading God's Word through medicine and education. Education about sustainable farming practices is their most recent innovation. Informal and carried out by gifted individuals, these efforts make up what has been called the largest environmental self-help movement in the world.[46] The power of social networking, facilitated by digital technology and modern transportation, is bringing health, healing, and hope to millions around the world. Holistically integrating economic, social, and environmental sustainability, microenterprise and entrepreneurial non-profit groups make up the great untold story of missions today.

Ethical Questions Concerning Sustainable Missions

Environmental stewardship is not simply a popular response to the advancing environmental degradation of the earth. Rather, it is and always has been a central component of the biblical story, even if at times it has been a forgotten thread in contemporary expressions of the Gospel.[47] In light of the centrality of environmental sustainability in Scripture,[48] numerous questions must be asked regarding missiological approaches that place limits on this ecological imperative.

First, is it possible today to serve Jesus with integrity and neglect the environment? Christopher Wright claims that it is essential to link fidelity to Jesus with care of creation. Yet large segments of the Christian church have serious reservations about doing so. Grizzle and Barrett have done a service to the church by mapping out Christian responses to environmental issues. Their conceptual model of "pluralistic stewardship" leaves room for significant differences among communicants yet encourages respectful dialogue.[49]

Second, is the time right for asking to what extent the question of missional integrity and care for the earth inform the Lausanne Covenant? One definition of integrity is "the quality or condition of being whole or undivided; completeness" (*American Heritage Dictionary*, 4th ed.). Integrity, according to psychologist Henry Cloud, is revealed in a person or an organization that connects authentically, is oriented toward the truth, works in a way that gets results and finishes well, embraces and deals with the negative, is oriented toward growth, and is transcendent.[50] None of these aspects of integrity can be true of a missionary whose work is being undermined by environmental degradation. If the environment is being degraded, then connections become impaired and integrity is lost. If the way of life of a people is unsustainable, then a missionary practitioner must acknowledge this fact and be oriented to the truth of the context. No matter the soul count success of an evangelist, if local habitats are being destroyed the missionary endeavor will not end well. If environmental degradation is burdening a community, this negative factor must be acknowledged and engaged. Communities cannot grow if the natural capital upon which they depend is in decline. To ignore creation is akin to ignoring the transcendent. If Cloud's approach to integrity is accepted, then environmental stewardship must be prominent in a missionary ethic of serving Jesus with integrity.

Third, as Robert Goudzwaard states, the impoverishment of the southern hemisphere is "at least partially caused by the enrichment of the North."[51] He goes on to cite a letter written by southern churches to those in the north which says in part:

> Next to the pain and suffering in the South, there are threats in the North. We heard about poverty, coming back in even your richest societies; we received reports about environmental destruction also in your midst, about alienation, loneliness and the abuse of women and children. And all that, while most of your churches are losing members. And we asked ourselves: is most of that not also related to being rich and desiring to become richer than most of you already are? Is there not in the Western view of human beings and society a delusion, which always looks to the future and wants to improve it, even when it implies an increase of suffering in your own societies and in the South? Have you not forgotten the richness that is related to sufficiency?[52]

These are challenging and difficult words to hear, and a common response is to mount a defense by pointing to all that is good and right in what Christians have done.[53] But at this moment in history perhaps it is time for us just to listen. How should we respond to these arguments? Will a more holistic mission practice help us answer such questions?

Fourth, how might consideration of environmental sustainability be implemented in missionary practice? One practical way is through use of environmental impact assessments. Conducting environmental impact assessments has the added virtue of addressing a growing concern on the part of suppliers of funds, both governments and foundations, which are now demanding rising standards of environmental accountability. Harry Spaling, Janelle Zwier, and David Kupp discuss the practical problems these expectations pose for missionaries seeking funding and have pioneered a community-based assessment process in the context of faith-based communities.[54] Their work offers a significant approach to a subject that lies at the intersection of what were formerly seen as separate entities—one environmental and the other missional.

Fifth, what are the consequences if we do not address environmental stewardship in the practice of mission? The choice before us is stark: we must care for the earth or we could all die. If we care about giving a cup of cold water or feeding the hungry or clothing the naked or healing the sick, then today we must think of all of these things while holding the environment also in mind.[55] Tight linkages bind together biodiversity and food production, ecosystem disturbance and emerging diseases, conservation biology and safe fresh water supplies, medicines and nature. No longer can we afford to overlook the creational context of iconic missions passages such as Matthew 25. The good news is that many in the church understand this fact and are acting on it.

Finally, who will pay for neglect of the environment? Those involved in the front lines of missionary practice already know the answer. The poor pay the highest cost, something I (Michael) witnessed when I worked for World Vision. The burden that falls on the poor is the reason why partnerships such as the Micah Initiative have been formed. The Micah Initiative is active precisely because human environmental degradation is putting the poor of the world at increased risk, lacking adequate food, unable to obtain clean water, and subject to economic displacement. The literature on this topic alone is voluminous.[56] Several book-length treatments of the subject from a Christian perspective are now available, including two that explore the ethical implications of climate change.[57] One of the most effective ways to serve the poor is by helping to protect the ecosystems upon which they depend.

Conclusion

This chapter began with the assertion that in the near future the state of the environment across the earth could compare closely to the state of the environment in Haiti. We cannot conclude by leaving such a picture at the forefront, because we are profoundly hopeful that Christians around the globe are acknowledging their failure to address environmental sustainability and are beginning to serve God's creation with integrity.

Plant with a Purpose, previously known as Floresta, is a Christian nonprofit organization that was created to address deforestation in Haiti. Deforestation there is without question one of the root causes of its people's poverty. Scott Sabin, director of Plant with a Purpose, described Port-au-Prince back in 1995; the description he gave then is not dramatically different from the CNN reports following the 2010 earthquake. Like Jared Diamond, Sabin witnessed the effects of environmental degradation on the population of the capital city:

> It looked as if the tide had come in over the cinderblock-and-iron architecture and stranded garbage and rubble on every horizontal surface. Human beings spilled out

onto the broken streets, in every sort of dress imaginable. A naked man walked past a gentleman in a pin-striped suit, who was picking his way through debris. People filled each alley and turned every sidewalk into an impromptu market. Rotting fruit and raw sewage odors combined with the smell of frying meat and exhaust. UN convoys of white SUVs and armored personnel carriers passed frequently.[58]

Sabin did not go to Haiti out of concern for the environment. He went to Haiti to minister to the poor in the name of Jesus. Yet he quickly discovered that to minister effectively to the poor he could not neglect the environmental crises that were among the root causes of poverty in his mission field. He states, "I had no intention of devoting my life to environmental issues. Yet somewhere on that trip, it dawned on me that they were foundational."[59]

Sabin is not the first missionary practitioner to awaken to the biblical as well as pragmatic necessity of environmental stewardship. In the twelfth century Francis of Assisi, now known as the patron saint of ecologists, paved the way for the contemporary holistic approach modeled in the triangle of sustainable missions. States Diana Bass, "By drawing connections between economics, creation, peacemaking, and political organization, the medieval Francis anticipated much contemporary thinking on the web of relationships that make up a global ecology."[60] At the dawn of the modern missionary era, the efforts of William Carey stand out. The remarkable thing about Carey is how ignorant we are, by and large, of the details of his life outlook, preparation, and actions. We do know that Carey was a distinguished amateur botanist. In this he was typical of many parson-naturalists of the nineteenth century. He specialized in horticulture, and it can be said that "like his preaching and his translations work, [his horticultural efforts had] the same motive, to enrich men with life's best."[61] Today we could add a growing group of environmentally minded missionary and development workers. Heading the list would be Peter and Miranda Harris of A Rocha International, Martin and Bonnie Price of ECHO, Ed Brown of Care of Creation, and Cal and Ruth DeWitt of the Au Sable Institute.[62] The approaches followed by St. Francis, Sabin, and the rest offer us significant illustrations of the triangle of sustainable mission in practice. Their environmental ethic, shaped and inspired by passionate faith in Christ and his mission to the poor, give witness to the love of the Creator for the whole of creation. Such an approach serves Jesus with integrity and bespeaks a vibrant faith for many generations to come.

Questions for Discussion

1. Should mission agencies commit to creation care ministries? The missionary task has often been defined as taking the Gospel of salvation to those who have not heard. How does the task of creation care relate to this task?
2. Missionaries of an earlier generation were accused of ignoring the social implications of their preaching. Now it appears they are being accused of ignoring the ecological implications. Are these legitimate charges against missions? Should missionaries be more responsible for the full implications of what they preach?
3. Do the churches in the Global South have a legitimate claim that Christians in the Global North are being enriched at

the expense of the environment and needs of people in the Global South?
4. To what extent should missionaries and mission agencies be engaged in transformational ministries that include responsibility in addressing environmental stewardship?

Notes

1. Jared Diamond, *Collapse: How Societies Choose to Fail or Succeed* (New York: Penguin Books, 2005).
2. J. Matthew Sleeth, *Serve God, Save the Planet: A Christian Call to Action* (White River Junction, Ver.: Chelsea Green Publishing, 2006).
3. This is not the place for a detailed exposition of this thesis. One can survey some of the literature, with arguments pro and con, in the following: Steven Bouma-Prediger, *For the Beauty of the Earth: A Christian Vision for Creation Care* (Grand Rapids: Baker Academic, 2001); Thomas Homer-Dixon, *The Upside of Down: Catastrophe, Creativity, and the Renewal of Civilization* (Toronto: Knopf Canada, 2006); Douglas J. Moo, "Nature in the New Creation: New Testament Eschatology and the Environment," *Journal of the Evangelical Theological Society* 49 (2006): 449–88, note 21, available online at www.wheaton.edu/CACE/resources/onlinearticles/MooNature.pdf; Jeff Rubin, *Why Your World Is About to Get a Whole Lot Smaller: Oil and the End of Globalization* (Toronto: Random House Canada, 2009); James Gustave Speth, *The Bridge at the Edge of the World: Capitalism, the Environment, and Crossing from Crisis to Sustainability* (New Haven: Yale Univ. Press, 2008).
4. Bill Moyers, *Earth on the Edge*, DVD (Films for the Humanities and Sciences, 2006).
5. Christopher J. H. Wright, *The Mission of God: Unlocking the Bible's Grand Narrative* (Downers Grove, Ill.: IVP Academic, 2006), 417.

6. Mission, according to Wright (*The Mission of God*, 416), "is not truly holistic if it includes only human beings . . . and excludes the rest of creation."
7. David J. Bosch, *Transforming Mission: Paradigm Shifts in Theology of Mission* (Maryknoll, N.Y.: Orbis Books, 1991); J. Andrew Kirk, *What Is Mission? Theological Explorations* (Minneapolis: Fortress Press, 2000); Waldron Scott, *Bring Forth Justice: A Contemporary Perspective on Mission* (Grand Rapids: Eerdmans, 1980). The contemporary expression of this emphasis is the Micah Network (www.micahnetwork.org), a group of over 330 Christian relief, development, and justice organizations from 81 countries first formed in 1991.
8. Raymond E. Grizzle and Christopher B. Barrett, "The One Body of Christian Environmentalism," *Zygon: Journal of Religion and Science* 33, no. 2 (1998): 234.
9. Robert D. Putnam, *Bowling Alone: The Collapse and Revival of American Community* (New York: Simon & Schuster, 2000), 66.
10. Nan Lin, *Social Capital: A Theory of Social Structure and Action* (Cambridge: Cambridge Univ. Press, 2001), 3.
11. Most definitions of sustainability identify this sector simply as "economic." But Grizzle and Barrett ("The One Body of Christian Environmentalism," 237), opt for the term "subjectionist" to emphasize that on this view "the non-human environment is to be brought into subjection for the purpose of facilitating human expansion."
12. Steven C. Hackett, *Environmental and Natural Resources Economics* (Armonk, N.Y.: M. E. Sharp, 1998), 315. The point was succinctly expressed by Senator Gaylord Nelson, "The economy is a wholly owned subsidiary of the biosphere;" quoted by Anthony D. Cortese, "Sustaining God's Creation: The Role of Higher Education" (paper, annual meeting of the National Association of Schools and Colleges of the United Methodist Church, Broomfield, Colo., July 28, 2008), 1. See also Paul Hawken, *The Ecology of Commerce: A Declaration of Sustainability* (New York: HarperCollins, 1993).

13. W. Dayton Roberts, *Patching God's Garment: Environment and Mission in the 21st Century* (Monrovia, Calif.: MARC, 1994). There are many threads to this story and we list these mission agencies as illustrative of some of the earliest responders. A number of denominations could be cited as well.
14. Ronald J. Sider, "Biblical Foundations for Creation Care," in *The Care of Creation: Focusing Concern and Action*, ed. R. J. Berry (Leicester, Eng.: Inter-Varsity Press, 2000), 43–49.
15. Loren Wilkinson, "The Making of the Declaration," in *The Care of Creation*, ed. Berry, 50–59.
16. The Council of Christian Colleges and Universities Global Stewardship National Conference, Gloucester, Mass., October 16–20, 1996.
17. The term "natural capital" refers both to the species of the biosphere that provide material goods and to the services, such as clean air, water, and soil that the biosphere supplies. The concept was detailed by Paul Hawken, Amory Lovins, and Hunter Lovins, *Natural Capitalism: Creating the Next Industrial Revolution* (Boston: Little, Brown, 1999), and Gretchen C. Daily, ed., *Nature's Services: Societal Dependence on Natural Ecosystems* (Washington, D.C.: Island Press, 1997).
18. Fred Van Dyke, David C. Mahan, Joseph K. Sheldon, and Raymond H. Brand, *Redeeming Creation: The Biblical Basis for Environmental Stewardship* (Downers Grove, Ill.: InterVarsity Press, 1996), 26–27.
19. Glenn Ricketts, "History of Sustainability Management," *Academic Questions* 23, no. 1 (January 19, 2010): 20–53.
20. Scott, *Bring Forth Justice*, 6. Images summarize important understandings of the ethical implications of these topics, but we are not aware of any study of the iconography of sustainability, creation care, missions, or their interactions.
21. Andres R. Edwards, *The Sustainability Revolution: Portrait of a Paradigm Shift* (Gabriola Island, B.C.: New Society Publishers, 2005).
22. Scott Campbell, "Green Cities, Growing Cities, Just Cities? Urban Planning and the Contradictions of Sustainable Development," in *Readings in*

Planning Theory, ed. Scott Campbell and Susan S. Fainstein (Oxford: Blackwell, 2003), 435–58.
23. The Brundtland Report was published as *Our Common Future* (New York: Oxford Univ. Press, 1987). The full report and its definition of sustainability can be found at various Web sites, including www.worldinbalance.net/intagreements/1987-brundtland.php.
24. John Mackay, *Ecumenics: The Science of the Church Universal* (Englewood Cliffs, N.J.: Prentice Hall, 1964), 175.
25. Darrell L. Guder, "Incarnation and the Church's Evangelistic Mission," in *The Study of Evangelism: Exploring a Missional Practice of the Church*, ed. Paul W. Chilcote and Laceye C. Warner (Grand Rapids: Eerdmans, 2008), 178.
26. Bryant L. Myers, ed., *Working with the Poor: New Insights and Learnings from Development Practitioners* (Monrovia, Calif.: World Vision, 1999).
27. Alister McGrath, *The Reenchantment of Nature: The Denial of Religion and the Ecological Crisis* (New York: Doubleday, 2002); Michael S. Northcott, *The Environment and Christian Ethics* (Cambridge: Cambridge Univ. Press, 1996), 312; Michael S. Northcott, "The Spirit of Environmentalism," in *The Care of Creation*, ed. Berry, 167–74.
28. This literature is scattered; we are not aware of a comprehensive survey. In addition to works already cited, the following give some flavor of a (mostly) Protestant literature: Dave Bookless, "Towards a Theology of Sustainability," in *When Enough Is Enough: A Christian Framework for Environmental Sustainability*, ed. R. J. Berry (Nottingham: Apollos, 2007); Calvin B. DeWitt and Ghillean T. Prance, eds., *Missionary Earthkeeping* (Macon, Ga.: Mercer Univ. Press, 1992); Allan Effa, "The Greening of Mission," *International Bulletin of Missionary Research* 32, no. 4 (2008): 171–76; Willis Jenkins, "Missiology in Environmental Context: Tasks for an Ecology of Mission," *International Bulletin of Missionary Research* 32, no. 4 (2008): 176–84.
29. Roberts, *Patching God's Garment*, 97.
30. James Houston, *I Believe in the Creator* (Grand Rapids: Eerdmans, 1980), 205.

31. Jonathan R. Wilson, "Evangelicals and the Environment: A Theological Concern," *Christian Scholar's Review* 28 (1998): 298–307.
32. Ronald J. Sider, "Biblical Foundations for Creation Care," in *The Care of Creation*, ed. Berry, 44.
33. Peter Harris. "Why Creation Is Waiting for the Christians: A Manifesto," *Crux* 45, no. 1 (2009): 12–21. Harris mentions the consternation he faces when fund-raising in North America for a "Christian environmental mission." See his *Kingfisher's Fire: A Story of Hope for God's Earth* (Oxford: Monarch Books, 2008), 167–68.
34. Randolph B. Haluza-DeLay, "Churches Engaging the Environment: An Autoethnography of Obstacles and Opportunities," *Human Ecology Review* 15, no. 1 (2008): 71–81; available at www.humanecologyreview.org/pastissues/her151/haluzadelay.pdf.
35. There are several surveys of this literature. For recent coverage of a broad range of Christian denominations, see Allan Effa's and Willis Jenkins's articles cited in note 26. For a comprehensive survey of responses made by the Christian church to ecological and other social issues via formal statements, see Mark Ellingsen, *The Cutting Edge: How Churches Speak on Social Issues* (Grand Rapids: Eerdmans, 1993).
36. Calvin DeWitt and Dave Bookless, "To Strive to Safeguard the Integrity of Creation and Sustain and Renew the Life of the Earth," in *Mission in the Twenty-first Century: Exploring the Five Marks of Global Mission*, ed. Andrew F. Walls and Cathy Ross (Maryknoll, N.Y.: Orbis Books, 2008), 84–104.
37. John Jefferson Davis, "Ecological 'Blind Spots' in the Structure and Content of Recent Evangelical Systematic Theologies," *Journal of the Evangelical Theological Society* 43, no. 2 (2000): 273–86.
38. In his *Pollution and the Death of Man: The Christian View of Ecology* (Wheaton, Ill.: Tyndale House, 1970), Francis Schaeffer reprints the famous essay by Lynn White, Jr., "The Historical Roots of Our Ecologic Crisis," and responds to it.

39. See Colin Gunton, *The One, the Three, and the Many: God, Creation, and the Culture of Modernity* (Cambridge: Cambridge Univ. Press, 1993); Darrell W. Johnson, *Experiencing the Trinity* (Vancouver: Regent College Publishing, 2002); John R. Wood, "Biophilia and the Gospel: Loving Nature or Worshipping God?" in *Living in the LambLight: Christianity and Contemporary Challenges to the Gospel*, ed. Hans Boersma (Vancouver: Regent College Publishing, 2001), 153–76.
40. Anthony Campolo, *How to Rescue the Earth Without Worshiping Nature* (Nashville: Thomas Nelson, 1992), 113.
41. Thomas L. Friedman, *Hot, Flat, and Crowded: Why We Need a Green Revolution—and How It Can Renew America* (New York: Farrar, Straus & Giroux, 2008).
42. Roberts writes (*Patching God's Garment*, 98): "Speaking as the 'MK' ('Missionary Kid') son of missionaries to Asia and as one who has spent most of his own life as a missionary in Latin America, I think I can state without fear of contradiction that most missionaries go overseas with plenty of their own cultural baggage, but with very little ecological perception."
43. For one of us—John—this chapter marks the closure of a professional circuit involving all three facets of the sustainability triangle. John began as a short-term student missionary to Alaska in 1967. He worked for four years with a prison ministry in Seattle, Washington—Job Therapy, The M-2 Program. His thirty-year academic career found him teaching biological and environmental sciences, most recently as the academic dean at the Au Sable Institute of Environmental Studies. It was in the Au Sable Forums that many of these ideas were first explored. See www.ausable.org/or.fora.cfm.
44. For more on the implications of these phenomena for the interface of missions and the environment, see the essays in *The Gospel and Globalization: Exploring the Religious Roots of a Globalized World*, ed. Michael W. Goheen and Erin G. Glanville (Vancouver: Regent College Publishing, 2009).

45. "Mashup" is a neologism for the combination of two or more digital platforms. The most recognizable is Craigslist, built on the Google map platform. More examples can be found by googling "mashup."
46. Paul Hawken, *Blessed Unrest: How the Largest Movement in the World Came into Being, and Why No One Saw It Coming* (New York: Viking, 2007).
47. DeWitt and Prance, *Missionary Earthkeeping*, vii–viii.
48. Wright, *The Mission of God*, 397–420.
49. Grizzle and Barrett, "The One Body of Christian Environmentalism."
50. Henry Cloud, *Integrity: The Courage to Meet the Demands of Reality* (New York: HarperCollins, 2006).
51. Bob Goudzwaard, "Climate Change and the Rapid Dynamic of Globalization," in *The Gospel and Globalization*, ed. Goheen and Glanville, 242.
52. The letter, written in the context of the World Alliance of Reformed Churches in December 1999, is available at www.warc.ch/update/up101/03.html.
53. The wide-ranging and lively discussion of this subject may be entered at many points. We suggest: Don Brandt, ed., *God's Stewards: The Role of Christians in Creation Care* (Monrovia, Calif.: World Vision, 2002); David S. Koetje, ed., *Living the Good Life on God's Good Earth* (Grand Rapids: Faith Alive Christian Resources, 2006); and David Warners and Larry Borst, "The Good of a Flourishing Creation: Seeking God in a Culture of Affluence," *Perspectives on Science and Christian Faith* 57, no. 1 (2005): 24–33.
54. Harry Spaling, Janelle Zwier, and David Kupp, "Earthkeeping and the Poor: Assessing the Environmental Sustainability of Development Projects," *Perspectives on Science and Christian Faith* 53, no. 3 (2001): 142–51.
55. See Eric Chivian and Aaron Bernstein, eds., *Sustaining Life: How Human Health Depends on Biodiversity* (Oxford: Oxford Univ. Press, 2008), and Fred Van Dyke, "Between Heaven and Earth—Evangelical Engagement in Conservation," *Conservation Biology* 19, no. 6 (2005): 1693–96.

56. For climate-related actions being taken by Christian relief and food aid agencies, see John Wood and Geoff Strong, "A Primer on Climate Change," *Faith Today* (January/February 2008): 18–22.
57. Michael Northcott, *A Moral Climate: The Ethics of Global Climate Warming* (Maryknoll, N.Y.: Orbis Books, 2007); Nick Spencer, Robert S. White, and Virginia Vroblesky, *Christianity, Climate Change, and Sustainable Living* (Peabody, Mass.: Hendrickson, 2009).
58. Scott C. Sabin and Kathy Ide, *Tending to Eden: Environmental Stewardship for God's People* (Valley Forge, Pa.: Judson Press, 2010), xii.
59. Sabin and Ide, *Tending to Eden*, xv.
60. Diana Butler Bass, *A People's History of Christianity: The Other Side of the Story* (New York: HarperOne, 2009), 140.
61. See Dennis E. Testerman, "Missionary Earthkeeping: Glimpses of the Past, Visions of the Future," in *Missionary Earthkeeping*, ed. DeWitt and Prance, 26.
62. The details of these individuals' stories can be found at the respective organizational Web sites or in Peter Harris, *Under the Bright Wings* (London: Hodder & Stoughton, 1993), and Edward R. Brown, *Our Father's World: Mobilizing the Church to Care for Creation* (Downers Grove, Ill.: IVP Books, 2008).

Part V:

Integrity in Recruitment and Representation

13

Truth and Storytelling: It Is Important to Get the Facts Straight

JOHN MCNEILL

A long personal odyssey has led me to the subject and tentative conclusions presented here. Permit me to briefly highlight the journey. But before I do so, a disclaimer is needed. In this chapter I will discuss the work of Francis and Edith Schaeffer and the famous community that they established in Huémoz, Switzerland. I personally have benefited in incalculable ways from their work and their sacrificial hospitality. The thinking of Francis Schaeffer has influenced me greatly. His attempt to live out his faith in all spheres of life is an example that has had great impact on many people and one that I have tried, with varying degrees of success and failure, to follow. My great debt to the Schaeffers should be clear before reading the following, which might otherwise be misinterpreted as being unnecessarily critical.

Two signposts, one distant and one recent, give orientation to my journey. The first is located where my small part in the story of the evangelical Christian world began just over forty-one years ago when I arrived at L'Abri in the Swiss village of Huémoz as a twenty-one-year-old recent graduate from university. Uncertain what to do next, I had left Canada with my backpack and guitar and was wandering on the hippie trail, my university-honed atheism a bit ragged on the edges. Very recently a second signpost flashed by in a faculty meeting at the college where I now teach, a college acutely sensitive to the economic hard times that we are in. We were discussing what we as faculty could do to help the college survive, and some promotional material was read to us during the discussion. My reaction was to suggest that we moderate the inflated language in the material we had just heard. Some affirmative body language from others showed me that I was not the only one in the meeting to think this way, but my reaction did not move the group to any decision about changing our advertising slogans.[1] Clearly I had developed a higher than normal level of intolerance for exaggeration.

My sensitivity to overblown publicity extends to the classroom. For years I have warned my "Missions Issues" students to beware of missionary stories. I have watched hype in operation for decades and in many years of raising missionary support have seen a variety of reasons why it is used. Its destructive potential has been fairly obvious. When hype is used in missionary storytelling and fund-raising, it can become like an addiction in a context of competition for mission resources and the attention of potentially generous donors. Good stories lead to better support, and missionaries are often known for the stories they tell. If your stories do not match up, you can expect less support.[2]

My entry into the missionary story occurred in the above mentioned village in Switzerland. As an undergraduate I had made many switches of major, from engineering through pure sciences to psychology with some other minor detours. But I

13—John McNeill

had been careful to complete all the prerequisites for medical school, wanting to keep that door open as well. Having gotten on the waiting list, but just missed a place at a medical school of my choice, I decided to take time off to travel the world and think about the future. What was planned as a brief visit with a university friend in Huémoz led me to an encounter with the Savior and a complete change of life direction.

The first very brief published report of my part in the greater missionary story of L'Abri appeared in 1969, including a picture of Christel's and my wedding in a collage on the cover of Edith Schaeffer's book *L'Abri*.[3] As newlyweds we found it exciting to be part of something greater than ourselves, but I was troubled by the factual inaccuracy of being labeled as a medical student. I often half-consciously wondered why it was that my story came out as it did. Knowing that I had never been at medical school, but only in pre-med studies, I concluded that I must have exaggerated the details when I told someone about myself, and that my distortion somehow had been passed on to Edith Schaeffer. This got filed in my mind as a reminder to myself to rein in my tendency to exaggerate stories to make them more interesting.

As I learned the ropes in the evangelical Christian world I had discovered a widely held but often unstated and sometimes disregarded general principle: "truth matters." It was clearly in the background of the careful attention that teachers such as Francis Schaeffer gave to the Scriptures. Biographer Barry Hankins refers to the "infallibility of Scripture, something Schaeffer had insisted on since his conversion," as one theme that was emphasized consistently by Francis Schaeffer throughout his life.[4] In an environment influenced by teaching such as this, how could the details of my life have been deliberately or even carelessly changed or exaggerated? Surely no one among the leaders of L'Abri would have gotten my story wrong. The fault must have been mine.

Storytelling

As humans, we tell stories and make stories, but we are also made by our stories. They place us in a context greater than ourselves, giving us meaning.[5] Stories are our main vehicles for communicating what is most important to us. On the one hand we have Jesus, a great teller of stories and parables. On the other hand we have our "fishing stories" where the catch gets bigger with each retelling. How can we tell stories and still be careful about their truth content?

Part of telling stories is to select what to tell and what to leave out. All storytellers select on the basis of the point that they are trying to make. John selected certain specifics from the life of Jesus for his Gospel, based on his intent in writing (John 20:30–31, 21:25). He wanted to help his readers to believe in Jesus and selected accordingly, realizing that he could have included much more if he had wanted to give the complete story of what Jesus had done on earth. Selection is unavoidable in writing stories, and as long as the selection does not badly skew reality, it is not a problem. But the writer should be aware of the danger of warping reality and should take measures to minimize distortion. I think we see such efforts being made in the New Testament where, mixed with stories of the heroics of people like Paul, we also find texts minimizing their importance and emphasizing that they are merely servants (1 Cor. 3–4, 2 Cor. 12).

Telling "fish stories" involves selection, but also exaggeration and changing of details, something that is acceptable if the hearers are aware that the story is fictional. This approach to storytelling should not be accepted, though, when stories are being represented as factual.

Although I was capable and may have been guilty of exaggeration about myself, I have since discovered that a number of other factors probably contributed to the inflation of my story of entry into the Christian world. Edith Schaeffer herself seems to have exaggerated for a variety of reasons. If this was the case, she was probably perceived as a spiritual heroine and thus virtually beyond criticism: a kind of aura emanating from the teaching that she and her husband were associated with may have provided them with a shield of protection because they were seen as unique spiritual figures.

Heroes

In a 2008 interview on the PBS program *Fresh Air*, Frank Schaeffer, the son of Francis and Edith, explained his strong desire to free his father's memory from the hero worship that had grown up around him in evangelical circles.[6] The adulation that put him above criticism for many admirers made him seem inhuman to his son. Over a period of about ten years, beginning in the early 1990s, Frank published three novels that were at first represented as fiction.[7] He has since admitted that they contain much autobiographical material,[8] something that was always evident to people who knew the Schaeffers personally. Although the novels are well written and amusing, the "L'Abri family" tended to look on them as a kind of unmentionable scandal, skeletons in the closet.[9] Without my pretending to know where the biography ends and the fiction starts, it is clear to me that the father in the novels is no angel and that through him Frank is debunking the superhuman hero myth that surrounded his father. Referring in the PBS interview to his more recent book *Crazy for God*, Frank denied that it was an expose of his father. Instead, he said, he was "trying to rescue his father from a lot of people who worshiped him as a cult figure."

Now, I feel free to criticize my own father, even having gone through a period of time when I felt the necessity of doing so thoroughly. Nor have I avoided or been spared the heat of criticism from my own children. But I personally had to overcome great internal resistance to read what Frank had written about his parents: I felt that I was being unfaithful to his father, to his memory, to his service in the kingdom. This resistance was not simply personal. My wife, with whom I have discussed this project in detail, has often tried to discourage me from continuing. A good and respected friend commented that, while he understand why I had written what I had, he wished that it could be done without criticism of a very respected Christian leader. In one library, where I had gone to borrow some books on this subject, I was even discouraged from reading the books that Frank had written about his family. A library staff member felt that they were disrespectful and unworthy of attention.

When we reach such a point, have we not elevated the senior Schaeffer couple from the category of normal fallible mortals to that of untouchable spiritual heroes? Why do people do this kind of thing? Quoting Ernst Becker on the place of heroes in culture, Joseph Scimecca observes that the burden of our mortality and the fear of meaninglessness cause us to grasp for meaning. Heroes and the systems of thought that we build around them help us to identify with something bigger than ourselves that soothes our insecurity and comforts us.[10] Jesus is unquestionably the ultimate hero, but we like to create mediators between what we perceive to be his untouchable heroic status and our very incomplete selves.

We want to be like him, and we create heroes who appear to be much more like him than we are.[11] Then we become unwilling to criticize those heroes because the criticism would shake our security system. Frank Schaeffer saw how this process had captured his father. He wrote: "One of the mysteries of human need is that religious leaders must become more than the sum of their fallible, sometimes awful, parts, because other people need them to be more. This does not make the religious leader a hypocrite; it just shows that the rest of us are desperate."[12]

Clearly tied to the hero theme is the elitism, mentioned above, that was part of the mentality within the growing L'Abri family. The tendency for the community at L'Abri to see itself as not only unique but also as better than others has already been mentioned in note 9.[13] This problematic tendency can be found within evangelicalism more generally, but the L'Abri version of it was unique. The environment that such elitism generated lent support to hero worship of its founders. It is germane to ask: Is the evangelical world widely involved in generating and accepting hero worship, or is hero worship simply a problem caused by a few overzealous people?

Exaggeration

My assumption in continuing this discussion is that exaggeration by changing or inflating details of a story for dramatic effect is unacceptable when telling what is presented as a factual account. A couple of biographies of the Schaeffers illustrate ways that exaggeration might occur. The biographies I mention are popular rather than scholarly, the type that might be found on a church book table or in a church library and therefore might be read by larger numbers of people. The authors, L. G. Parkhurst and

Sam Wellman, supply many of the same details that appear in more recent and more critical biographies.[14] The overall impression given, however, is not the same. The difference in effect is achieved by a selection of which material to present and which to leave out. The struggles discussed and the inevitable victories are ones that we can identify with, although the victories in our own lives might not be quite as inevitable. But not mentioned in either of these two popular accounts are some of the longer-term, seemingly insoluble, and more secret struggles that we all deal with.

In his PBS interview Frank Schaeffer talked about his father's battle with depression, something that is not mentioned by either Parkhurst or Wellman. Therefore the picture they give is out of focus, to put it mildly.[15] To present only victories in battle, without putting them into the context of an ongoing struggle with other problems that were not so victoriously and decisively resolved, amounts to exaggeration. Both biographies read like Hollywood movies in which we know that the hero is eventually going to win. Evangelicalism, along with the culture in which it is so deeply embedded, likes a good story of a hero with a happy ending. As for myself, the part of me that resonates with this cultural theme rejoiced as I read both stories. I enjoyed the resolution of a simple theme and the victory of my heroes. But my critical faculty, knowing of other struggles which we all experience, felt sometimes abandoned, sometimes cheated. Maybe heroes like the Schaeffers really do not have the same struggles that others have, or maybe some part of their story has been hidden. Simplification, by manipulating the context of a story, can shade into exaggeration.

Given that their general cultural environment and their specific sub-cultural context encouraged hero formation and possible hero worship, the question must be asked: To what extent did the Schaeffers themselves contribute to this? Frank Schaeffer talks about evangelicals venerating his father, but was there anything that either Francis or Edith Schaeffer did that may have added to the problem?

Edith Schaeffer was very much the storyteller of L'Abri, and a good, almost inexhaustible, one at that. But she edited the story, emphasizing some parts while ignoring others, changing the context for the story and causing the kind of exaggeration mentioned above. Both in his PBS interview and in *Crazy for God*,[16] Frank Schaeffer refers to things that his mother insisted should never be talked about or mentioned in public. His father's strong tendency to depression was one such subject. Here we see exaggeration by elision.

I have noted how my own story got changed in the telling. Could the writer of *L'Abri* have had a part in changing the details? Personal communications from a variety of people closely linked to L'Abri confirm that Mrs. Schaeffer had a tendency to exaggerate by changing details.[17] One of my correspondents mentioned having taken her to task on the subject. It is hardly surprising that she might exaggerate; that tendency is widely distributed in the human race. Her idealism and the desire to make a good story that would fulfill her ideal could have been contributing factors. Duriez writes, "Fran's proneness to anger and depression ... did not sit easily with Edith's tendency to cling to flighty ideas of what her imagination had pictured as ideal."[18] It is easy to see how pressure to conform to an ideal could have led to unconscious, or even conscious, editing of the account of their work to make it more closely match her ideal as she presented their story to the public. One specific direction that this exaggeration might take is hinted at in remarks from Frank's book *Crazy for God*. He notes the snobbery that was part of the mentality of the L'Abri family, with a related excess of respect for people who were seen as being of higher status.[19] Medical doctors were one group seen as being more important. If this was the case, the transformation of a new convert from a pre-med to a medical student would be a simple piece of exaggeration-driven social climbing that made that convert seem more important and enhanced the story of L'Abri, showing how it was reaching people of potential influence, wealth, and relatively high social status.[20]

Pragmatism

Francis and Edith Schaeffer had a great burden to bring the message of salvation in Christ to a lost world. The desire to do this effectively was a central motivation for their lives and work. Frank mentions, in his PBS interview, memories from his childhood in which much of what his parents did in daily life was driven by a hidden agenda: how they would turn conversations from some other theme to the subject of conversion to Christ. They had a very pragmatic approach to their calling. In an interview with Colin Duriez, Francis Schaeffer stated, "I'm only interested in an apologetic that leads in two directions, and the one is to lead people to Christ, as Savior, and the other is that after they are Christians, for them to realize the lordship of Christ in the whole of life."[21]

Hankins has noticed a similar pragmatism in Schaeffer, who, when given an example that contradicted one of his generalizations in philosophy, responded, "I was just making a point."[22] In an article on Schaeffer and scholarship, Hankins noted: "The idea of writing history without a political agenda—that is, merely to get the story straight—was difficult for Schaeffer to grasp."

Later in the same article Hankins wrote that at the end of his life Schaeffer was at odds with contemporary Christian scholars because he thought that their work should result in "an undiluted and useful apologetic for the Christian-Right side of the early culture wars."[23] In their presentation of their own story, a similar pragmatism seems to have been at work. Frank Schaeffer tells how it was forbidden to him and his siblings to mention publicly the struggles his father experienced. Any such talk would have meant "letting our side down" in the ongoing battle to present a good image for the purposes of evangelism.[24]

It is easy to see how the zeal that the Schaeffers shared, combined with their pragmatic approach to achieving their goal, along with the idealism of Edith Schaeffer, could result in the writing of a story that might enhance some details while suppressing others in order to promote their evangelistic agenda. Such a story would be encouraging to potential supporters, and it would fit right into the cultural pattern of heroic stories with happy endings.

Truth and Context

Exaggeration and pragmatism can wreak havoc on the facts. Even if isolated details are correct, their placement in an inaccurate context can greatly distort the overall picture. Postmodern scholars have taken the idea of the connection of truth to context to an extreme, leaving them skeptical about any possibility of objective truth. Such skepticism is a logical result of the misuse of human reason, autonomous or otherwise, but is not a necessary conclusion given different presuppositions. Critical realist thinkers accept that truth is always tied to context. Instead of ending in skepticism, however, they conclude we can know truly, but we must accept that our knowledge is at best only approximate, and our approach to truth gradual and fallible.[25]

Hankins found a tendency in Francis Schaeffer to idealize the founding fathers of the United States as having been uniquely and decisively influenced by Christian values.[26] In my period of studying with and reading Schaeffer I have thought there was a similar idealization of certain of the reformers. The critical realist idea of truth can provide conceptual protection against the idealization of a group or a period of history, and it should help in avoiding the pitfall of hero worship.[27] No one and no group has a monopoly on truth; all have some access and all need others to improve their grasp on it. Both personal giftedness and cultural perspective help, on the one hand, and limit and hinder, on the other, in the search for truth. In many ways Francis Schaeffer was conscious and critical of his culture and subculture, and he was ahead of his time in discussing intellectual movements that were later clearly identified as postmodern. But epistemologically he appeared to be stuck in modernity, accepting certain specific theological formulations of rationalist theologians as final, and accepting the formulations produced by the U.S. founding fathers as being a political model for all times and places. A critical realist would see the same formulations as approximations to final truth, as stopping points in the ongoing process of gaining a better grasp on truth, theological or political. Schaeffer was depending on the adequacy of human reason to define truth precisely—a dependence that his cultural analysis criticized. Ironically, having questioned the Enlightenment and pushed it to its logical conclusions,[28] he then, Hankins observes, "fought against postmodernism with the modern weapons of enlightenment reason."[29] His investment in enlightenment reason, because it did not have the epistemological humility of critical realism, became a prop under his idealization of specific historic periods and groups and under the exaggeration and pragmatism discussed above.

Does Any of This Matter?

Why bother to write about any of this? Does it not simply show that the accounts coming from L'Abri have been enhanced, polished, and exaggerated in ways that all of us do when we tell stories? Does it really matter? I suggest that it does, for several reasons.

When we tell stories as Christians, we communicate some life-changing truths. We need to be careful how we do it. Perhaps we can develop ethical guidelines for our storytelling. On one side, we have an obligation to our hearers and to the facts to treat them with respect and honesty. Our story, be it about ourselves or someone else, should represent the facts in a balanced way so that our hearers are not misled due to our having misrepresented the situation either by a too radical selection of facts or by actually having changed details. On the other side, we need to be sensitive to our subjects, the people about whom we are telling a story. Are we treating them with respect, or are we using them for our own purposes? During my time in the former Soviet region I heard many stories that included names and places. Some people think that after the political changes of the 1990s giving such specifics is no longer a problem. I have always disagreed, refusing to give names, and recent developments from the region indicate that too many personal details might leave people there as vulnerable as they once were under the Soviet regime. We owe it to those whom we include in our stories to protect both their privacy and their safety. Jenell Williams Paris describes the ethical standards of anthropological research as being broadly compatible with Christian ethics.[30] I suggest that we might use them to help us in developing ethical guidelines for Christian storytelling.

On a personal level, for many who met and worked with the Schaeffers, they were models, mentors: father and mother in the Lord. Those who got closest to them probably noticed that they really were mere mortals and therefore did not fall into the trap of idealizing them. Many others, my wife and I included, were close enough to be influenced, but not close enough to see their failings. Edith Schaeffer, for example, was a woman of prodigious energy. Frank refers to her energy as superhuman.[31] Hurvey Woodson is quoted by Duriez as remembering how incredibly hardworking she was: "I was always impressed with the amount of endurance she had, because there were times when she would not go to bed for a couple of days. Yes, she would not sleep but work right through the night. She had an enormous amount of stamina and drive. She just worked constantly."[32]

How does a young co-worker or a new believer imitate someone like her? Doing so is especially difficult if some of her faults are hidden, her strengths are highlighted, and she is idealized. Presenting such a picture through misguided idealism/pragmatism as part of an effort to win more people to Christ can misfire. The rosy picture may be effective in the short term, but it does not help for long. People soon see that they themselves have faults. In a good case, they may subsequently become more realistic and understand that the picture they were given of the "heroes" was false or at least overblown. In a worse case, they may end up trapped in a lifestyle of hypocrisy, pretending to be someone they cannot be. Or they may abandon their faith, deeming themselves to be unworthy because they cannot live up to the (falsified) model that was presented as representative of the truth.

Concerning our understanding of and participation in truth, we are all broken pots in the process of being remade, and Francis Schaeffer, in his writing and his life, showed that he was aware of this. But the story of L'Abri published widely did not always reflect such awareness. The elitism of the L'Abri family, which saw itself as better than the rest of the Christian world, did not help its converts to get an accurate sense of the incompleteness of real life and of L'Abri specifically. Truth is lived out in a personal and cultural context, one that does not resemble either our idealistic dreams or the separatist zeal of the 1930s fundamentalism that influenced the Schaeffers.[33] Each period in the history of the church and each branch of the church today struggles to find and express truth, working with cultural forces and grappling to formulate things adequately for its own circumstances. Concerning the deep mysteries that God has revealed, we all, in the words of Paul, see a poor reflection in a mirror (1 Cor. 13:12).[34] No individual or group and no period in church history has gotten it all right. We have adequate knowledge for finding our way back to God and for having some idea about how God's kingdom works, but there is much that we do not know. The conclusion for Paul was to focus on the essentials–faith, hope, and especially love—something that the Schaeffers were strong at teaching and practicing.

But another part of Paul's message in the context is the degree to which we need one another. Because our knowledge of the deep mysteries of God is at best partial and our gifts differ, we need one another, both within local bodies of believers and across the whole spectrum of the church in the world. This need for one another is a message that can be diluted or lost when people are not open about their weaknesses and are not aware of their limitations at the level of both their own personal life and their cultural setting. When we make people into heroes and manipulate history to maintain the myth of heroes, truth suffers. We make it look as though truth is fully formulated in us or in our group, when in fact we are stumbling along like everyone else. Living with a hero myth ultimately takes us farther from the truth, for we can only really get closer to it as we approach it in humility and help one another.

Questions for Discussion

1. Can you think of personal heroes you have had? How did they become heroes in your mind?
2. What were the positive effects in your life of your heroes?
3. Can you think of negative effects of hero worship from your own experience?
4. What boundaries would you set for yourself to assure that you have an appropriate attitude to people who have a hero role in your life?
5. What steps can you suggest for a leader to take to prevent an unhealthy or dangerous abuse of the status of hero?

Notes

1. In our discussion, a distinction was made between what we actually are as a college and our aspirations and dreams for what we might become, which is what our advertising was talking about. This distinction seemed to satisfy most of those present, but left me still protesting inwardly. My objection persists because the consumers of our advertising may not understand the context, that is, that we are presenting aspirations, not facts.

2. An example: in the early 1990s, immediately after the collapse of the Soviet Union, I was already working in the region and began to focus on Russia, as I still do. A colleague told me that her mission was recruiting as many candidates for the region as possible because they were "cash cows." The collapse of the "evil empire" gave such a compelling backdrop to any missionary storytelling/fund-raising that millions of dollars rolled in for workers there, and the percentage that supported the home office was gratefully received. She was sure that the numbers of people being recruited were greater than the need and the specific work available to be done. Whenever I have mentioned this story in the company of experienced mission workers there have been affirmative nods and parallel examples given both from the Soviet region and other parts of the world.
3. Edith Schaeffer, *L'Abri* (Wheaton, Ill.: Tyndale House, 1969), 211.
4. Barry Hankins, *Francis Schaeffer and the Shaping of Evangelical America* (Grand Rapids: Eerdmans, 2008), 23. For the enduring concerns that occupied Francis Schaeffer's thought and teaching, see *The Complete Works of Francis A. Schaeffer: A Christian Worldview*, 6 vols. (Carlisle: Paternoster, 1982).
5. Christian Smith, *Moral, Believing Animals: Human Personhood and Culture* (New York: Oxford Univ. Press, 2003), 64.
6. Frank Schaeffer, "Pro Life–and in Favor of Keeping Abortion Legal," interview on PBS's *Fresh Air* (December 9, 2008); available at www.npr.org/templates/story/story.php?storyId=97998654.
7. Frank Schaeffer, *Portofino* (1992), *Saving Grandma* (1997), and *Zermatt* (2003); all published by Carroll and Graf, New York, N.Y.
8. Frank Schaeffer, PBS interview, "I started writing obliquely about my family in my novels." For a comment on the thinly veiled biography in *Portofino*, see his *Crazy for God: How I Grew Up as One of the Elect, Helped Found the Religious Right, and Lived to Take All (or Almost All) of It Back* (New York: Carroll and Graf, 2007), 384. Schaeffer has posted a number of reviews and comments on his books on his Web site, www.frankschaeffer.com.

9. Those who had been through L'Abri and became "part of the work" were called part of the "L'Abri family." It was interesting that this family was defined in some vague but definite way as distinct from the body of Christ at large. In his PBS interview Frank Schaeffer also mentions the sense of identity as a special group that was part of the mentality at L'Abri. This probably reflects an ongoing effect of the theological separatism that was part of the ethos in which the Schaeffers trained and worked as a young couple. Separatism clearly emerged again in Francis Schaeffer's later years. See details provided in Hankins, *Francis Schaeffer*, 15–16, 147–49.
10. Joseph A. Scimecca, "Cultural Hero Systems and Religious Beliefs: The Ideal-Real Social Science of Ernst Becker," *Review of Religious Research* 21, no. 1 (1979): 63.
11. If we understood this better we might be more compassionate toward other groups that create their own mediator-heroes. I do not say this to justify any hero worship, but only to make a point about our general human vulnerability that makes us willing to create heroes in the first place.
12. Frank Schaeffer, *Crazy for God*, 103.
13. One illustrative example is found in "The Mark of the Christian," which is Appendix II to Francis Schaeffer's *The Church at the End of the Twentieth Century* (Wheaton, Ill.: Inter-Varsity Press, 1970). The story is told there (pp. 151–52) of a church that split in two, not on the basis of a bitter disagreement, but in order to serve its members and region more effectively. Having been part of the church planting team in the story, I know it well and still today maintain contact with the church that my wife and I helped to start. The church is given as a positive example, which it was and still is. But it never was and is not today categorically better than others. The mentality existed, however, that L'Abri was the place to be, and if you could not be there, then at least go to a work or church started by "L'Abri people."
14. L. G. Parkhurst, Jr., *Francis and Edith Schaeffer: Christian Missionary Apologists Who Challenged a World of Skeptics to Faith* (Minneapolis:

Bethany, 1996); Sam Wellman, *Francis and Edith Schaeffer: Defenders of the Faith* (Uhrichville, Ohio: Barbour, 2000).

15. Colin Duriez, discussing Francis Schaeffer's early public popularity, notes that the advertising used for a reception at Harvard "in its excitement... anticipated an unfortunate American evangelical tendency to hype up the streetwise pastor-intellectual"; see his *Francis Schaeffer: An Authentic Life* (Wheaton, Ill.: Crossway Books, 2008), 163. Douglas R. Groothius positions Hankins's and Duriez' volume within a quarter-century of reflection on Francis Schaeffer's thought and apologetics; see www.denverseminary.edu/news/francis-schaeffer-and-the-shaping-of-evangelical-america-and-francis-schaeffer-an-authentic-life.

16. Frank Schaeffer, *Crazy for God*, 138.

17. E-mails from three individuals who were very much insiders at L'Abri confirm the presence of exaggeration in her telling of the L'Abri story.

18. Duriez, *Francis Schaeffer*, 36. Frank Schaeffer, *Crazy for God* (42–43), also refers to his mother's idealism.

19. Schaeffer, *Crazy for God*, 51, 80, 211.

20. Frank Schaeffer (ibid., 122) refers to another aspect of L'Abri subject to exaggeration, the "life by faith" that supposedly involved only praying to God and trusting him for finances. He explains how this actually worked out and how the needs of L'Abri were, in fact, very well and clearly communicated to potential supporters.

21. Duriez, *Francis Schaeffer*, 218.

22. Hankins, *Francis Schaeffer*, iv.

23. Barry Hankins, "'I'm Just Making a Point': Francis Schaeffer and the Irony of Faithful Christian Scholarship," *Fides et Historia* 39, no. 1 (2007): 24, 34.

24. Frank Schaeffer, PBS interview.

25. Paul Hiebert, *Transforming Worldviews: An Anthropological Understanding of How People Change* (Grand Rapids: Baker Academic, 2008), 258–60, 274–76.

26. Hankins, "'I'm Just Making a Point.'"

27. The creation of a hero might serve some short-term pragmatic purposes for a group, but what happens when the "followers" discover that the hero that has been created is to some extent a fraud? They might be driven to doubt their leader's opinion about other things, including his or her testimony about the things of God. In such a case, a false hero could interfere with or even block communication of the truly heroic story of a Father who sent his Son as a sacrifice for the sins of the world.

28. Schaeffer criticized pretentions that autonomous human reason had the ability to give complete definition to truth. In contrast to autonomous human reason, a Christian critical realist would see reason as useful, but in need of the support of (1) God through the ongoing and indwelling work of the Holy Spirit and (2) a local and worldwide body of other reasoning people in order to get closer and closer to full truth by careful and diligent work.

29. Hankins, *Francis Schaeffer*, 237.

30. Jenell Williams Paris, "A Pietist Perspective on Love and Learning in Cultural Anthropology," *Christian Scholar's Review* 35, no. 3 (2006): 380.

31. Frank Schaeffer, *Crazy for God*, 111.

32. Duriez, *Francis Schaeffer*, 142.

33. Included here is the idea that "our" particular splinter group has (finally) gotten a monopoly on the truth.

34. For my students in the former Soviet region, I use a slightly different analogy. In the era of industrially made mirrors, few of us see the kind of bad reflection Paul might have seen in looking at himself in a battered bronze shield. But dirty bus windows are an everyday experience in Eastern Europe, and trying to find a bus stop and an address through one of them is an experience that many have shared. Our knowledge, even of the mysteries of God that are revealed, is at best partial and incomplete.

14

Ethical Issues in Missionary Filmmaking: Cinematic Tropes of Power and Perspective

CURTIS A. WILKINSON

When we decide to watch a film we enter into a negotiation. Filmmakers vie for our "suspended disbelief" as we choose to accept or reject their created cinematic representations. No film could ever pretend to be a complete and true representation of its subject, but the mimetic nature of film does give it the quality of being truth-full. This "truth pursuit" is of special and critical concern to the nonfiction filmmaker. Nonfiction film uses codes and conventions which force the audience to consider the way it looks at the events and objects that pass before the camera: to see it, in a word, as signifying what it appears to record.[1] Critique and criticism of the codes and conventions used in nonfiction film emerge most prominently in scholarly discourse and debate surrounding the ethics of documentary film and ethnographic filmmaking. The literature of these two fields offers fertile ground for discussion of ethical issues in missionary filmmaking.[2]

SERVING JESUS WITH INTEGRITY

From its inception, film has been used to document the truth of daily life and cultures around the world. As early as 1895 August and Louis Lumière were making nonfiction films in France. The two brothers also trained several camera operators to travel the world to make films and give film showings.[3] In the third decade of the twentieth century, Robert Flaherty became the "father of documentary" through his collaborative filmmaking effort with the Inuit Kabloonak. Though *Nanook of the North*, released in 1922, became a box office success, it later came under attack for its use of staged events and reenactments.[4] Cinéma-vérité ("cinema of truth"), Kino-Pravda ("film truth"), observational cinema, direct cinema, and third/fourth cinemas dot the timeline of film history as filmmakers, anthropologists, and film theorists have proposed new philosophies for telling the truth through the medium of film.[5]

In various ways each of these nonfiction approaches to filmmaking has made a contribution, but overall they can be generalized as promoting two basic ethical principles. First, the pursuit of truth through nonfiction filmmaking should be done as objectively as possible and without bias. As Walter Goldschmidt suggests, ethnographic film is "film which endeavors to interpret the behavior of people of one culture to persons of another culture by using shots of people doing precisely what they would have been doing if the camera were not there."[6] Filmmakers must submit themselves to an intentional act of self-examination and scrutiny of the influences brought to the process. Self-reflexivity allows us to examine the motivations, blind spots, and misconceptions that influence the representations to be created. All films must pass through this detailed ethical review, which Bill Nichols refers to as "axiographics," pointing out that an indexical bond exists between the image and the ethics that governed its production.⁷

Second, the literature suggests that filmmakers need to allow the subjects of their films to participate in the creative process and to provide input into their own filmic representation. For filmmakers to grant their subjects access during the filmmaking process is a submissive act. Doing so allows an intertextual authorship to emerge and creates a world in which the filmmaker and the subject are less clearly separated and in which reciprocal observation and exchange increasingly matter.⁸ Developing a collaborative link and loyalty with the subject of a film can help filmmakers avoid some of the common ethical weaknesses found in missionary films.

Tropes of Power

The word "trope" is a literary term that denotes a recognized theme or motif. In cinematic tropes we come to understand the meaning of shots, compositions, and their juxtapositions through their repetition. These filmic conventions become second nature for our interpretation of film and many times they go by unnoticed. Several cinematic tropes frequently found in missionary filmmaking need to be deconstructed and exposed as conventions that convey a message of hegemony.

The first cinematic trope might be titled "enter the liberators." This shot sequence includes a series of images where the missionary leader and entourage arrive in the village with the necessary food, medicine, and supplies to rescue the native community. Often this sequence includes a shot of the high tech vehicle in which the missionaries arrive, especially if the door or side panel includes the name of the sponsoring organization. The scene presents a triumphant image and mimics cinematic portrayals of an army general arriving in a village after the fighting has ceased. Sadly, many of these photo opportunities are staged for the cameras. Ministry leaders are whisked in and out just long enough to capture the touching moment on film.

A second trope of power is the constant visual presence of "superior technology." Often this sequence visualizes the landing and unloading of an airplane or helicopter. At times it is represented by shots of heavy duty equipment easily doing a job that would take ten peasant farmers all day to accomplish. Any form of technology that drills a well, reroutes a river, immunizes cattle, or makes bricks is a visual feast for missionary filmmaking. Productivity through technology equals ministry success.

A third trope is the visualization of power through placement or positioning of people and through shot composition. Missionary leaders are placed up front, before the crowd, often with an interpreter by their side. They are shown passionately teaching or advising the local community. The shots tell us that they have come to impart knowledge, and we are convinced that the people are truly enjoying this opportunity to learn. This shot convention is most successful when four things are present: a missionary, a local, a ministry activity that the missionary is performing for the local's benefit, and in the background a full color banner or logo of the ministry.

These stereotyped images challenge us to reconsider the way we make filmic representations of ministry. How can filmmakers begin to visualize servanthood and submission? Do we film national leadership in up-front positions? Are they filmed in the roles they assume when the camera is not there? Do we posture outside visitors as "listeners" and "learners"?

Dramatic Simplification

A filmmaker was asked to produce a film promoting the ministry of a Christian radio station in a large city of Central America. When he arrived in town, he asked the taxi driver if he could listen to the local Christian radio station. The taxi driver smiled and quickly tuned to a Christian station. After a few minutes of listening, it was obvious to the filmmaker that the radio station did not belong to the mission organization he had come to work for. He asked the taxi driver if there was another Christian station. The taxi driver responded that there was and quickly tuned in the frequency. Again the station did not belong to the ministry he had come represent. Finally, after going through a half dozen Christian radio stations, the taxi driver switched the radio to the AM bandwidth and finally found the faint signal of a Christian radio station that sounded three decades out of date. That week a film was shot to promote that Christian radio station, and no mention was ever made regarding the realities of Christian radio in that Central American city.

Ethical acts of omission are hard to avoid in filmmaking. The dramatic thrust in a film is often heightened through a process of simplification, forcing a binary opposition between two characters or issues. Films by nature are distillations of time and space, and they often achieve greater dramatic effect if there is only one hero and one villain. Telling a mission organization's story loses its punch if you communicate to the audience that 100 other organizations are doing the same work in that city. Though most filmmakers will avoid overtly communicating a lie in their films, they do face ethical dilemmas centered around decisions of whether to omit details in order to simplify a story line for dramatic effect.

Exoticism

A minimal expectation for filmmakers drawn to the mission field and to cinematic representation of culture and customs is that they be conscientious and be clearly conscious of negative representations and stereotypes produced due to ignorance, racism, and prejudice. A greater temptation for missionary filmmaking is an aesthetic prone to producing representations marked by exoticism.[9] Filmmakers' and viewers' fascination with the context and subject of a film can take on a quality of consumption. The result can be compared to Gauguin's artistic treatment of the natives of Tahiti, creating a mythic portrayal of a non-existent reality. The participants of such films are exploited as they are objectified for the fascination of an outside audience.

Filmic stereotypes abound all over the globe. It is not long before these depictions become a bit comical. Binyavanga Wainana offers some tongue-in-cheek tips on how to write about Africa: "Never have a picture of a well-adjusted African on the cover of your book, or in it, unless that African has won the Nobel Prize. An AK-47, prominent ribs, naked breasts—use these. If you must include an African, make sure you get one in Masai or Zulu or Dogon dress."[10]

It is not hard to fall into exploiting a subject in this way. That is why collaborative filmmaking, which is dependent on trust, is essential as a first step to truthful filmmaking. Trust creates a safe place for the mutual exchange of ideas and information. Building trust represents a bridge to collaboration and an openness to express the story from the subject's perspective.

Voice and Agency

The concept of voice and agency represent issues of perspective and power both inside and outside the film. Who gets to speak in the film? Will it be narration delivered by a booming "voice of God" narrator? Who determines what we will see and hear? Who determines when we see and hear it? Assertion of control and agency is something that comes naturally for the Western filmmaker.

In missionary contexts around the world people find themselves with limited or no access to the "tools of discourse." To find oneself liberated from a "culture of silence" and to suddenly emerge as a thinker and producer of ideas is to be transformed.[11] As Paulo Freire suggests in *Pedagogy of the Oppressed*, one thereby ceases to be a subject that is acted upon, and instead becomes one who acts upon and transforms his world. In so doing one moves toward ever new possibilities of fuller and richer life individually and collectively.[12]

In collaborative filmmaking it is the outside voice that must surrender control. The assumption of inequity between the filmmaker and the "insider" with whom he wishes to collaborate must be subordinated. Listening and various exercises designed to produce film content must come only after initial trust has been established. Penny Woolcock, director of *Tina Goes Shopping* (1999) and *Tina Takes a Break* (2001), spent months interviewing the subjects of her films in pursuit of an accurate portrayal of life and reality in a Leeds housing estate. Collaboration suggests an alliance with the subject, assuring that the film will not exploit or misrepresent.

Ideologically, participatory filmmaking investigates the possibility of bringing the representation process directly to the personal level of the subject. It raises the question of self-reflection—how does one represent one's self and to whom? Many film theorists understand this question to be vitally important for the ontological understanding of self. Yet the outsider may find insiders to be puzzled about the value of such an exercise. Individualism and the high priority placed on the "self" are qualities prized in the West, but they are often criticized by the Two-Thirds World. This observation alone offers motivation enough for pursuing alternative, collaborative perspectives through film as articulated by the inside voice.

In an image-based society the image creator advances to the position of stakeholder. Recent films have focused on this fact, for example by placing the camera in the hands of marginalized children. Examples include *Born into Brothels* (dir. Briski and Kauffman, 2002), *The Wooden Camera* (dir. Ntshaveni Wa Luruli, 2003), and *Cidade de Deus / City of God* (dir. Meirelles, 2002). To be an image maker is to make a statement that says, "I am not blind to what is happening. I see the injustice, and I also see beauty. I will not be defined by your image of me, but by my own." These words are not the language of a victim, but of a protagonist. Paraphrasing Augusto Boal in *Theater of the Oppressed*: Why would anyone want to be a member of the chorus or a supporting actor when they can be the protagonist?[13]

Commodification of the Great Commission

A review of the content of many missionary films makes it apparent that a commodity is being vended. The underlying message is that if you truly want adventure, if you truly want to be at the center of God's will, if you really want a great life, it is time to sign up for missionary duty. According to the films it appears to be all about "you," and every mission organization can provide the country destination and time duration that fits you best. Videos demonstrate people "just like you" hugging street children, riding camels, and tasting local fare. Loyalties postured are clearly aligned with North American audiences and their needs. The local film subjects and their country and community merely serve as the context for your visit. It appears that language skills are not necessary, nor is it necessary to possess any real vocational skills. All the film requires of you is a willing heart.

The missions experience is commodified in film form in such a way that discerning consumers can easily determine where the most attractive experiences are to be obtained. The prevalent film style is that of VH1, MTV, and the music video. These missionary films adopt the four major characteristics of the music video: elevation of the importance of "feeling states," downgrading of any formal use of plot, use of disjunctive editing to obliterate time and space, and creation of self-reflexive dream states.[14] The idea is to get the overall vibe of the missionary experience as opposed to asking the film to provide hard data and solid content able to inform intelligent decisions.

Conclusion

Missionary filmmaking represents a philosophy of film production that merits ongoing investigation. In reality, its further development will come only through experimentation, fieldwork, and actual film projects. The pursuit of self-reflection and collaboration demonstrates an ideology that values the dignity and perspective of the subject, and the introspection necessary to expose the biases that often go unnoticed by North American audiences. Learning to listen to the people we represent through film allows missionary filmmakers to put Philippians 2 into practice as we carry out our craft. It is motivated by the ethical assumption that although wealth may reside with the filmmaker, the truth is not similarly owned. Filmmakers can posture themselves as the eager pupils of the "insider" voices they seek to represent with accuracy, and in doing so they can find who really knows what needs to be conveyed on film.

An intentional manifesto for ethical missionary filmmaking is much needed today. In reality, filmmaking is costly and time consuming. Most often those who make films do not have the budget or permission to spend the time with their subjects that would be necessary to represent them well. On paper, idealism runs high, but there are ways to promote these ideals and they merit consideration and implementation. To that end, here are some suggested best practice principles to be considered for ethical missionary filmmaking:

- Conventions and production styles never force a false or disingenuous reading. Missionary filmmaking is to be implemented utilizing a cautious aesthetic that pursues truthful representations objectively.
- Filmmakers expose personal biases and agendas to a process of self-reflection. "Outside" voices understand the importance of listening to their inside collaborators and value the listening process as an exercise in self-reflection in pursuit of a better film.
- Local participants, customs, and celebrations are not represented for mere audience interest and entertainment. Filmmaking adopts a philosophy that resists creative choices that exoticize the subject.
- Subjects are allowed access to the process of creating their filmic representation. Images and representations are the

products of collaborative preplanning, filming, and edit room evaluation. There is a commitment to rethinking and reshooting these representations after discussion and evaluation.
- Participants develop a confident voice spoken to an audience that listens. Central to the motivation behind collaborative filmmaking is facilitating the growth and development of an independent voice.

Taking a collaborative approach to missionary filmmaking may seem naive and idealistic to some, but the accusation does not weigh heavily enough to justify abandoning the effort. As Lucien Taylor observes of David MacDougall's work and writing, "what becomes incontrovertibly true ... is that if [filmmaking] is not, in the end, participatory and self-reflective, then it is not human."[15] Few would argue against the value of such an endeavor; perhaps the greater challenge lies in undertaking the research and developing the methodology that would actually bring about truly collaborative missionary filmmaking.

Notes

1. Dai Vaughan, *For Documentary: Twelve Essays* (Berkeley and Los Angeles: Univ. of California Press, 1999), 84–85.
2. "Missionary filmmaking" includes many styles and genres, including indigenous-based narrative fiction. For the purposes of this chapter, it is limited to the "pray, give, go" application used by mission organizations to increase prayer support, raise funds, and recruit new missionaries.
3. See Erik Barnouw, "Prophet," *Documentary: A History of the Non-fiction Film* (New York: Oxford Univ. Press, 1993), 3–30.
4. See Barnouw, "Explorer," *Documentary*, 33–48.

5. For discussion of these terms, see Susan Hayward, *Cinema Studies: The Key Concepts* (New York: Routledge, 2006).
6. Walter Goldschmidt, "Ethnographic Film: Definition and Exegesis," *PIEF Newsletter* 3, no. 2 (1972):1.
7. Bill Nichols, *Representing Reality: Issues and Concepts in Documentary* (Bloomington and Indianapolis: Indiana Univ. Press, 1991), 77.
8. David MacDougall, *Transcultural Cinema* (Princeton: Princeton Univ. Press, 1998), 38.
9. Ella Shohat and Robert Stam, *Unthinking Eurocentrism: Multiculturalism and the Media* (New York: Routledge, 1994), 21.
10. Binyavanga Wainana, "How (Not) to Write About Africa," *Developments* 34 (2006):30; available at www.developments.org.uk/articles/how-not-to-write-about-africa.
11. Hayward, *Cinema Studies*, 215.
12. Paulo Freire, *Pedagogy of the Oppressed* (New York: Continuum, 1989), 12.
13. Augusto Boal, *Theater of the Oppressed* (London: Pluto Press, 1979), xiv.
14. Ken Dancyger, *The Technique of Film and Video Editing: History, Theory, Practice* (Oxford: Focal Press, 2002), 187–90.
15. Lucien Taylor, "Introduction," in MacDougall, *Transcultural Cinema*, 3.

15

The Missionary and the Camera: Developing an Ethic for Contemporary Missionary Photographers

GABRIEL B. TAIT

Missionaries were early adopters of the camera. They quickly recognized the potential photography offered for communicating with home constituencies. By means of photographs they could introduce the people with whom they worked in remote corners of the world and do so with an immediacy that went beyond words printed on a page. Today the study of missionary photography is a useful tool for missiologists who wish to peer more deeply into missionary motivations and attitudes. Photographic records (mostly prints and postcards) are spectral ships that transport viewers to colorful times, places, and peoples. They extend our vision, but simultaneously they direct, limit, and fix our view. We see the world and life as viewed by the photographer through the camera's lens. Rarely can we speak with confidence about things beyond the camera's field of vision or activities that were going on outside the borders of the scene captured on film. We see what the photographer decided we should see. The picture shows us what the photographer thought would be important for us to see or thought we ought to be shown or considered acceptable for us to view or simply thought would interest us.

Visual anthropologist John Collier (1961, 1) rightly reminds us that "the camera is not ... a cure-all for our visual limitations, but ... an extension of our perception." Therefore, photographs are not neutral, because the choices that the photographer makes flow from his or her culture and from who the photographer is as a person. Beyond the question, "What is a photograph?" the issue of perception raises important missiological questions. What values and perceptions are revealed that affect missionary photographers' representations of culture and communities? To what extent do photographs perpetuate biases behind the camera? Should we promote a code of ethics for missionary photographers? If taken seriously, these questions can reshape the way Christian photographers see and represent the people they photograph. But before I present a suggested code of ethics for missionary photography, I want to focus the issues involved by relating an incident in which I was involved as a member of a mission team.

Recording a Missional Encounter

As the team of eleven marched through the thigh-high grass, minutes away from their Wednesday evening church service, sounds in the distance caught their attention. It was not music from the newly constructed church in Nijro, Tanzania, that our short-term mission team had finished working on hours earlier. Nor were the sounds coming from the multitude of chickens, goats, or cattle freely walking around the affluent suburban community, about six miles from the city center of Arusha. As the muffled sounds grew louder and louder, the team became concerned, but they continued to move toward the church. What were the sounds? Where were they coming from? As they walked on, clearing the brush and ducking the thorns, the leader of the pack, Laura, nearly stumbled over a child, one of four children crying in the grassy field. The children were sitting in front of a one-room shanty, their faces soiled, their hair disheveled, and two of them, twins, were wearing only shirts and rags for diapers. The oldest sat calmly eating a sugarcane stalk. He watched us as we looked for their parents. He was only about four years old. Our interpreter asked the young boy, "Where is your mother? Where is your father?" The child did not answer. This story and many others like it play out in many communities around the world each day. Children are left unattended while the parent or parents are away. The thought came to my mind that if the adage is true that "it takes a village to raise a child," what is the big deal?

Viewing these seemingly abandoned children through my camera lens, I realized that I had several ethical decisions to make. How should I record this moment? Should I photograph them as they were, in their natural context, keeping in mind what others might think? Do I embellish the image by asking the children to stand in places or to do things they would not normally do? Do I use the photographs? Do I ask God for his direction? Or do I make images that represent others in the image of God? How could I maintain the dignity of the little children, while also representing their culture? What would the implications be if I published the photos? Many more questions can be asked when we are taking photographs of others. Ultimately, it is important to ask ourselves: Ethically, where does the line fall for us between representation and exploitation? Additionally, we must weigh the value of the image against our Christian convictions. Will the image injure others?

Questions to Ask

Visual anthropologist Karl Heider (2004, 426) reminds us that "'taking photographs,' 'shooting film,' ... are not totally inadvertent metaphors for a process that raises daunting ethical issues." Photographs are a powerful form of visual communication that "simulates both intellectual and emotional responses—they make us think as well as feel" (Lester 2006, 65). Perhaps their power to engage us is one reason why we are so vested in the images we view and take.

Each time we pick up our cameras, whether a trusty SLR (35mm camera) or a video camera, we consciously and unconsciously make decisions. We may ask such questions as "What are we going to show?" "How are we going to [re] present it?" "Who is our intended audience?" and "Why should the audience care about this particular subject matter?"

Henri Cartier-Bresson (1979, 11–24), who is considered the father of modern photojournalism, would say these questions begin the process of photographing "the decisive moment." In capturing this decisive moment the photographer seeks to record on film the most significant interaction or representation or emotional moment of an event or tableau so as to inform viewers and have the maximum impact. It is important to note that this decisive moment will vary from photographer to photographer, depending on the photographer's aesthetic and ethics. These points must be considered if we are going to use our cameras effectively to tell the stories of the communities we visit and serve.

The same was true for photographers in the past. They, too, had to make critical ethical decisions on how to photograph others and what to show about the distant cultures with which they came in contact. Whether professional or amateur, the photographer's images bid for the viewers' attention in the hope of transporting them to another place and time. Christraud Geary suggests: "As a method of recording their time in the 'exotic' fields of Africa, many missionaries made photographs and published images [that] are deliberate constructions of the missionary experiences along the lines of a pervasive narrative and a one-dimensional ideological representation of the other, which permeated the colonial discourse"(Geary 1991, 50). We must ask: Do we do the same with our images today?

Looking Back

We can learn much by looking back at missionary photographs from 75 and 100 years ago that will be helpful to us as we seek to construct a code of ethics for missionary photography today. Specifically, we find our attention called first to the personal and cultural perceptions and intentions that the photographers brought to the act of taking photographs. Second we can note the photographers' diligent attention to the skills and techniques of the craft of photography as they composed scenes for photographic representation. But, third, we can examine what ingredients are present when photographs "work," when they show mutuality, relationship, honor, and respect for God's intention that people should show forth his image.

Beginning with the first of these, not surprisingly people construct their understandings of new encounters based on their past experiences. In traveling from Europe and the United States to Africa during the middle of the nineteenth century, many missionaries' perceptions of what they saw were largely shaped by their past and the historical information they studied. They were also influenced by the outlook of their mission agencies. Although nineteenth-century missionaries sought to spread the Gospel of God's love, their photographs often betray an unbiblical equating of evangelizing with "civilizing." Nicholas Thomas (1994, 126) observes, "One of the central features of this propaganda was the narrative of conversion, which contrasted former savagery with a subsequently elevated and purified Christian state."

Historically a perception existed that people on the continent of Africa were "heathens" and "savages" and needed to be civilized (Tiénou 1991, 297; Johnson and Seton 2002). Furthermore, many missionaries' understanding of culture was imbued with the ideas that Africa was a "dark" land, with "dark" people, who had "dark" thoughts about religion. Missionaries were thus obligated, and enthusiastic, to be bearers of needed light. An example of the attitude is found in Methodist author-photographer Frank Deaville Walker's 1911 book, *Call of the Dark Continent* (31): "The picture of early life in South Africa would be dark indeed were it not relieved by the presence of Christian missionaries, who championed the cause of the natives. Some of these ambassadors of the Gospel wandered far in their efforts to make Christ known to the heathen." This focus on the poor Africans and their need to be reached by dominant culture missionaries from the West (i.e., white Americans and Europeans) was a common theme in missions, and it clearly shows through in the photographs they took and staged. Thus, who the missionaries were and the cultural assumptions they carried with them because of who they were made a difference in the photographs they produced.

15—*Gabriel B. Tait*

These issues can be conveniently examined utilizing the International Mission Photography Archive, a searchable online database that provides ready access to a sizable body of early missionary photographs (http://digitallibrary.usc.edu/impa/controller/index.htm). In it one can find the two photographs discussed below as well as many other photographic representations of cultural—and possibly personal as well—assumptions about power, position, privilege, and prerogatives.

In the first image, four unidentified indigenous women carry missionary Aagot Kjeldseth of the Norwegian Missionary Society in a filanjana to church. The women are believed to be her students at the Antsahamanitra Girls' School, but this information is not known for certain. It appears that they are walking through a garden that was planted at the school. Kjeldseth is dressed in all white and carries an umbrella to keep off the sun. Four of the six students accompanying Kjeldseth wear "Western style" hats. All of the women are dressed in what can be noted as Western clothes. Kjeldseth is wearing shoes but the indigenous women are not. We can appreciate the aesthetic value of the image. It is properly composed from the photographer's point of view, but something appears jarringly out of order. The photo portrays a person who has servants, apparently students from her school. The servants are carrying the leader. What message does this send if we are seeking to develop leaders and break down hierarchical structures of privilege? Barring a physical ailment, this image appears to be contrary to God's word. Jesus reminds his leaders to embrace the posture of a servant, teaching that "whoever wants to become great among you must be your servant, and whoever wants to be first must be slave of all" (Mark 10:42–45 NIV).

Aagot Kjeldseth rides a filanjana (palanquin) on her way to church, Antananarivo, Madagascar, ca.1896.

On the mission field converts were expected to go through a transformation process. In the second photograph we see an example of transformation—and conformity—made visible. The photograph comes from the senior secondary school at Wesley College, Ibadan, approximately eighty miles inland from the coastal city of Lagos. The school aimed to train students in literacy, safety projects, disaster relief, and fish-farming in rural areas (Nigeria 2003). This formal group portrait of a missionary with scouts in uniforms presents the Western ideal of organization and discipline. Aesthetically, the image is well composed, and it highlights the level of discipline. As with many colonial photographs, differences are evident, especially surrounding the subjects' clothing and the power distance. The missionary is the leader of the pack, dressed in white Western priestly regalia. This look often symbolizes purity. He is sitting front and center and is wearing shoes. The Boy Scout students are dressed also in Western-style uniforms, which feature their green short-sleeved jumpers and khaki shorts with beret and group scarf. Interestingly enough, they are not wearing shoes. What outlook does this image project? For whom is this image intended? These are questions that we must address in regard to our own photographs as well.

Formal group portrait of missionary with scouts in uniforms, Nigeria, 1929.

Craft and Aesthetics

If two people look at a photograph, one will be likely to see elements another does not. In part this is due to the fact that, as Jay Ruby (1976, 5) rightly says, photographs can be seen as both a "record of reality" and "aesthetic objects." Each photograph captures a moment in time that cannot be duplicated and each has an element of beauty or aesthetic quality inherent to it. The "twin" or even multiple character of photographs means that once the photographer releases the picture, she or he also releases control over its interpretation.

Artistic control shows up possibly most strongly at the point of a photograph's composition, before the shutter is snapped. To obtain a properly composed photograph the photographer takes into consideration many issues such as where a person is positioned in the frame, the angle at which the photograph is taken, the balance of the photograph, how space is divided, the direction of line(s), and the overall design quality and visual strength of the photograph. Composition and framing are important because they give structure to the image that results. With respect to image composition Terrance Wright (2004, 55–56) observes that "Everything within the broad range of the camera's format, from foreground to far distance, as long as it is in the camera's line of sight, will appear in the photograph. As the photograph changes position the alignment between close, near and distant objects changes, creating different picture effects in the images." Therefore, to obtain a striking or particularly illuminating image requires forethought as well as technical proficiency.

Photographic proficiency involves intentionally expanding one's knowledge and experience with regard to lighting and the properties of light, cameras and lenses, shutter and film speeds and their digital equivalents, depth of field, and many other facets of the craft of photography. The missionary photographer, as distinct from the missionary snapshot taker, has an obligation to keep abreast of developments in the field and to continue honing her or his photographic skills.

Finally, people must be instructed on ways to interpret photographs that can enlarge their understanding of what they see. One step that can be taken is to find images that highlight positive relationships between missionaries and those missionized. These

15—Gabriel B. Tait

images can be used as models for budding missionary photographers; they can also be used to guide viewers of missionary photography toward more informed and generous readings of missonary photograpic images. Space does not allow us to expand upon this topic, but the interpretation of images falls within the field of ethical concern for missionary photographers.

Ethics for Missionary Photography

I first touched a camera as a budding photographer in the mid-1980s. Since those days the issue of photo ethics has arrested me, figuratively and literally—for I have been arrested twice while working as a photojournalist for two of this nation's top newspapers. In each case, both editors and attorneys highlighted the personal and professional photo ethics that were shown during the ordeals. Photo ethics prevailed. The charges were dropped and expunged from my record.

Ethics is often a set of peer-developed rules gleaned from particularly challenging experiences. Those who have the opportunity to participate in a community engaged in ethical reflection find it encouraging to watch the way professionals think through issues of concern in their vocation. This process aids participants in developing appropriate responses to issues of crisis and in governing themselves accordingly. Tom Wheeler (2002, 70) provides a comprehensive description: "Ethics presupposes a human being's awareness of right and wrong, and evaluates human conduct as reflective of moral values. More specifically, ethics refers to a discipline, theory, or other system that seeks to provide moral guidelines by integrating or balancing personal values with institutional or community obligations."

John Willigen, in *Applied Anthropology* (2002, 59–60), highlights a code of ethics for the field of anthropology. His code is not meant to serve as a comprehensive list of specific ethical guidelines for researchers or practitioners, but it does offer a framework for further discussion. Willigen asserts that professional anthropologists need to maintain a high ethical standard in their work, presenting six areas that a statement on professional ethical responsibility must cover. Below we will adapt his list to create a missionary photography ethic.

- As researchers, we owe full disclosure and confidentiality to our subjects.
- As researchers, we owe the utmost integrity and dignity to our subjects.
- As researchers, we should not prejudice communities for personal gain.
- As researchers, we will remain up-to-date in our skills.
- As researchers, we will make every effort to prevent distortion.
- As researchers, we will make every effort to communicate with the public and provide useful information that will influence their lives.

In the field of visual anthropology, Karl Heider (2004), John Collier (1961), Jay Ruby (1981), and others have championed the need for a strong visual ethics, albeit focused largely on film. Heider devotes an appendix in *Seeing Anthropology: Cultural Anthropology Through Film* (2004, 28–34) to the American Anthropological Association's code of ethics, which he adopts. Photojournalism itself has a strict code of ethics which is highlighted in the work of Paul Martin Lester (2006; see also Lester and Ross 2003). Missionary photography, however, appears to lack a formal statement of ethics.

Having said that, is a separate code of ethics for missionary photography necessary? Why can missionary photographers not just adopt the anthropologists' ethical code? Apart from the need, touched on above, for practitioners of a discipline or craft to develop codes of ethics that address issues specific to their work and circumstances, the answer is quite simply that the Bible expects even more of Christ's followers. As the apostle Paul says, we must go beyond looking at people from a human point of view to seeing them from God's point of view (2 Cor. 5:16). In that spirit, here are six points of reflection for an ethics of missionary photography.

As missionary photographers we will view those we photograph as created in the image of God (Gen. 1:27).

Genesis provides the foundation for humankind. Humanity—in its diversity of ethnicities, languages, cultures, rituals, and so forth—was created and blessed for God's purposes. If the notion of *imago Dei* is taken seriously, we see God's instruction to rule over creatures of the sea and fields, but not over one another by exploitation, even exploitation with a camera. If we are unable to appreciate the uniqueness of God's creation, we need not engage in photographing that subject. Authentic relationship acts to break down cultural and ideological differences.

As missionary photographers we seek to understand the culture and gain the subjects' consent before taking photographs. This includes gathering detailed field notes and information for photograph captions.

Can you imagine a person walking into your house without being invited, taking a seat in your favorite chair, and then leaving without acknowledging you as host? But do not missionary photographers too often act in an analogous manner? Are they careful to show regard for others when they enter their culture and community? Developing an understanding of a society's culture and customs and of the community order are good first steps in gaining access and finding a welcome there. We can accomplish this by asking questions and seeking to learn about the community. Who are the leaders? What are their social structures? How does the kinship system function? Are they materialistic, paternalistic, and so on? The missionary photographer should seek to locate one or more informants who will assist him or her in understanding the culture and its structures.

As missionary photographers we will appreciate the privilege of being a part of the community we are photographing (Gen. 23:1–20).
     When God promised the land for his nation (Gen 12:1–3, 15:7), Abraham did not acquire it by conquering the inhabitants. Instead, he stood alongside his allies in war (Gen. 14), and they offered him some land (Gen. 23:5–6). Likewise, we must appreciate being in diverse and unfamiliar communities. When we come as learners, God can reveal a great deal about those we are observing and about ourselves.

As missionary photographers we understand we are not paparazzi. Neither we as photographers nor mission agencies will be allowed to exploit our photographs of subjects. If the photographer cannot show the photograph to the indigenous community for their approval, it should not be used.

15—*Gabriel B. Tait*

In the narrative of David and Mephibosheth, David asks, "Is there anyone still left of the house of Saul to whom I can show kindness for Jonathan's sake?" (2 Sam. 9:1 NIV). As we enter into various cultures near and far, let us seek ways to honor the community. As participant observers, we should appreciate the fact that we are guests and that the community makes sacrifices in allowing us into their contexts.

As missionary photographers we will not manipulate our photographs.

Given current technological advances in processing of photographs, we will not alter photographs for personal gain either, for example, by adding clothing or by disfiguring the indigenous people to make them appear more "exotic" or "worse." During a recent conversation a former missionary to northern Kenya admitted that one of his photographs was manipulated to add a top to cover the breast of a Kenyan woman. He altered the photograph because he thought the sponsoring mission organization would not approve of a picture with a woman's breast exposed and that the original image would not have been permitted to be printed in the missionary's newsletter. If the missionary photographer cannot allow supporters to go along on the journey, then the photo should not be submitted.

As missionary photographers we will allow the love of Christ to define relationships and our representation of others.

This point should seem obvious for Christ's followers.

Solving the Riddle

We can now go back to the story of the children in the field. As I have shared this story with people around the world, I have often been asked what happened to the family. Did you take the photographs? How did you use them?

In the end the result was that half of the team continued on their way to the church, while the other half stayed with our interpreter and me. We went to the local *duka* or community store and purchased beans, bread, rice, and water. Then we contacted the neighbors, hoping to find the parents, but were unsuccessful. After we prayed with the children, read the Bible in their language, treated the thorns in their feet, gave them water, and fed them bread and beans, the mother returned. She had been away nearly four hours getting her hair braided. The mother had carried the youngest child, who was still nursing, with her.

Laura holds one child as short-term mission team members attempt to calm the other children.

The mother's return solved our ethical dilemma. We used the photographs in our newsletter but only after receiving the mother's permission. As we as missionary photographers consider appropriate ways to photograph others, we must always have the Golden Rule in mind, "Do to others what you would have them do to you" (Matt. 7:12 NIV).

Colonialism in Africa (and on other continents) had a long history and its effects are real. They are real both from the former colonizers' position as well as from the perspective of the oppressed. When we fervently consider how we represent others through the lens of a camera, we open up a wonderful opportunity for dialogue and for our appreciation of the communities we serve. In missions we have a distinct responsibility to consider the effects our photographs will have, for they represent others as well as ourselves.

Conclusion

As we have seen in this chapter, a "colonial gaze" was etched upon the representations, including missionary representations, that came out of Africa. As missionary photographers today, we have the weighty responsibility and eminent privilege of entering into people's lives with a camera. But we must also accept responsibility for people's interpretation of the photographs and ask how our images will be interpreted when we are not around. The camera is an extension of our perceptions. If our perceptions are shaped by and filled with respect for the local community, then our images will resemble the fullness that the culture has to offer.

Questions for Discussion

1. What is photography's role in missions?
2. Is there a need to safeguard cultures? Who gets to participate?
3. What are important first steps in developing a code of ethics for mission photography?
4. Who gets to participate in the process of developing a code of ethics?
5. How might our efforts to develop a code of ethics for mission photography serve to advance missions?

Photographic Sources

Aagot Kjeldseth rides a filanjana (palanquin) on her way to church, Antananarivo, Madagascar, ca.1896. Everybody in the picture seems to be dressed up. The garden may be at Antsahamanitra Girls' School. The wall in the background is very typical and made of dark red soil. Aagot Kjeldseth was a missionary in Madagascar, 1896–1907. She was a teacher at Antsahamanitra Girls' School, 1896–1898. In 1898 she married Thomas Joergensen, 1874–1957. Antsahamanitra Girls' School was established in 1872 by Johanna Borchgrevink, 1836–1924, and led by her until 1912. Hundreds of Malagasy girls were taken care of and given education during this long period. Source: Mission Archives, School of Mission and Theology, Stavanger, Norway. Collection: A-1079 Jørgensen, Aagot and Thomas. Used with permission.

Group portrait of missionary with scouts, Nigeria, 1929. Formal group portrait of missionary with scouts in uniforms. Methodist missionary work in West Africa had begun in 1811 with Coke's mission to Sierra Leone. A second station was opened on the River Gambia in 1821 and on the Gold Coast in 1834. Source: (Wesleyan) Methodist Missionary Society collection, School of

Oriental and African Studies, University of London. Used with permission of the Methodist Publishing House.

Mission team tends to children in Nijro, Tanzania, July 2007. (Gabriel B. Tait; © Mission with Visions)

References

Cartier-Bresson, Henri. 1979. Introduction to *The Decisive Moment.* In *The camera viewed*, vol. 2, *Photography after World War II*, ed. Peninah R. Petruck, 11–24. New York: Dutton.

Collier, John, Jr. 1961. *Visual anthropology: Photography as a research method.* San Francisco: Holt, Rinehart, and Winston.

Geary, Christraud M. 1991. Missionary photography: Private and public readings. *African Arts* 24 (2): 48–100.

Heider, Karl G. 2004. *Seeing anthropology: Cultural anthropology through film.* Boston: Allyn & Bacon.

Johnson, Samantha, and Rosemary Seton. 2002. 'Fields of vision': Photographs in the missionary collections at the School of Oriental and African Studies, London. *International Bulletin of Missionary Research* 26 (4): 164–68.

Lester, Paul Martin. 2006. *Visual communication: Images with messages.* 4th. ed. Belmont, Calif.: Thomson Wadsworth.

Lester, Paul Martin, and Susan Dente Ross. 2003. *Images that injure: Pictorial stereotypes in the media.* 2nd. ed. Westport, Conn.: Praeger.

Ruby, Jay. 1981. Seeing through pictures: The anthropology of photography. *Camera Lucida* 3:19–32; available at http://astro.temple.edu/~ruby/ruby/seethru.html.

Scouting facts: Nigeria. 2003. www.scoutbase.org.uk/library/hqdocs/facts/pdfs/fs260056.pdf.

Thomas, Nicholas. 1994. *Colonialism's culture: Anthropology, travel, and government.* Princeton, N.J.: Princeton Univ. Press.

Tiénou, Tite. 1991. Invention of the "Primitive" and stereotypes in mission. *Missiology* 19 (3): 295–303.

Walker, Frank D. 1911. *The call of the dark continent: A study in missionary progress, opportunity, and urgency.* London: Wesleyan Methodist Missionary Society.

Wheeler, Tom. 2002. *Phototruth or photofiction? Ethics and media imagery in the digital age.* Mahwah, N.J.: Lawrence Erlbaum Associates.

Van Willigen, John. 2002. *Applied anthropology.* 3rd. ed. Westport, Conn.: Bergin & Garvey.

Wright, Terence. 2004. *The photography handbook.* 2nd. ed. London: Routledge.

Part VI:

Integrity Through Intentional Accountability

16

Holding Missionaries Accountable: A Proposed Code of Ethics for Missionaries Based Upon the Code of Ethics of the American Anthropological Association

DOUGLAS HAYWARD AND

PAUL E. LANGENWALTER II

Missionaries and anthropologists have much in common. Both are interested in people and usually work across cultural, subcultural, or ethnic boundaries. They carry with them a desire to help those peoples with whom they work that includes many forms of assistance. Indeed, both missionaries and anthropologists often develop deep bonds of loyalty to and concern for the well-being of the people with whom they work and study. During the twentieth century this relationship was drawn closer by the growing recognition of the value of anthropology and has only increased as more evangelicals have become professionally trained anthropologists (see esp. Whiteman 2008). The close association of anthropology and missions is reflected in a story once told about an African president who wanted to celebrate his country's emergence from colonial authority by commissioning a statue of a larger-than-life Black man breaking the bonds of his slavery. At his feet are three fearful men fleeing for their lives. One is a colonial officer with a copy of his tax records, another is a missionary with his Bible, and the third is an anthropologist fleeing with his notes on African leadership styles.

Still there is a divergence of perspectives between missiologists and anthropologists in purpose. Anthropologists focus on the study of culture to explore and understand it as a dynamic process that is integrated into a broad range of social and natural settings. In the majority of their research projects their work does not include attempts to transform the cultures of those they study. In fact, they often seek to preserve traditional cultures and to protect them from outside intrusions and change. On the other hand, missionaries always seek to transform culture through the introduction of Christ and a Christian worldview to different people groups. Such is the nature of the Great Commission. This fundamental difference in goals, along with differences in perspective, personalities, and beliefs, has resulted in ambivalence and often rejection by the members of both groups, one of the other. Still, the histories and activities of the two groups have close parallels. This chapter explores a beneficial facet of the professional activities of both groups, namely, the way in which ethics are articulated into the activities of the two groups. The groups' differences in articulation follow from historically separate responses to political and moral binds that simultaneously confronted both groups in the mid-twentieth century and have resulted in distinctive approaches between modern missions and anthropological activity.

In spite of their differences the two disciplines share a common core of concern for adherence to a high ethical standard. Codes of ethics, however, can take a number of forms. They range from statements of general principles imbuing the beliefs of an organization to quite specific definitions of ethical conduct. In addition, they may include procedures for grievance, redress, and discipline. Organizational statements on ethics may be designed to address a narrow topic, such as personal conduct, or they may attempt to provide a comprehensive statement that encompasses the entire range of activities in which the organization is involved. Most organizations within the mission field gravitate toward the general, basing their discussions on institutionally adopted articles of faith and Scripture. Anthropologists tend to be more specific, including procedures for grievance and discipline in the same or parallel documents. Our concern is twofold: how are ethical concepts expressed and how accessible are they to interested parties? Concise expressions of ethical conduct juxtaposed with statements of grievance and disciplinary processes make it easier to identify and guard against potential abuses. Accessibility lends power to ethical codes by providing transparency and making it easier to determine accountability and effect correction.

Background

The need for such codes of ethics arose early during the colonial era, particularly during the nineteenth and twentieth centuries when missionaries and anthropologists often had cozy relationships with the governments of their home countries and with colonial administrators. Each readily called upon the other for support in their work and shared their work with their governments. Missionaries eagerly sought the support of colonial authorities against recalcitrant village leaders or to persuade the authorities to pass and enforce laws intended to end practices that they opposed. Anthropologists likewise sought the support of governments in order to gain access to particular people groups and willingly shared their studies with administrators in an attempt to promote more orderly and humane treatment of indigenous peoples. In fact, in the final years of the colonial era, Ruth Benedict, under contract by the U.S. government, did a study of Japanese culture in order to provide the War Department with a better understanding of the Japanese people as a militaristic and hostile enemy. E. E. Evans-Pritchard even went so far as to join the British army during World War II in order to lead a band of irregular troops in North Africa to fight the Italians. It was during this period that he wrote his ethnography on the Sanusi.

With the collapse of colonialism following World War II, Western governments resorted to new stratagems for using missionaries and anthropologists. One such strategy was that of sending spies into an area under the cover of doing research as anthropologists or as ministers and missionaries. In other instances anthropologists and missionaries have been called upon by their governments to provide vital information regarding politically unstable regions. For instance, during the height of the Cold War a well-known mission agency with the IFMA would allow CIA agents to come to its mission headquarters to interview furloughing missionaries upon their return from politically vulnerable countries. While there is credible evidence that missionaries and governments have sometimes worked together in such secret collaborations, it has also been very evident that some missionary agencies have openly collaborated with the government of the countries in which they work in order to promote what they believe to be the well-being of the people living there. Perhaps one of the most obvious examples of this is the friendly relationship between Cameron Townsend (SIL/Wycliffe) with the Mexican government, and the continuing policy of SIL to work with local governments and educational administrators on behalf of the people of the nation. Indeed, SIL has been (falsely) accused of not only having an open and friendly relationship with national governments, but also of engaging in hidden CIA and international business connections with more sinister implications.

Likewise, anthropologists such as T. E. Lawrence have functioned in duplicitous roles, gathering data for the government or one of its many agencies. Some anthropologists were even more blatant in their governmental roles, as was the case of F. E. Williams in Papua, who served the colonial administration as a government-paid anthropologist. Indeed, many anthropologists have agreed to work openly and willingly with the government to prepare studies that would not only ensure the success of a project but would also advocate for the Western perception of what they concluded was the well-being of the people.

During the recent and ongoing Iraq war, the military discussed having "embedded" anthropologists serve with the troops in order to guide military action and decision making. Likewise, no USAID project is supposed to be funded and approved without a cultural impact study done by a qualified anthropologist showing how the project will influence the people of the target area. In a similar vein, anthropologists are called upon in carrying out federal and state laws which require that the discovery of human remains, and often religious artifacts, found to be of Native American origin be reported to the appropriate Native American descendants. Although often inconsistently enforced, similar laws and similar calls upon anthropologists are the convention in Western nations.

Steps Taken by Anthropologists

Over the years, then, the work of anthropologists and missionaries has been a subject of concern. Whether their work was in active collaboration with government, was simply used by government and large multinational corporations, or was promulgated by religious zeal, the outcomes have often been judged to be detrimental to the well-being of target communities or have been challenged by human rights advocates. Charges have been leveled that former and current practices have compromised the ability of future scholars, researchers, or missionaries to engage in legitimate work. In a vigorous attempt to address these criticisms, the American Anthropological Association (AAA) has formulated a very explicit set of guidelines to serve as a code of ethics for AAA members who engage in research. During the past several years AAA annual meetings have included multiple symposia exploring the ethics of such activities by its membership. Codes of ethics are common among scientific societies, particularly those in the social sciences. A survey of thirty-four international, national, and regional anthropological societies (table 1) revealed that all but one had published codes of ethics readily accessible to their membership and all interested parties (posted on Web sites). Numerous regional societies and smaller agencies have similar codes or subscribe to the codes of larger umbrella agencies. Even the American Association of Petroleum Geologists has a code that defines ethical conduct between peers, between scientist and client, and in the use of information developed in professional research. These codes provide a mechanism for clarifying and articulating domains of ethical conduct in the profession, including at the individual, group, and institutional levels. They are a ready resource covering professional conduct in specific contexts and can aid all parties in identifying misconduct when it occurs.

Hallmarks of anthropological codes of ethics include consideration of responsibilities to the public, to colleagues, to clients, to persons and groups being studied, and to the use and conservation of information (Society for American Archaeology 1996). The emergence of the concept of stakeholders in anthropology clarifies the set of individuals, groups, peoples, and organizations that should be viewed. Originally the term was applied in the business community to identify individuals, groups, and organizations that could affect the actions of an organization, or could be affected by those actions, because of a direct or indirect association with the activities of the organization (Freeman and Reed 1983). The term has come to be applied in a parallel a manner by archaeologists as legal and ethical considerations have transformed the handling of culturally sensitive remains and artifacts within the scientific community. Essentially the point of this concept is to balance the rights and needs of all parties in as fair and evenhanded manner as possible (cf. Bruning 2006). The term was first applied to a people being studied, or their descendants, and to the archaeologists who considered themselves as stewards of the public heritage. Subsequently the term has become global, including all persons, groups, peoples, and organizations (private, public, governmental, and nongovernmental) who are directly or indirectly touched by any given project (cf. Zimmerman 2005; Zimmerman et al 2003).

With regard to the public, anthropologists are concerned that research be carried out in a transparent manner, that provision be made for public access to information gathered for educational purposes, that impacts of anthropological research be considered relative to communities where they occur, that community standards be considered, and that the public be served. The parts which deal with standards and conduct between peers and client-professional relationships generally follow expectations common to business practices, seeking for open, positive interactions that will benefit working relationships, provide for successful outcomes, and ultimately benefit the field. Standards in this area are wide-ranging, including issues of competence and the nature of personal and business relationships between peers, anthropologists and their clients, informants/respondents, and research communities and students. In general, principles of honor, the principle of "do no harm," honesty, and equity are foundational to the various codes. Some examples are as simple as giving students credit for their part in project efforts through acknowledgment or authorship. Others are concerned with fair play and are aimed at avoiding abuse of the persons, communities, and peoples studied whether through deliberate or inadvertent manipulation, misrepresentation of purpose and goals, betrayal, or similar deceits.

One of the most important domains of anthropological codes of ethics relates to what happens after the research is finished. This concern revolves around the use and conservation of information, and sometimes collections, that are the product of professional activity. A concern among ethnographers focuses on the principle of "do no harm," involving consequences for individuals and peoples studied arising from the use and dissemination of information gathered. In the past, such information has been used to engage in genocide, as well as ethnocide, not to mention disenfranchisement and forced acculturation which have had negative consequences for the peoples studied. This part of ethical concern extends to the broader arenas of military and intelligence services' use of anthropologists in various contexts. For archaeologists, this domain involves the concern that archaeological specimens be preserved for future research and education, along with the supporting documentation (e.g., records, notes, photographs, sketches, and maps). Among the processes required in anthropological codes of ethics, when applicable, are the production of research designs, considerations of project impacts, consultations with all stakeholders (such as individuals and communities affected by the research, clients, project personnel, and governmental and nongovernmental agencies) who have direct, indirect, or historical interests in a given project prior to the execution of the project.

What of the Missionaries?

Similar domains of concern have been expressed among evangelical missionaries, especially during the emergence of the postcolonial era over the past half century. The *Lausanne Covenant* (ICWE 1974) articulates biblical precepts and standards to define the scope and goals of modern missions by identifying imperatives, problem domains, and their associated needs that should be addressed by the missionary enterprise. Subsequently, the *Manila Manifesto* (SICWE 1989) reaffirmed and expanded on the *Lausanne Covenant*. These widely available documents provide vision, ideology, purpose, and scope for modern missions activities. Each superbly expresses the evangelical view of the Great Commission in our contemporary world. Like many anthropological ethics codes, the *Lausanne Covenant* and *Manila Manifesto* identify and define responsibilities along with domains of action, seek unity, and look to suppress self-serving and useless actions within the missions community. Other parts provide clarification of priorities, such as the spread of faith as foundational and that works must flow from faith, along with the implication that individuals who engage in missions need to be healthy in both the moral and social sense of the word. Together, both documents are inclusive in the identification of stakeholders. They address broader levels of concern, but are not designed to provide more than general instruction in conduct which would help in avoiding ethical binds and problems or inresolving such problems when they do occur. Codes of ethical conduct that articulate responsibilities and obligations remain the domain of the agencies and organizations engaged in missions activity. By and large, these agencies and organizations are responsible for providing remedies to ethical breaches within their sphere of influence. Considering the dynamics within the missions community, those whom they serve, and other stakeholders, broader oversight may be desirable.

Some mission agencies and missionary societies have sought to clarify their own position in respect to ethics in ministry. By comparison to anthropology, however, these statements are little publicized and often are not readily available. More often they are integrated into missionary training programs or candidate orientation seminars and in contractual agreements. Even then, they are usually limited to the conduct of relations between the agency and its missionaries. A survey of forty mission agencies with long-term, mid-term, and short-term workers (table 2), drawn from tables 6, 7, and 8 of the *Mission Handbook* (Weber and Welliver 2007), was conducted through Web site examination and direct contact via a letter of inquiry describing our project. Our letter asked a number of questions regarding organizational ethics. The first asked whether the "organization [had] a formal code of ethics (or conduct)," and if so, we requested a copy. The second noted that "if your organization does not have a code of conduct, that would be useful information as well." The third and fourth questions were more narrowly targeted. The third focused on training, asking, "Are the missionaries and personnel in your organization informed about expected standards of ethical conduct, and if so, how?" Question four was aimed at identifying the level at which ethical problems are addressed within the organization: "Are there cases where the ethical conduct of personnel is left up to the individual's discretion?" This last question was posed in a fashion that required a more complex response than simply identifying the body or official charged with oversight of ethical issues.

The primary goals of the Web site examination and subsequent survey were to determine whether the agencies had specific codes of ethics or conduct and to determine the codes' accessibility. If an agency lacked an identifiable code of ethics, we attempted to learn whether elements of a code were present in other instruments produced by the agency. Table 2 summarizes the outcome of the data collection phase of the study. Twenty percent of the agencies responded to the letter inquiry, and all of the agencies maintain Web sites or are attached to one belonging to a parent organization. The results revealed that seven of the eight agencies that responded to the letter of inquiry have instruments identifiable as codes of conduct. These range from moderately to relatively comprehensive codes of conduct readily accessible from the agency. One respondent indicated that the agency lacked a specific instrument but addressed ethical concerns in a number of its documents.

Examination of the various Web sites revealed that most have elements of ethical conduct that might be found in general church documents (not missions specific), resolutions, manuals, handbooks, adherence to various covenants, or other sources. Although most do not seem to have a specific document addressing ethical issues, all of those whose Web sites are informational beyond the level of advertising and fund-raising include elements of ethical conduct in documents appearing under various titles (e.g., "Position Statement," "Core Values," "Mission Statement," and "Doctrines"). Some Web sites provide targeted statements of ethical policy, such as those concerning sexual conduct. Though there are exceptions, overall mission agencies lack comprehensive policies assembled into an instrument that can be used by the public or by members and employees of the agencies, not to mention those whom they serve, that will enable them to understand the ethical parameters by which the agencies operate. Consequently, it is difficult to understand how ethical guidance is provided and ethical concerns are handled by most agencies.

Most agencies did not respond to our requests for information (including an earlier telephone survey). Three agencies identified themselves as members of CrossGlobal Link (CGL). CGL does have a code that is binding for members (www.crossgloballink.org/Integrity). Interestingly, informal inquiries showed that workers for some CGL member agencies were unaware of the CGL code. One agency is known to have a detailed code of ethics that is not openly circulated. The World Evangelical Alliance did create the *Singapore Covenant* in 1994, followed up by the *Granada Covenant* of 2006, calling for its members to adhere to the highest standards of personal holiness and accountability. But the primary focus of these documents is on godly behaviors rather than ministry practices. These observations are by no means an indication of the absence of such codes within the surveyed agencies, just that their accessibility is problematic for outsiders. All of the surveyed agencies are assumed to operate under the authority of Scripture, with some ethical policy based on legal, practical, and business considerations. When viewed from the public side, however, the processes of articulating what constitutes an ethical lapse, along with the procedures for grievance, redress, and discipline, appear to be largely inaccessible or are unclear. It is our sense that internally most agencies are unclear in their policy and processes for relating Scripture (whether specifically moral instruction or otherwise) to specific points of application. This lack of clarity raises the question of how individual staff or members of the communities served by an agency can identify ethical misconduct, be protected, and receive appropriate redress when they are victims of misconduct by those who are charged with care for their spiritual and physical needs.

Range of Ethical Concern Compared

In comparison to the range of ethical issues of concern to anthropologists, the scope of missions' apparent ethical concern is much less robust. The greatest contrast is the general lack of documents containing specific codes of ethical behavior or that even enumurate all the individuals and communities—the stakeholders—whose lives are impacted by the agency, be they converts and others served, the missionaries and their families, or agency personnel, to name a few. How do outsiders determine if an agency is functioning appropriately at all levels? How can ethical standards be adequately accessed for training, information, and reference? How can victims among the organization's personnel and their families, as well as the individuals and communities served, be educated about the realm of ethical lapses and gain redress? These and questions like them are hard, but such problems exist. Some existing problems include the use of guilt and manipulation to proselytize, placing converts who live in hostile environments at risk, misuse of information, and insufficient care for missionary families. The last is known to include grossly inadequate retirement/pension income for missionaries coming off the field, not to mention problems in preparation of missionaries for working on the field or support services when they come home.

Reentry can be particularly difficult for missionary families, parents and children alike. Missionaries and their families, particularly those on the field for periods of years or decades, often evidence problems related to culture shock (commonly shared by anthropologists) and need additional support upon reentry to their culture of origin in the form of social and psychological services which are often not available or are insufficient in scope. The children of missionary families are sometimes further affected by insufficiencies in their education and even problems of molestation. "Missionary care" upon reentry is even more important for missionary children when their parents return home. In the context of publically available information on ethics, it is appropriate to point out that archaeologists seem to place more forethought and preparation into the care of a stone artifact and what will happen to it after it is studied, than is evident in the consideration that most mission agencies seem to have for those whose lives they touch.

The failure of evangelical missions agencies to openly, systematically, and aggressively address the ethics of the missionary enterprise has prompted us to propose that missional ethics statements be formulated and adopted by all agencies and groups involved in mission endeavors. We present here a model for use by evangelicals in the hope that it will stimulate further discussion and refinement. It is our desire that the process of ongoing reflection and refinement will assist mission agencies to represent better the intent and purpose of their missional activities, as well as to clarify the ethical guidelines that support the kinds of activities and associations they carry out.

It is our hope that this effort will help to standardize policy on ethical conduct across the field in a way that reflects Scripture and assists missiologists in applying ethical principles to specific issues. Also, we hope to encourage provision of informed ethical reflection, open and accessible to all, that will serve as a basis for common conduct, act to allay the concerns of groups and individuals outside of the field of mission endeavor, and provide to all a basis for identifying possible misconduct.

In search of these guidelines, we next examine the Code of Ethics of the AAA, and then propose a code of ethics for consideration by contemporary mission agencies.

Code of Ethics of the American Anthropological Association

In its preamble, the Code of Ethics (henceforth CE) of the AAA acknowledges that in the course of doing research, misunderstandings, conflicts, incompatible values, and competing agendas will arise, forcing anthropologists to make difficult ethical choices regarding their work. The purpose of a code of ethics is to give guidelines to researchers in the field, but the AAA recuses itself from the task of adjudicating any claims for unethical behavior since it does not exercise regulatory power over its members.

The introduction to the CE declares that the mission of the AAA "is to advance all aspects of anthropological research and to foster dissemination of anthropological knowledge through publications, teaching, public education, and application." It further asserts that generating and appropriately utilizing knowledge about the peoples of the world is a worthy and honorable task. The CE, therefore, requires that scholars give due consideration to gathering and disseminating such information in the most ethical manner. In fact, it advocates that training about codes of ethics relating to anthropological work be included in anthropological training as part of the curriculum.

In Section III the CE offers specific guidelines for engaging in ethical research. These include:

Guidelines with respect to anthropologists' self-representation. According to the CE, anthropologists must be open about the purpose of their research, the potential use of their study, its possible impact upon the community being studied, and even the sources of their funding. They must also be alert to conflicting ethical demands placed upon them by individuals, communities, government representatives, and their own supporting agencies as they become guests, responsible members, and trusted friends in their host societies.

Guidelines with respect to safeguarding the well-being of their host communities. Anthropologists must avoid doing any harm or wrong to their host communities through their research. They must respect the safety, dignity, and privacy of their informants, their families, and their communities. Anthropologists must adhere to the obligations of openness and informed consent from those who share information with them. Informed consent does not require written or signed consent, but rather willingly shared communication given in a spirit of openness and honesty.

Guidelines in respect to reporting research results. Anthropologists bear the responsibility to report their findings honestly and accurately without deception or known misrepresentation. They must seek to preserve opportunities for future fieldworkers to follow them in the field and be willing to share their data with other researchers with reasonable requests for access. Anthropologists also need to be aware of the social and political implications of their studies and of any potential harm these studies may cause to the people with whom they work or their colleagues.

Guidelines in respect to teaching anthropology. As teachers, anthropologists must not discriminate on the basis of sex, race, social class, religion, or other criteria irrelevant to academic performance. Teachers need to acknowledge the work and contributions of students and research assistants, and encourage the highest levels of ethical standards for their students. Teachers of anthropology also need to beware of exploitation or serious conflicts of interest which may result from close and often extended periods of contact with trainees and to refrain from sexual liaisons with students whose work is under their supervision.

Proposed Code of Ethics for Evangelical Missions

Much that has been covered above can serve as a guide for the missiological community. While the CE of the AAA is discipline focused and perhaps not always relevant to missions, the next section seeks to build upon the example of the AAA to provoke similar reflection by missionaries. What follows is a proposed code of ethics for missions following the example set by the AAA and using seminal guidelines already set forth by the CrossGlobal Link ethical guidelines statement.

Introduction

The task of presenting the Gospel of Jesus Christ to the world has assumed a wide variety of forms. Not all mission agencies attempt to fulfill every aspect of the missionary enterprise, choosing instead to represent their faith and show God's grace to the nations in one or another specifically focused way. However differently the mission statements of missionary agencies may be, throughout the history of missions the goal of missions has been broadly identified as:

- Giving opportunity to the members of every tribe and nation to hear the claims of Jesus Christ that through faith in him humanity can experience forgiveness of sins and reconciliation with the God of creation.
- Forming local bodies of believers into communities of faith where they can worship God in a culturally appropriate manner, receive further instruction in the Word of God, and find support and encouragement in their desire to follow godliness and righteousness.
- Promoting godliness, righteousness, and Christian values through exemplary living expressed in such activities as improving living standards, enhancing health care, offering quality education for all segments of the populace, and advocacy for the poor and oppressed of this world.

In keeping with these goals it is of the utmost importance that mission agencies give careful attention to performing their tasks with the highest standards of godliness, righteousness, and ethical standards.

Ministry Standards for Missions

Evangelical missions are hereby called upon to conduct their missionary activity in keeping with the following guidelines for ensuring openness, honesty, and integrity in the service of Jesus Christ.

I. Integrity in Message
The task of missions must be focused on conveying the truths of the Word of God through proclamation, through deeds of righteousness, and through the powerful example of godly living. It must not be diverted into pursuing political agendas, economic hegemonies, or regional interests. The kingdom of God must be understood in terms of God's reign in the hearts of individuals and not in terms of the formation of civil governments.

Evangelical missionaries must not enter into any covert alliances with governments or government agencies to promote political causes, undermine government authority, or promote organized rebellion. In fulfillment of their prophetic role of speaking out against evil, corruption, and exploitation, evangelical missionaries must not be silent in the face of evil. They must speak out and respond to such situations in a manner that is wise, discreet, and appropriate in promoting peace, justice, and godliness, not political or hegemonic interests.

II. Integrity in Finances
Mission agencies need to be fully transparent in respect to the manner in which they raise funds, give a proper accounting of

the funds they receive, adhere to reliable receipting and reporting of funds donated, and make responsible audits available to all donors.

Missionaries need to take care in the administration of funds to avoid using them to exert undue influence over national ministries, churches, agencies, and individuals.

III. Integrity in Relationships
Evangelical missions embrace the need to present the living dynamic of God's offer to all humanity in every part of the world including those areas where this message has never been heard, where it has become confused or relegated to some form of "dead orthodoxy," and where it has lost its transformative powers for provoking godliness and righteousness in the pursuit of God. Therefore, in the presence of existing churches or competing missionary activities, evangelical missionaries shall seek to pursue the following ministry strategies:

- In respect to the charges of proselytism from other branches of the Christian church, evangelical missions will not seek to foster change in religious affiliations through competitive programs or vitriolic attacks on others, but rather will seek to foster renewed relationships to Jesus Christ however those can best be attained.
- Evangelical missions will seek to be faithful in teaching the Word of God and in instructing inquirers regarding what the Word of God proclaims, including clarification of how alternative mission messages differ from their own. All believers and inquirers have a right to know what competing faith traditions offer to their followers and what they teach.
- Whatever else may transpire in the competition between denominations for followers, evangelical missionaries must

demonstrate the highest levels of ethical behavior and Christian grace toward those with whom they disagree.
- In respect to opposing faiths, including those that are not Christian, evangelical missionaries must demonstrate an attitude of respectful disagreement, and when it is necessary to engage in a conflict of faiths, evangelicals must rely on the power of the Holy Spirit, not on any contrived power plays or deceptive strategies.
- Evangelical missionaries are further encouraged to refuse to engage in "triumphalistic displays" of victory by using the testimonies of new converts from another faith to their own in ostentatious "displays of power or efficacy" or through public campaigns that insult other faiths or promote religious conflict.

IV. Integrity in Morals

In this section we follow the ethics statement of the IFMA/CrossGlobal Link document. It is very clear.

> Missionaries sent out by a member mission will be expected to maintain holiness in their marital relations, in their use of time and money, in their relations with people in the countries where they serve, and in their personal habits. Each CrossGlobal Link member mission is expected to hold not only its missionaries, but its officers and board as well to these high standards. Christlikeness is the model for every level of every CrossGlobal Link member mission. (www.crossgloballink.org/Integrity)

V. Integrity in Missionary Practices

It is common practice throughout the world for people to make judgments about others based on their behavior. The way people see and interpret the conduct they observe influences how they relate to others. This involves trust, respect, and confidence, and, for missionaries, their acceptance and the acceptance of their Gospel message. Conduct that is seen as betrayal may lead to a loss of confidence in mission workers and resultant loss of faith. We therefore recommend that:

- Evangelical missionaries who seek to represent the Gospel in countries or regions that are hostile to the Gospel may choose to represent themselves as business persons, teachers, or other professionals, but in choosing this access route to ministry, such individuals must first ensure that they have the full qualifications required for their primary source of identification. They must be prepared to fully engage and perform the duties of their chosen profession as "kingdom professionals" and not just as cover careers for evangelistic purposes.
- Evangelical missionaries must never resort to coercion, bribery, promises of gain, or causing unreasonable guilt or fear to win converts to the Christian faith. It is important that new converts be brought to Christ voluntarily, without the pressures of overt or subtle forms of coercion. We acknowledge that part of the Gospel includes the fear of God, fear of retribution, and loss of fellowship with God for all who reject his claims, but these truths must always be balanced by the message of love, truth, and hope in God's offer of salvation.
- In full recognition that the Gospel sometimes requires significant changes in the social and cultural practices of a people and that sometimes resistance to the Gospel message is primarily due to social barriers, evangelical missionaries must become sensitive to the social implications of the

message they bring. They must do everything in their power to overcome social resistance to the Gospel by offering constructive, transformative solutions that will promote greater godliness and righteousness within the entire community.
- Inasmuch as the proclamation of the Gospel both in word and deed will have significant implications in transforming the lives of individuals, entire societies and even local environments, missionaries must be willing to engage in their ministries in a manner that wisely and biblically addresses such issues as care of creation, justice, peace and reconciliation.
- In those areas of ministry that come under attack from warring parties, missionaries must demonstrate the highest levels of discernment as to their own involvement. Their highest priority ought to be protecting innocent believers from the evils of conflict. Missionaries must be very careful if they engage in supporting either side of a conflict. Missionaries have been called upon to be both peacemakers and those who can rise up to love their enemies.
- In those areas/nations openly hostile to the proclamation of the Gospel by evangelical missionaries and where the distribution of the Scriptures is forbidden, or where communities of believers are not free to meet for worship, it may be necessary to violate human laws in order to follow the mandate of the Gospel. Missionaries and agencies that embrace such strategies must be willing to accept the legal consequences of their activities. In the same manner that peaceful demonstrators have protested human rights abuses, they must never resort to violence in the pursuit of their evangelistic objectives, and they must strive to pursue the highest standards of personal godliness in keeping with the holy character of God.

- In full acknowledgement that converts to the Christian faith often make their choices during times of personal crisis, when they are emotionally vulnerable or physically in need, evangelical missionaries must refrain from exploiting people at such times by ensuring that the "ministries of mercy" they offer are not subtly coercive, but flow from a genuine desire to meet human needs.

VI. Integrity in Missionary Care, Recruitment, and Representation
Those who elect to serve Christ by joining in the Great Commission need to do so through the exercise of free will. Those who train, support, and serve with them should be prepared to provide for the spiritual and corporal needs of the servants. We recommend that:

- Individuals who enter the mission field must do so freely and willingly in answer to a personal conviction that they are called by Christ. Teachers, pastors, administrators and their associates should never use overt or subtle forms of coercion (e.g., guilt or shame), abuse their offices, or engage in deceit when recruiting into the mission field. Anything but a voluntary commitment is a weak foundation for such service and is likely to fail or cause emotional harm to those who lack a genuine call to service.
- Preparation for the mission field must be based on a comprehensive education that is preparatory for those who work in cross-cultural contexts. Students, interns, and trainees must receive training which prepares them to work in the organizational, cultural, and spiritual contexts where their service takes them. Teachers and mentors should encourage participation in mission-related activities, and acknowledge their students/trainees' contributions. Students and trainees

should be encouraged to hold themselves to the highest standard of ethical conduct.
- Teachers, mentors, administrators, and their associates should always disclose the hazards and risks that mission workers will face in a given region, nation, or sociocultural context. Students and workers must be informed prior to making a voluntary decision so as to avoid the pitfalls of entrapment. Students and workers must receive education and training that will prepare them to meet the hazards and risks inherent to service in some contexts.
- Mission agencies should be prepared to provide for the care and well-being of the dependents of mission workers serving in the field. The agency and its administrators, supervisors, and boards of trustees assume legal as well as moral responsibility for the protection, health, and basic needs of dependents, particularly the safety and education of dependent children.
- Missionaries who are confronted with charges of moral failure or who are dismissed or transferred or experience a significant change in duties should have access to a clearly defined appeals policy in the event they disagree. In cases of charges of moral failure, the rights of both the accused and the accusers must be carefully addressed.

VII. Integrity in Reporting Standards for Missions

Adherence to honesty and the avoidance of deceit are foundational to sharing the Gospel. Therefore we propose:

- Evangelical missionaries shall refrain from reporting conversions that never took place, inflating the number of people reached by their efforts, or miscounting the number of people to whom they have ministered. Furthermore, supporting

agencies for all missionary activities need to require accurate and responsible ministry reports from their members and to make serious attempts at confirming such reports.
- As missionaries seek to raise support for their ministries, letters to supporting churches need to reflect honestly what is happening in the ministry. Stories about converts and the ministry must sustain the dignity of those individuals who are featured in their reports, and show sensitivity toward their future safety and well-being.
- Mission agencies, national churches, missionaries, and their supporters and supporting churches need to foster open, cooperative, and fully transparent relationships in working together as partners in order to ensure the highest standards of ethical behavior and kingdom values.

Inasmuch as the Evangelical Missiological Society (for which this proposal has been written) is not a regulatory agency, nor does it have the power to enforce these guidelines for ethical behavior, we nevertheless call upon mission agencies and individual missionaries to carry out their ministries in accordance with these principles, and to hold their colleagues accountable for their own behaviors.

Conclusion

This chapter has reviewed the Code of Ethics of the American Association of Anthropology and has suggested a number of ethical guidelines for missionaries. Our review the AAA's ethical guidelines has shown that although accusations of unethical behavior still plague anthropologists, at least for the AAA, having a thoroughly worked out code of ethics has emboldened anthropologists to become self-policing in their research and augmented their willingness to expose unethical behavior on the part of their colleagues. It is the writers' hope that a similar set of guidelines for missionaries would embolden missions to hold other missionaries and mission agencies to the highest standards of Christian ethical behavior. Furthermore, it would be a powerful tool in the hands of missionaries and mission agencies as they seek to respond to the (often false) allegations of those who oppose missions. To be effective, these guidelines need to be discussed in depth by mission executives, taught in missionary training curricula, and further refined and perfected utilizing the shared wisdom, experience, and goals of a host of missionaries and mission agencies engaged in furthering the cause of the Gospel of Jesus Christ.

Questions for Discussion

1. Do mission agencies really need a code of ethics to explain to their critics what they do, or should critics and criticism simply be ignored?
2. Do you agree with the authors of this statement regarding the goal of mission?
3. How might this document put unnecessary restrictions on missionary activities in today's very complicated world?
4. What suggestions would you make to improve or strengthen this declaration?

References

Bruning, Susan B. 2006. Complex legal legacies: The Native American Graves Protection and Repatriation Act, scientific study, and Kennewick Man. *American Antiquity* 71(3):501–21.

Freeman, R. Edward, and D. L. Reed. 1983. Stockholders and stakeholders: A new perspective on corporate governance. *California Management Review* 25(3):88–106.

International Congress on World Evangelization (ICWE). 1974. *The Lausanne Covenant*. www.lausanne.org/covenant.

Register of Professional Archaeologists. n.d. *Code of Conduct*. www.rpanet.org/displaycommon.cfm?an=1&subarticlenbr=3.

Second International Congress on World Evangelization. 1989. *The Manila manifesto*. www.lausanne.org/all-documents/manila-manifesto.html.

Society for American Archaeology. 1996. *Principles of archaeological ethics*. www.saa.org/AbouttheSociety/PrinciplesofArchaeologicalEthics /tabid/203/Default.aspx.

Weber, Linda J., and Dotsey Welliver, eds. 2007. *Mission handbook: U.S. and Canadian Protestant ministries overseas 2007–2009*. Wheaton, Ill.: EMIS.

Whiteman, Darrell. 2008. Anthropology and mission. An uneasy journey toward mutual understanding. In *Paradigm shifts in Christian witness: Insights from anthropology, communication, and spiritual power*, ed. Charles E. Van Engen, Darrell Whiteman, and J. Dudley Woodberry, 3–12. Maryknoll, N.Y.: Orbis Books.

Zimmerman, Larry J. 2005. Consulting stakeholders. In *Archaeology in practice: A student guide to archaeological analyses*, ed. Jane Balme and Alistair Paterson, 39–58. London: Blackwell.

Zimmerman, Larry J., Karen D. Vitelli, and Julie Hollowell-Zimmer, eds. 2003. *Ethical issues in archaeology*. Walnut Creek, Calif.: AltaMira Press.

Table 1. **Representative Anthropological Societies with Codes of Ethics**

American Anthropological Association
American Association of Physical Anthropologists
Archaeological Institute of America
American Association of Museums
American Cultural Resource Association
American Institute for Conservation
Association of Social Anthropologists of Aotearoa/New Zealand
Association of Social Anthropologists of the UK and Commonwealth
Australian Anthropological Society

Australian Archaeological Association
Australian Association of Consulting Archaeologists
Brazilian Association of Anthropology
Canadian Archaeological Association
Canadian Association of Archaeologists
European Association of Social Anthropologists
European Association of Archaeologists
Florida Anthropological Society
International Council of Monuments and Sites
International Council of Museums
International Union of Anthropological and Ethnological Societies
Institute for Archaeologists
National Association for the Practice of Anthropology
Ontario Archaeological Society
Registry of Professional Archaeologists
The Royal Anthropology Institute
Society for American Archaeology
Society for Applied Anthropology
Society for Archaeological Sciences
Society for the Anthropology of Consciousness
Society for Historical Archaeology
Society of Ethnobiology
UNESCO
Pacific Coast Archaeological Society
World Archaeological Congress

Table 2. **Mission Agencies Included in the Census**

Agency	Response	Other	CGL*
Africa Inland Mission International			Y
Assemblies of God World Missions			
Association of Baptists for World Evangelism (ABWE)		1	
Baptist Bible Fellowship International			

Baptist International Missions, Inc. (BIMI)			
Campus Crusade for Christ, Intl.			
Christian and Missionary Alliance			
Christian Churches/Churches of Christ			
Church of God (Cleveland, TN) World Missions	Y[a]		
Church of the Nazarene, World Mission Department		2	
Church World Service			
Churches of Christ			
CMF International			
Educational Services International		N	
Evangelical Covenant Church—Covenant World Mission	Y		
Free Methodist World Missions			
Global Outreach International			
Global Partners/Wesleyan World Missions			
Habitat for Humanity International			
Heifer International	Y		
Leader Treks			
Mennonite Central Committee (MCC)	Y	3	
Mennonite Mission Network			
Mercy Ships			
Mission to the World (PCA), Inc.	Y		
Missionary Ventures International			
Network of International Christian Schools			
New Tribes Missions			Y
On The Go Ministries/Keith Cook Evangelistic Association			
Operation Mobilization			

Presbyterian Church (USA) Worldwide Ministries		6	
Samaritan's Purse			
Southwest Baptist Convention International Missions Board		3	
TEAM (The Evangelical Alliance Mission)	Y		Y
United Church of Christ—Wider Church Ministries		5	
United Pentecostal Church Intl., Foreign Missions Division			
World Gospel Mission			
Wycliffe Bible Translators, Inc.	Y		
Youth for Christ/USA—World Outreach		4	
Youth With A Mission	N		
International Red Cross		Y	

1 In *Principles and Practices Handbook*; privacy policy on Web site.
2 Identifies sources.
3 Agency level code; also in position statement and elsewhere.
4 Manual level; guidelines for supervisors and missionaries, some ethics.
5 Resolution calling for ethical conduct and definition of practices.
6 Addresses sexual conduct.
a Embedded in policy manual.
Y Yes.
N No.
* CrossGlobal Link.

Index

A

abuse, 15, 32, 45, 89, 96, 101, 129-30, 142, 189, 200, 274, 304, 345, 350, 365-66
    financial. *See* financial.
    power, 77, 79, 82-83
    sexual. *See* sex.
    substance. *See* substance.
    victim of abuse, 15, 17
accountability, 27-28, 33-45, 75-76, 79-81, 83-84, 86-88, 90-94, 97-100, 102, 121, 157, 179-80, 226, 275, 341, 345, 354
    communal, 3
    financial. *See* financial.
    holistic, 37
    lack of accountability, 36, 236
    local, 37
    mutual, 18, 37-38, 90
    organizational, 83
    processes, 34, 36-37, 39-40, 44
    requirements, 34, 42
    secular meaning of accountability, 35
    structures, 37, 41, 44, 80-81
Ackerman, Richard, 170
addiction, 101-02, 118-20, 290
    hidden, 79, 83, 95
Adeney, Miriam, 251-52
Africa, 251, 254, 314, 325-26, 337

North Africa, 346
Africans, 32, 326, 344
> leaders, 32

agnosticism, 20
Algerian, 190
Alzheimer's, 75
American, 15, 33, 49, 54-55, 57, 62, 94, 142, 243-44, 250, 252, 255, 326
American Society of Missiology, 80
Americans, 54, 243-44, 252, 326
> assumptions, 55
> families, 49

Anabaptist village, 6
Anglican, 268
> evangelical, 95

anthropology, 332, 343-44, 349, 352, 359
> anthropologist, 61, 64, 310, 322, 324, 332-33, 343-48, 350-51, 355-59, 368
> cultural, 32

apologetics, 2
Arab, 53-54
Ardagh, David, 161
artist, 14, 61
Asia, 56, 91
> Central, 77

Axxess Church, 7
Australia, 87
authority, 20, 77, 90, 96, 101, 134, 140-41, 146, 148, 158, 167, 183, 191, 213, 344, 361

B

Bader-Saye, Scott, 15
baptism, 182, 195, 241
Baptist, 61
Barrows, Cliff, 84

Bass, Diana, 277
Becker, Ernst, 294
belief, 2, 13, 52, 60, 62, 68, 120, 130, 138, 183, 210, 344-45
    genuine, 13
    mythical, 13
believer, 15, 17, 22, 34, 43, 59, 97, 99, 103, 132, 134, 136, 138-40, 184, 190, 226, 229-32, 237-41, 246-47, 268, 302-03, 360, 362, 365
    community of believers. *See* community.
belonging, 13, 17, 128, 353
benevolence, 17, 20, 255
Bible, 17, 49, 63, 70, 132, 141, 183, 197, 211-12, 241, 333, 336, 344
    Gospel. *See* Gospel.
Bible study, 14, 17, 241
biblical
    criticism, 2
    narrative, 16
    pattern, 20
    standards, 33, 142, 182
body of Christ, 11, 13, 31, 43, 99, 102, 140, 232, 237, 239, 241
    global, 31
Bonk, Jonathan, 251
Bosnians, 37
Boyatzis, Richard, 161
Boyd, Brady, 172
Britain, 55-56
Brown, Ron, 149
Brussels, 81
Bryant, Anita, 50
Buddha, 57
Buddhism, 58, 68
    Theravada, 68

C

California
    Modesto, 84
calling, 84, 145, 150, 208, 215, 226, 228-29, 232, 234, 298, 354
Campbell, Scott, 265
Campolo, Tony, 269
Canada, 28, 43, 87, 243, 270, 290
capitalism, 55
Carey, William, 277
Carlson, Paul, 269
Carnes, Patrick, 110, 119
Cartier-Bresson, Henri, 324
Cecil, Brad, 7
charismatic, 93
Chawga, Stephen P., 163
Chinnawong, Sawai, xviii
Christendom, 10
Christian
    Christian America. *See* United States of America.
    community, 2, 6, 251
    evangelical, 50, 52, 55, 58-60, 62, 289, 291
        conservative, 50
        culture, 15
        preachers, 50
    leaders, 58, 65, 77-78, 82, 98, 101, 142, 219, 294
    mission. *See* mission.
    persecution of Christians, 56
    perspective, 62, 276
    traditions, 6, 10, 19
Christians, 2, 5, 7, 12, 15, 50, 52-54, 56-64, 66, 106, 108, 113, 119, 134, 140-141, 148, 204, 212, 234, 243, 252, 269, 274, 276, 278, 298, 301
    conservative church, 51
Christianity, 2-5, 7, 12-13, 15, 55, 58-61, 67, 94, 123, 133, 243, 247, 251

Christianity Today, 106
church
    community. *See* community.
    global, 31, 35
    growth of church, 5
    leaders, 22, 45, 58, 139-140, 233
    local, 56, 58, 85, 96, 98-99, 102, 197, 231, 233-234, 241, 246
    members, 4, 132, 209, 234, 248, 272
    planting, 40, 114, 211, 225-27, 230-34, 236-38
Church of Jesus Christ of Latter-day Saints. *See* Mormonism.
Clinton, Robert, 77
Cloud, Henry, 273
CNN, 276
college, 203, 290
    campus, 22, 269
    students, 14, 51
Collier, John, 322, 332
Collins, Jim, 157
colonialism, 28-30, 32-33, 337, 346
    colonial pattern, 32
    colonial rule, 29, 32
    enterprise, 32
Colorado
    Colorado Springs, 172
    Denver, 14
communication, 111, 164, 181, 184-85, 188, 210, 215-16, 239, 270, 297, 324, 359
    honest, 99, 102, 162
    indirect, 39, 156
    intercultural, 39
    international, 88
communism, 58
community, 2, 4-8, 11, 13-14, 16-19, 57, 83, 100, 102, 139-141, 155-156, 194, 207, 234, 238, 241, 248, 250, 253, 268, 271, 273,

275, 289, 295, 311, 317, 323, 331, 334-36, 349-50, 358, 365
    Christian. *See* Christian.
    church, 7, 11
    committed, 16
    community of faith. *See* faith.
    convictional, 5-6
    faithful, 7, 9
    kingdom community. *See* kingdom of God.
    local, 239, 251, 255, 312, 337
    of believers, 4, 22, 36
    visible, 16
confession, 19, 76, 95-96
congregation, 1, 4, 14-16, 20, 69, 207, 246, 272
    diverse, 20
consumerism, 3, 8, 244
    consumer culture, 20
    spiritual, 3-4
contextualization, 68, 190, 239-40
conversion, 5, 7, 9, 12, 14, 20, 51, 57, 68, 133, 231, 291, 298, 326, 367
    convert, 4-6, 9, 12, 51-52, 55, 58, 89, 135, 239, 298, 303, 328, 355-56, 363-64, 366, 368
conviction, 2, 4-5, 9, 12, 14, 17, 76, 129-130, 134, 136-37, 139-40, 143, 162, 173, 231, 324, 366
Cornelius, 136
corruption, 58, 133, 260, 361
Corwin, Gary, 160, 244, 250
Cosmopolitan, 107
Coulter, Ann, 55
Craik, Rebecca, 146
creation, 11, 22, 89, 111, 120, 192, 263-64, 266-69, 271, 273, 275-78, 317, 333, 360, 365
credibility, 3, 34, 84, 87
critical realism, 2
criticism, 2, 85, 163, 206, 293, 294-95, 309, 348, 369

cross, 8, 21, 44, 198
cross-cultural
    conflict, 35, 39
    ministry. *See* ministry.
    partnerships, 27, 29, 44
    training, 39
CrossGlobal Link, 78, 180, 354, 360, 363
cruciform sacrifice, 8
culture
    consumer culture. *See* consumerism.
    cultural context, 39, 303
    cultural intelligence, 35
    different, 30
    dominant. *See* dominant culture.
    modern marketing, 7
cynicism, 34
Cyprian of Carthage, 12

D

Daniels, Gene, 244-45
David, 335
demonic, 78-79
    attacks, 77
Denver. *See* Colorado.
Denver Seminary, 172
denominations, 13, 58, 135, 251, 268, 270, 362
    in United States. *See* United States of America.
dialogue, 9, 12, 18, 28, 30-31, 35-36, 38, 40-41, 86, 88, 273, 337
Diamond, Jared, 259-60, 276
discipleship, 19-20, 90, 101, 130, 264
discourse, 3, 52, 55, 58, 268, 309, 315, 325
    interreligious, 52
diversity, 79, 192-94, 333
divine intervention, 76, 137
doctrine, 13, 60, 134, 183

dominant culture, 3, 10, 62, 326
domination, 30, 38
Dominican Republic, 259
donor, 29-30, 34, 45, 189, 290, 362
    agencies, 45
Dowsett, Rose, 89
drunkenness, 19
Duriez, Colin, 297-98, 302

E
ecclesiology, 230, 240
economic crisis, 43
education, 111, 113-15, 122, 272, 351, 356, 358, 360, 366-67
Edwards, Andres, 264
Egypt, 10
Ekstrom, Bertil, 89
Elmer, Duane, 141, 146
emerging church, 15
English, 51, 162
eschatological hope, 20
ethical
    approach, 69
    evangelism, 5, 8-9, 12, 15-16, 20, 22
    evangelist, 21
    outreach, 8
    problems, 53, 226, 353
ethnicity, 55, 190, 193
    assumptions of ethnicity, 55
ethics
    definition of ethics, 2, 5
    dynamic process of ethics, 2
    modern loss of ethics, 1
    practicing, 2, 5
Eucharist, 11, 18-20
Europe, 13, 81, 243, 269, 325

European Union, 81
evangelical, 1, 9, 15, 50, 52, 55, 57-66, 70, 77, 87, 93, 95, 97, 180, 182-83, 190, 193, 229-30, 232-34, 260, 263, 267-68, 289, 291, 293, 295, 297, 343, 351, 356-57, 363
    critics, 62
    leadership, 15
Evangelical Missiological Society, 78, 80, 368
evangelism
    countercultural, 8
    credibility of evangelism, 3
    direct, 18
    ethics of evangelism. *See* ethical.
    faithful, 6
    goals of evangelism, 4
    holistic, 5, 10
    integrity of evangelism, 3
    leader, 77
    methods of evangelism, 4
    opportunities, 1
    overseas, 53
    peaceful, 7
    performance of evangelism, 2, 14
    practice of evangelism, 4-6, 14
    strategies, 7
    successful, 6
    techniques, 4
    welcoming, 12
    witnesses, 7
evangelist, 4, 9, 14, 21, 84, 273
    ethical. *See* ethical.
Evans-Pritchard, E. E., 346
exaggeration, 85, 188-89, 290, 292-93, 295-99, 301

F
faith, 2-4, 6-7, 9-10, 17, 49, 59, 61-65, 69-70, 101, 107, 137,

164, 183, 190, 194-95, 198, 203-04, 230, 233, 236, 262, 266, 278, 289, 302-03, 345, 352, 360, 362-64, 366
    community of faith, 6, 194
    public expression of faith, 61
    quality of faith, 4
faithfulness, 5, 7, 90, 94, 101, 191, 227
Falwell, Jerry, 50
family, 7, 12, 16-17, 20, 49, 77, 79-80, 82-84, 87, 92-93, 98-101, 112, 121, 156, 190, 234, 237-238, 245, 261, 293-95, 298, 303, 336
    American. *See* Americans.
    breakdown, 83
    difficulties, 77
Farrell, Hunter, 250
favoritism, 207, 209
fear, 11, 13, 53-54, 61, 67, 94, 228, 233, 294, 364
fidelity, 93, 273
film, 49-50, 53-54, 309-18, 322, 324, 330, 332
filmmaking, 309-15, 317-19
financial
    abuse, 85
    accountability, 27, 31-34, 36, 40, 42, 44, 46, 180
    assistance, 45
    compliance, 28-29, 41, 43
    deception, 83
    disparities, 28
    issues, 81
    misconduct, 77
    mismanagement, 77, 82, 94
    regulations, 28, 34, 43
    reporting, 37
    requirements, 28, 41-42
    resources, 33, 43, 199
Fiorina, Carly, 159
Flaherty, Robert, 310

Florida, 261
    Miami, 87
    Orlando, 78
forgiveness, 59, 95-96, 98, 100-01, 254, 360
    sin. *See* sin.
Francis of Assisi, 277-78
fraud, 36, 40
freedom, 3, 19, 29, 61, 171, 181, 184, 227-28
    of religion, 65
Friedman, Thomas, 270
Fuller Theological Seminary, 109
fund-raising, 187, 204, 290, 354
funds, 30, 36, 43, 45, 99, 102, 200, 204, 219, 235, 275, 361-62

G
gay, 49
    anti-gay, 49
Geary, Christraud, 325
gender confusion, 79, 101
George Washington University, 173
Germany, 77, 87
global
    church. *See* church.
    credibility, 87
    financial world, 43
    mission. *See* mission.
    movement, 42, 84
    networks, 81, 83, 91
    North, 78, 278
    South, 78, 278-79
    theologies. *See* theology.
Global Connections, 82
God
    as Creator, 51, 267, 278, 316
    as Father, 10, 20, 195, 230

    as heavenly Father, 38, 44
    as King, 16, 226-27
    character, 6
    existence, 51
    grace of God, 10, 14, 43, 59, 76, 78, 99, 200, 202, 227, 360
    greatness, 54
    heart of God, 28
    image of God, 90, 264, 323, 333
    mystery of God, 18,
    ongoing work of God, 7
    people of God, 7, 186
    power of God, 8
    provision, 43
    reign of God, 13, 16, 361
    relationship with God, 14, 44
gods, 8
Goldschmidt, Walter, 310
Goleman, Daniel, 161
Good News, 7, 9, 10, 20, 129, 268, 275
Google, 84
Gospel, 4, 10, 22, 128-30, 133-42, 145, 148, 183, 188, 191, 193, 200, 228-30, 232, 235, 237, 239, 241, 261, 266-67, 271-72, 278, 292, 326, 360, 364-65, 367, 369
    message of the Gospel, 10
    proclamation of the Gospel, 9, 365
    transformative power of the Gospel, 22
Goudzwaard, Robert, 274
government, 32, 35-36, 42, 57, 132, 182, 275, 345-49, 358, 361
    corruption, 260
    foreign, 29
    invading, 29
    laws, 35
grace, 8, 10-11, 14, 18, 29, 43, 59, 63, 112, 123, 139, 162, 183, 188, 227, 248, 267, 363

provision of grace, 11
Graham, Billy, 84-85, 168, 269
    Billy Graham Archives, 85
    Graham Crusade, 84
Granada Covenant, 82, 89, 91, 97, 100, 354
Great Commission, 230, 316, 344, 351, 366
greed, 13, 19
Greenberg, Jerald, 214
Guatemala, 131
    Guatemala City, 131
Guder, Darrell, 265
guilt, 356, 364, 366
    from sin. *See* sin.

H

Hackett, Steven, 262
Hadith, 61
Haggard, Ted, 92-93
Haiti, 259-61, 276-77
    Port-au-Prince, 259
Hale, Thomas, 145
Haluza-DeLay, Randolph, 267
Hankins, Barry, 291, 298-300
Harris, Peter and Miranda, 278
Hart, Archibald, 109, 114
Harvey, Jerry B., 173
Hauerwas, Stanley, 14
Hay, Rob, 78
healing, 9, 12, 17, 19, 42, 119-20, 272, 275
heaven, 68, 100
Heider, Karl, 324, 332
hell, 68
hero worship, 293, 295, 297, 300, 304
Hiebert, Paul, 140
Hindu, 57, 136, 190

Hodge, Bob, 116
Hoffman, Harry, 77
holiness, 8, 17, 87, 90, 93-94, 98, 100, 354, 363
Holy Spirit, 2, 6, 21-22, 76-77, 93-94, 98, 100-02, 136, 140-41, 171, 215, 227, 229-30, 235, 239-41
    power of the Holy Spirit, 16, 363
homosexuality, 49
honesty, 22, 122, 132, 200, 301, 350, 359, 361, 367
hope, 7, 10, 32, 43, 67, 97, 212, 225, 260, 272, 303, 364, 369
hospitality, 13, 254, 289
    radical, 17
Hotchkiss, Lee, 170
Howard, David, 84, 95
humanity, 18, 20, 266, 268, 333, 360, 362
humility, 2, 10, 14, 21, 60, 84, 163, 239, 300, 304
    submission, 17
hypocrisy, 13, 302

I

identity, 2-3, 5, 7, 22, 39, 42, 53
    ethnic, 54
    religious, 54
idolatry, 8, 21
ignorance, 53, 59, 132, 314
imago Dei, 8, 333
immorality, 85, 109, 231
Indiana
    Zionsville, 272
indigenous, 29
    partnerships. *See* partnership.
    organizations. *See* organizations.
individualism, 3, 8, 20, 193, 316
individuality, 14
Indonesian, 190
injustice, 28, 142, 171, 200-02, 205-07, 209, 214, 216, 218, 316

inner city, 16
integrity
    in evangelism. *See* evangelism.
    in ministry. *See* ministry.
intelligent design, 62
intercultural
    communication. *See* communication.
    training, 28
interdependence, 18, 34
International Society for Frontier Missiology, 80
Internet, 78, 80, 101, 105-20, 122-23, 184, 216
Isaiah, 7
Islam, 51, 57, 59-61, 63, 65-66
    danger of Islam, 57
    ignorance of, 59
    Islamic school, 51
    parochial militant, 55
Israel, 10, 137

J

Jenkins, Philip, 243
Jerusalem, 136, 139-40
Jesus Christ, 3, 7-8, 10-11, 19, 33, 41-42, 61, 63, 94, 96, 162, 182, 190, 195, 198, 213, 226-27, 229-32, 238, 240, 266, 271, 273-74, 277-78, 292, 294, 327, 360-62, 369
    as head, 34
    as Lord, 19, 21, 29, 137, 162, 195, 195, 211, 226, 228, 230, 234, 238, 302
    as personal Savior, 3
    as sacrificial lamb, 42
    as Son of God, 10, 199, 271
    commitment to Jesus, 8
    dependence on Jesus, 11
    relationship with Jesus, 8, 44
    sacrifice of Christ, 20

Jews, 57, 135-36
joy, 6, 22, 247
judgment, 3, 34, 83, 146, 167, 170, 199, 210, 363
justice, 6, 166, 214, 218, 220, 264, 361, 365
    distributive, 202-03, 205, 207, 212, 214
    informational, 213, 215-16, 220
    interpersonal, 212-15
    organizational, 197, 199-200, 202, 215, 217-19
    procedural, 207-08, 212, 220

K
Kentucky
    Lexington, 87
Kenya, 335
    northern, 335
kingdom of God, 5-8, 11-12, 137, 159, 186, 191, 226, 235, 303, 361
    community, 12
Kjeldseth, Aagot, 327-28
koinonia, 234
Korea, 87

L
Lawrence, T. E., 347
leadership
    evangelical. *See* evangelical.
    styles, 40
        African, 344
    toxic, 82
Lester, Paul Martin, 324, 332
Lewis, Sinclair, 84
liturgical, 93
Lord's Supper, 20
love, 17, 19-20, 35, 53, 56, 94, 96, 99, 101, 103, 162-63, 166, 175, 189, 192, 194, 200, 210, 215, 219, 225-27, 232, 267, 278,

303, 326, 335, 364-65
Lumière, August and Louis, 310
lust, 19, 118-19, 226

M
MacDonald, Gordon, 94
MacDougall, David, 319
Mackay, John, 265
Macklin, Rob, 161
Majority World, 27, 30
Malawi, 244
Maranz, David, 32
marriage, 77, 79
    vows, 94, 101, 107-08, 109, 112, 182, 194
martyria, 5, 7
Maslin-Ostrowski, Pat, 170
Maxim, 107
McGavran, Donald, 229
McKee, Annie, 161
media, 34, 53, 216-17
    influence, 84
Melville, Herman, 166
Mephibosheth, 335
metanarrative, 10, 12
Methodist, 326
Micah Initiative, 275
ministry, 22, 28, 36, 53-58, 69, 75, 79-80, 82, 85, 87
    counterproductive styles, 56
    cross-cultural, 78, 179
        partnerships, 27, 29, 38, 44
    integrity in ministry, 85
    leaders, 31, 34, 38, 40, 312
    leaving, 120
    processes, 34
    programs, 40

        successful, 21, 204
missiologists, 52, 179, 190, 244, 321, 344, 357
missiology, 28-29, 40, 189
        reflection, 32
mission
        agency, 38, 79, 93, 114, 118, 129, 150, 156, 168-69, 181, 187, 195, 204, 346
        Christian, 32, 53, 245-46, 267
        community, 75-77, 79, 155, 179
        entities, 79-80
        evangelistic, 56
        field, 66, 70, 128, 134, 137, 142-44, 147, 149-50, 267, 277, 314, 328, 345, 366
        global, 28, 32, 45, 78, 256
                movement, 28, 78
        leadership, 121, 211
        models of mission, 1
        organization, 33, 122, 157, 174, 313, 317, 335
                multinational, 37
        partnerships, 27-28
        practitioners, 67
        short-term, 58, 132, 243-45, 250, 269-70, 322, 336
missionary, 95, 112, 114, 117
        short term, 244
Moabites, 10
modernity, 2-3, 10, 22, 263, 300
money, 31-33, 41, 85, 131-32, 186, 234-35, 245-46, 250, 363
Moody Bible Institute, 76
morality, 2-3, 5, 13, 101, 130, 142-43, 146, 227
        deficient, 14
Mormonism, 63, 65
        attitudes towards, 65
Moscow, 134
multiculturalism, 192
Muriu, Oscar, 250, 254

Murray, George, 156
musician, 14
Muslim, 53-60, 65-66, 136, 190
    as dangerous, 57
    doctrine, 60
    fear of Muslims, 53
    ministries, 58
    ministry to Muslims, 53-56, 58
    non-Muslim, 51, 57
        places of worship, 57
    scriptures, 60
    threat, 55
    viewpoint, 56
    worship, 60
mutuality, 17, 34, 36-39, 325
    genuine, 30
    holistic, 37
Myers, Bryant, 39, 266

N
Nader, Ralph, 54
Nairobi, 250
narcissism, 8
neocolonialism, 28-30, 44-45
New Jersey, 76
New York Times, 66
New Zealand, 87
Nichols, Bill, 310
Nigeria, 270
Nigerian, 190
nihilism, 20
non-believer, 17
non-violence, 21
North America, 55, 157, 232-33, 267, 269
Nouwen, Henri, 96-97

O

Ohio State University, 214
Operation Mobilization, 269
organization
    indigenous, 27
    mission. *See* mission.
    nonprofit, 43, 276
Osborn, David, 172
outreach, 7, 10, 17
    ethical. *See* ethical.
    evangelistic, 51, 261, 267

P

pacifism, 7
Panama, 272
Papua New Guinea, 271
parables, 33, 292
Paris, Jenell Williams, 301
Parkhurst, L. G., 295-96
participation, 4, 89, 303, 366
Partners International, 38
partnership, 27, 30, 37-40, 83, 98, 100, 249-50, 275
    cross-cultural. *See* cross-cultural.
    diverse, 37
    healthy, 45
    indigenous, 37
    mission. *See* mission.
patience, 8, 14, 20-21, 40, 165, 215, 254
Paul, 34, 96, 138-39, 148, 226, 231, 235, 237, 246-47, 292, 303, 333
PBS, 293-94, 296-98
peace, 6-8, 10, 22, 54, 137, 143-45, 215, 233, 361, 365
    peaceful means, 7, 20
Pentecostal, 93

Perkins, John, 165, 167
Peter, 41, 135-38, 141
Peterson, Eugene, 93, 170
Pharisees, 42, 111
Philippines, 87
photography, 321, 330, 338
    ethical, 331-33
    mission, 322, 325, 331-33, 338
photojournalism, 324, 332
pluralism, 12, 192
politics, 56, 58, 269
    nationalism, 56
pornography, 19, 78, 101, 105-14, 116-20, 122
    hard-core, 107
    prevention, 111-15, 122
    soft-core, 107
postmodern, 9, 15, 63, 183, 299-300
    constructs, 2
postmodernity, 2, 61, 63-64
power
    abuse of, 77, 79, 82
    foreign, 30
    games, 77
    structures, 4
    struggles, 13
prayer, 54, 56, 60, 84, 86, 96, 98, 101, 138, 141, 158, 189-90, 255
    in school, 57
    letter, 56, 204
    teams, 80
Protestant, 58
purity, 84, 98, 100, 182, 328

Q
Qur'an, 61

R

race, 55, 193, 359
    assumptions of race, 55
racism, 62, 314
Rajendran, K., 89
Reagan, Ronald, 50
reconciliation, 7-8, 19, 211, 218, 360, 365
    of people to God, 7
redemption, 12, 22, 267
Regent University, 163
relations
    Christian-Muslim, 57
relationship
    accountable, 87
    covenant, 37, 234
    fractured, 20
    holistic, 21
    personal, 8
    with God. *See* God.
religion, 12, 49-50, 52-53, 55, 57-61, 63, 65-67, 69-70, 326, 359
    antagonism, 57
    assumptions of religion, 55
    oppression, 57
    religious differences, 54
REMAP II, 145, 148
repentance, 14, 96, 100
research, 29, 35, 78, 90, 101, 106-07, 115, 129, 155, 165-66, 199, 201, 246-47, 267, 302, 319, 344, 346, 348-51, 357-59, 368
    academic, 28
    educational, 150
    literature, 144
    social science, 35
restoration, 76, 81-83, 94-95, 100, 112, 115, 119-22
Reynolds, Thomas, 11
rhetoric, 3, 7, 58, 64, 244

Rhode Island, 62
Rickett, Daniel, 38
Rieger, Joerg, 32
righteousness, 6, 22, 198-99, 360-62, 365
Robert, Dennis, 169
Roberts, Dayton W., 262
Robinson, Bill, 166
Rogers, William, 61
Roman Catholic Church, 77, 95
Rowell, John, 37
Rowland, Randy, 159, 166
Ruby, Jay, 329, 332

S
Saint, Nate, 269
salvation, 3-4, 12-13, 19, 59, 63, 129, 134, 137-40, 183, 278, 298, 364
Sample, Steven, 159
Satan, 35, 191
Saudi Arabia government, 57
Schaeffer, Edith, 289, 291, 293, 297-99, 302
Schaeffer, Francis, 268, 289, 291, 293, 297-98, 300, 303
science, 62-63, 173, 197, 290
    scientific rationale, 3
    scientific reasoning, 2
Scimecca, Joseph, 294
Scott, Waldron, 264
Scripture, 10, 33-34, 44, 49, 60-61, 63-64, 84, 99, 130, 135-38, 140, 148, 236, 239, 241, 261, 272, 291, 345, 355, 357, 365
    authority of Scripture, 16, 141, 355
    scriptural values, 36
Scum of the Earth Church, 14-21
    congregation, 14-15, 20
secular, 35, 44, 55, 61, 203-04, 211, 215, 263-64
    humanists, 61

    patterns, 44
    values. *See* values.
seekers, 9, 13, 253
self-actualization, 3
self-awareness, 93
self-defense, 127
self-interest, 13, 21
sex
    abuse, 77
    addiction, 110, 119
    as good and created by God, 112
    before marriage, 107-08
    outside of marriage, 107, 109
    sexual defeats, 77
    sexual impropriety, 85, 109
    sexual sin, 79, 109, 112-14, 119
Shalhoub, Tony, 54
shalom, 6, 11, 130, 137, 143-46, 148-50, 245
shame, 12, 19, 62, 109, 119, 156
Shea, George Beverly, 84
short-term mission. *See* mission.
Simon, 41
sin, 4, 12, 19-20, 42, 77, 79, 93, 95, 112, 119-20, 142, 191
    confession, 76, 95
    forgiveness of sin, 360
    guilt of sin, 12
    of humanity, 261
    personal, 83
Singapore, 86-88, 100
Singapore Covenant, 82-83, 86-87, 89, 91, 97, 354
sinner, 19, 129
skeptic, 15
Skype, 92, 217
social action, 5, 267
social justice, 262

social welfare, 53, 70
socioeconomic status, 16
society, 3, 7, 9, 12, 16-17, 190, 259, 274, 316, 334
    status quo, 8, 201
Solomon, 207
soteriology, 3
South Africa, 326
Southwestern Baptist Theological Seminary, 164
spiritual development, 14
spiritual disciplines, 98, 101
spiritual leader, 87, 139-40
spirituality, 93, 110, 266
    dry, 77
stereotypes, 50, 53, 59, 61, 70, 314
stewardship, 227, 229, 245, 262, 271-75, 277, 279
Stivers, Robert, 264
submission, 60, 312
substance abuse, 19
Sufis, 59
Swaggart, Jimmy, 50
Swindoll, Chuck, 83, 86, 94, 97
Switzerland, 289-90

T

Tanzania
    Nijro, 322
Taylor, Hudson, 192
Taylor, William D., 93
Texas, 7
    Austin, 87
Thailand, 57-58, 68
theft, 36
theologian, 18, 140, 198, 264, 300
theological
    change, 82

presentation, 49
reflection, 28, 96
theology, 132, 140, 267
 global, 2
Thomas, Nicholas, 326
Tibet, 76
Timothy Networkers, 117
tolerance, 40, 146-48, 150
Townsend, Cameron, 347
Tozer, A. W., 172
training
 accounting. *See* accounting.
 cross-cultural. *See* cross-cultural.
 intercultural. *See* intercultural.
transformation, 14, 20-21, 36-37, 93, 101, 172, 298, 328
 adult, 35
 theological, 15
Trebesch, Shelley, 172
truth in Christianity. *See* Christianity.
Tucker, Lem, 167

U
unbeliever, 34, 130, 230, 232
unethical, 43, 52, 148, 158, 192, 229-30, 234, 240-41, 252, 357, 368-69
United Kingdom, 82, 263
United Nations, 263
United States of America, 8, 27-28, 38, 43, 51, 55, 76, 79-81, 87, 92, 203, 243-44, 248, 250, 263, 300, 325
 Americans. *See* Americans.
 Christian America, 3
 Christianity, 12
 denominations, 13
 middle-class evangelical, 15
 Midwestern, 51

unity, 20, 41, 138, 182-84, 192-94, 232, 352
University of Southern California, 159
unreached people group, 76

V
values
    scriptural. *See* Scripture.
    secular, 34
    worldly, 44
Van Dyke, Fred, 263
Vencer, Jun, 83, 86
violence, 8, 19, 54, 56, 79, 270, 365
    nonviolence. *See* nonviolence.

W
Wahabis, 59
Walker, Frank Deaville, 326
war, 54, 269, 334, 347
    Cold War, 346
    global war on terrorism, 43
    World War II, 269, 346
Ward, Ted, 160
Washington
    Coupville, 271
    Seattle, 159
WEA Mission Commission, 78-79, 82-84, 86, 89, 92-93
wealth, 29-30, 33, 35, 250, 252-53, 298, 318
    disparity of wealth, 30
Wellman, Sam, 296
Wenger Shenk, Sarah, 6
Wesley College, 328
Western, 132, 136, 140-41, 143, 190, 243, 274, 315, 327-29, 347-48
    accountability processes, 40
    civilization, 53

cultural standards, 28
cultures, 31, 133
ethical standards, 28
financial regulations, 34
funding policies, 34
government, 346
    accountability, 43
    regulations, 36
legal requirements, 33
secular methods, 44

Westerners, 32, 146, 255
Wheaton College, 85
Wheeler, Tom, 331
Willard, Dallas, 93
Williams, F. E., 347
Williams, Ken, 109, 113-14
Willigen, John, 332
Wilson, Grady, 84
Wilson, Jonathan, 267
Winter, Ralph, 128, 180
witness
    faithfulness in witness, 5
    false, 52, 241
    patient, 8
    verbal, 18
Woolcock, Penny, 315
Word of God, 29, 183, 360-62
World Evangelical Fellowship, 97-98
World Vision, 129, 262, 275
worldview, 1-3, 20, 143, 344
worship, 9, 41, 57, 60, 100-01, 228, 241, 253, 262, 360, 365
    liturgical service, 19
    seeker-sensitive, 9
    service, 17, 228, 232, 241, 271
Wright, Christopher, 273

Wright, Terrance, 330
Wuthnow, Robert, 243-44, 247
Wycliffe Bible Translators, 269

Y
Yale University, 65-66
young adults, 11, 14
youth, 15, 107
      subculture, 14
Youth With A Mission, 270
YouTube, 107

Z
Zehner, Edwin, 250
Zigarelli, Michael, 163

www.ingramcontent.com/pod-product-compliance
Lightning Source LLC
Chambersburg PA
CBHW071227070526
44583CB00017B/2080